365 Unique Chicken Recipes

(365 Unique Chicken Recipes - Volume 1)

Norma Wells

Copyright: Published in the United States by Norma Wells/ © NORMA WELLS

Published on November, 19 2020

All rights reserved. No part of this publication may be reproduced, stored in retrieval system, copied in any form or by any means, electronic, mechanical, photocopying, recording or otherwise transmitted without written permission from the publisher. Please do not participate in or encourage piracy of this material in any way. You must not circulate this book in any format. NORMA WELLS does not control or direct users' actions and is not responsible for the information or content shared, harm and/or actions of the book readers.

In accordance with the U.S. Copyright Act of 1976, the scanning, uploading and electronic sharing of any part of this book without the permission of the publisher constitute unlawful piracy and theft of the author's intellectual property. If you would like to use material from the book (other than just simply for reviewing the book), prior permission must be obtained by contacting the author at author@shrimpcookbook.com

Thank you for your support of the author's rights.

Content

365 AWESOME CHICKEN RECIPES 8

1. 'Oven Fried' Four Cheese Chicken 8
2. 30 Minute Chicken Manicotti Skillet............ 8
3. 5 Cheese Italian Crispy Chicken Sandwiches 9
4. A.1. Fried Chicken Wings 9
5. Achiote Chicken & Rice.................................10
6. Air Fryer Chicken Nuggets 10
7. Amazing VELVEETA® And Chicken Nachos..11
8. Andouille Sausage Jambalaya 11
9. Angel Chicken...12
10. Angel Hair Pasta Chicken In Roasted Poblano Chile Sauce 12
11. Angel Hair Puttanesca With Chicken 13
12. Apricot Pesto Glazed Chicken.....................13
13. Asian Chicken With Broccoli & Chickpeas 14
14. BBQ Cherry Cola Chicken Legs.................14
15. BBQ Chicken & Rice Dinner 15
16. BBQ Chicken & VELVEETA Casserole .15
17. BBQ Chicken Fingers..................................16
18. BBQ Chicken Soft Taco 16
19. BBQ Chicken Stir Fry 17
20. BBQ Chicken Strip Sandwich 17
21. BBQ Chicken And Blue Cheese Pizza 17
22. BBQ Chicken And Rice Skillet 18
23. BBQ Grilled Chicken Pizza With Feta.......18
24. BBQ Oven Baked Chicken Wings 19
25. Bacon & Cheese Stuffed Chicken Breast..19
26. Bacon, Corn, Salsa And Chicken Roll Up 20
27. Bacon Wrapped Chicken Appetizers..........20
28. Baja Grilled Chicken Quesadillas 21
29. Baked Chicken Tenderloin Recipe.............21
30. Baked Chicken Thigh Dinner 22
31. Baked Garden Ratatouille 23
32. Balsamic Chicken Wrap With Mozzarella.23
33. Barbecue Chicken Nachos...........................24
34. Basil Chicken Breasts...................................24
35. Basil Chicken With Roasted Tomatoes 25
36. Beer & BBQ Marinated Grilled Chicken Wings..25
37. Berry Sweet Chicken Salad Sandwich........26
38. Better Than Ever Slow Cooker Cacciatore 26
39. Bistro Chicken And Pasta 27
40. Bistro Chicken Pasta Salad..........................27
41. Blue Cheese, Chicken And Spinach Pizza.28
42. Breaded Chicken Salad With Berries.........28
43. Brined BBQ Chicken Legs..........................29
44. Broccoli, Cauliflower & Chicken Salad......29
45. Buffalo Chicken Party Sandwiches.............30
46. Buffalo Chicken Pinwheels..........................30
47. Buffalo Chicken Salad..................................31
48. Buffalo Chicken Tostada..............................31
49. Butternut Squash And Chicken Pot Pie 32
50. CATALINA® Asian Chicken Salad 32
51. Cacciatore Style Chicken Bake 33
52. Cajun Chicken Lasagna With Andouille Sausage...33
53. Caribbean Coconut Chicken Bites 34
54. Champion Chicken Parmesan 34
55. Cheddar Chicken And Potatoes..................35
56. Cheddar, Bacon And Vegetable Chopped Salad 35
57. Cheese & Chicken Empanadas 36
58. Cheesy BBQ Chicken Salad Pizza 36
59. Cheesy BBQ Chicken Wraps......................37
60. Cheesy Bacon Orchard Chicken 37
61. Cheesy Chicken & Salsa Skillet 38
62. Cheesy Chicken & Stuffing Skillet.............38
63. Cheesy Chicken BLT Club Sandwich 39
64. Cheesy Chicken Pot Pie...............................39
65. Cheesy Chicken Taco Casserole 40
66. Cheesy Chicken Tacos..................................40
67. Cheesy Chicken And Rice...........................41
68. Cheesy Chicken And Veggie Pasta Skillet.41
69. Cheesy Chicken Pepper Quesadillas 42
70. Cheesy Mac And Chicken Taco Soup 42
71. Cheesy Primavera Skillet 43
72. Chicken & Bacon Pot Pie 43
73. Chicken & Pepper Pasta Bake....................44
74. Chicken & Rice Casserole 44
75. Chicken & Rice With Asparagus................45
76. Chicken & Summer Squash Skillet 46
77. Chicken Bacon Ranch Pita Pizzas 46
78. Chicken Breasts In Sour Cream Sauce......47
79. Chicken Burritos El Grande 47
80. Chicken Cacciatore Pronto 48
81. Chicken Caesar Salad Pizza.........................48

82. Chicken Fettuccine Primavera 49
83. Chicken Fiesta Chili Dip 49
84. Chicken Harvest Salad 50
85. Chicken Harvest Stir Fry 50
86. Chicken Herb Quiche Squares 51
87. Chicken Italiano Skillet 51
88. Chicken Kiev 52
89. Chicken Lo Mein 52
90. Chicken Marsala Sandwiches 53
91. Chicken Milanese With Apple Salad 53
92. Chicken Nicoise Salad Recipe 54
93. Chicken Parm Snackers 54
94. Chicken Parmesan Spaghetti 54
95. Chicken Pasta Bowl 55
96. Chicken Pesto Cavatappi 55
97. Chicken Pho Recipe 56
98. Chicken Pie 57
99. Chicken Pot Pie Bubble Bread Bake 57
100. Chicken Ranch BLT 57
101. Chicken Rollatini 58
102. Chicken Salad Cuban Sandwich 58
103. Chicken Salad Sandwich Recipe 59
104. Chicken Salad Stuffed Zucchini 59
105. Chicken Stir Fry With Jicama, Tomatillos And Red Peppers 60
106. Chicken TV Dinner Roll Up 60
107. Chicken Taco Casserole 61
108. Chicken Thighs With Fennel And Dried Apricots 62
109. Chicken Tinga Recipe 62
110. Chicken Tortellini Soup 63
111. Chicken Waldorf Salad 63
112. Chicken And Dumplings In Green Salsa .. 63
113. Chicken And Ham Lemon Soup 64
114. Chicken And Peanut Stew 65
115. Chicken With Apple Walnut Stuffing 65
116. Chicken, Apple & Spinach Salad 66
117. Chicken, Broccoli & Pinto Beans Recipe .. 66
118. Chicken, Broccoli And Rice Casserole 67
119. Chicken Parmesan Bake 67
120. Chicken Parmesan Bundles 68
121. Chicken Parmesan Pasta 68
122. Chicken Penne Florentine Bake 69
123. Chinese Sweet And Sour Chicken Recipe. 69
124. Chipotle Chicken & Vegetable Skillet 70
125. Chopped Greek Chicken Salad 71
126. Cider Glazed Stuffed Chicken 71
127. Classic Balsamic Marinade For Chicken 72
128. Cobb Salad 72
129. Coconut Chicken Dippers 73
130. Cool Fruited Chicken Salad 73
131. Cordon Bleu Chicken Casserole 74
132. Cornbread Topped Creamy Chicken Bake 74
133. Cranberry Glazed Chicken Dinner 75
134. Cranberry Pecan Glazed Chicken Dinner .75
135. Creamed Chicken On Toast 76
136. Creamy Broccoli Stuffed Chicken Breasts 76
137. Creamy Chicken & Cheddar Rice Bake 77
138. Creamy Chicken & Corn Soup 77
139. Creamy Chicken Broccoli Stuffed Potato .78
140. Creamy Chicken Casserole 78
141. Creamy Chicken Mac & Cheese With Sour Cream 79
142. Creamy Chicken Pomodoro 79
143. Creamy Chicken Salad Pizza 80
144. Creamy Chicken Sausage And Pasta Skillet 80
145. Creamy Chicken Soup With Matzo 81
146. Creamy Chicken Cauliflower Pasta 81
147. Creamy Curried Chicken Salad 82
148. Creamy Garlic Chicken & Broccoli Mac & Cheese 82
149. Creamy Guajillo Chicken Pasta 83
150. Creamy Mexican Chicken Casserole 83
151. Creamy Mexican Chicken Pasta 84
152. Creamy Parmesan Chicken Salad 84
153. Creamy Salsa Verde Chicken 85
154. Creole Chicken Salad Sandwich 85
155. Crispy Baked Pesto Chicken 86
156. Crispy Cheddar Chicken Nuggets Recipe .86
157. Crispy Chicken Parmesan With Avocado Salsa 87
158. Crispy Chicken With Honey Dipping Sauce 87
159. Crispy Oven Baked Chicken Parmesan 88
160. Crispy Santa Fe Chicken 88
161. Crunchy Topped Chicken & Rice Casserole 89
162. Curried BBQ Chicken Thighs 89
163. Curried Chicken Bites 90
164. Curried Chicken Spread 90
165. Deep Dish Chicken Pot Pie Recipe 91
166. Dijon Balsamic Herb Chicken 91

167. Dijon Chicken Elegant 92
168. Dijon Chicken Salad Sandwich 92
169. Dijon Marinade 93
170. Doner Kebab (Turkish Style Kebab) Wrap 93
171. Double Chipotle BBQ Chicken Rolls 94
172. Easy 30 Minute Skillet Chicken Mac & Cheese 94
173. Easy BBQ Glazed Chicken 95
174. Easy Cheesy Chicken Bake 95
175. Easy Chicken & Pasta Skillet With Parmesan 96
176. Easy Chicken Cacciatore Recipe 96
177. Easy Chicken Parmesan 97
178. Easy Chicken Quesadillas 97
179. Easy Chicken Rigatoni 98
180. Easy Chicken Stir Fry Skillet 98
181. Easy Chicken À La King 99
182. Easy Chile Stuffed Chicken Breasts 99
183. Easy Enchilada Recipe 100
184. Easy Feta Chicken Bake 100
185. Easy Glazed Chicken Dinner 101
186. Easy Greek Grilled Chicken Salads With Feta 101
187. Easy Grilled BBQ Chicken 102
188. Easy Grilled Chicken Parmesan Dinner . 102
189. Easy Skillet Fried Chicken 103
190. Easy Weeknight Pasta Toss 103
191. Fiesta Chicken Enchiladas 104
192. Fiesta Chicken Skillet 104
193. Foil Pack Bruschetta Chicken Bake 105
194. Foil Pack Chicken & Broccoli Dinner 105
195. Four Cheese Bacon Chicken Pizza 106
196. French Country Chicken Casserole 106
197. Fresh Chopped Salad 107
198. Garden Herb Chicken 107
199. Garlic Chicken Primavera 108
200. Gorgonzola Waldorf Sandwiches 108
201. Grecian Pizza Bowl Salad 108
202. Greek Style Skillet Chicken 109
203. Greek Style Stuffed Chicken Breasts 110
204. Green Salad With Skillet BBQ Chicken .. 110
205. Grilled BBQ Chicken Breasts 111
206. Grilled BBQ Chicken Thighs 111
207. Grilled Bruschetta Chicken 112
208. Grilled Chicken Caesar Salad 112
209. Grilled Chicken Rolls With Spicy Sauce . 113
210. Grilled Chicken Salad On Crispy Tortillas 113
211. Grilled Chicken Salad With Avocado Dressing 114
212. Grilled Chicken With Mushroom Pasta . 114
213. Grilled Chicken With Strawberry Salsa ... 115
214. Grilled Chicken, Veggie And Pasta Salad 115
215. Grilled Hot Chicken Sausage Sandwich . 116
216. Grilled Italian Chicken Tacos 116
217. Grilled Spicy Teriyaki Drumsticks 117
218. HEALTHY LIVING Easy Chicken BLT Salad 117
219. Hearty Mexican Chicken Soup 118
220. Herb Crusted Creamy Jalapeño Stuffed Chicken 118
221. Homestyle Chicken Fajitas 119
222. Honey Mustard Pear Salad 119
223. Hot & Spicy Crispy Chicken Sandwich .. 120
224. Hot And Spicy Grilled Chicken Wings ... 120
225. Indian Baked Chicken 120
226. Indian Chicken Curry 121
227. Indian Chicken Curry Recipe 121
228. Italian Chicken & Tomato Pasta Toss 122
229. Italian Chicken Sausage & Brown And Wild Rice 123
230. Italian Chicken Sausage With Pasta 123
231. Italian Chicken And Ham Sandwiches ... 123
232. Italian Style Chicken Enchiladas 124
233. Jamaican Jerk Chicken Breasts 124
234. Jerk BBQ Chicken Salad 125
235. Kicked Up BBQ Chicken Chili With Beans 125
236. Kickin' Chicken Spread 126
237. Kung Pao Chicken Wings 126
238. Layered Chicken Taco Salad 127
239. Layered Chicken, Bacon & Avocado Salad 127
240. Layered Egg, Chicken And Pea Salad 128
241. Lemon Garlic Chicken And Pasta 128
242. Lemon Rosemary Chicken Salad Spread 129
243. Lemon Rosemary Chicken Salad Topper 129
244. Lime Chicken Salad Wrap 130
245. MIRACLE WHIP Awesome Waldorf Salad 130
246. Madras Curry Chicken 130
247. Mango Chicken Salad Sandwiches 131
248. Maple Mustard Roast Chicken Dinner ... 131

249. Marinated Italian Chicken Skewers 132
250. Marinated Zesty Chicken 132
251. Mediterranean Chicken & Hummus Wraps 133
252. Mediterranean Chicken Pasta 133
253. Mediterranean Chicken Recipe 134
254. Mediterranean Chicken Skillet 134
255. Mediterranean Chicken With Orzo And Feta 135
256. Mexican Chicken Casserole 136
257. Mexican Marinated & Broiled Chicken Breasts 136
258. Mexican Taco Soup With Chicken........... 137
259. Mini Butter Chicken Pies 137
260. Mini Chicken Patties With Spring Green Salad 138
261. Miracle Whip Chicken Skillet 138
262. Mulligatawny Soup 139
263. Mushroom Smothered Chicken & Green Bean Skillet 139
264. Mushroom Stuffing Chicken Roll Ups 140
265. Nana's Smothered Chicken Skillet With Cheese 140
266. One Pan Chicken 'N Noodles 141
267. One Pan Chicken, Tomato And Pepper Pasta 141
268. Onion & Feta Greek BBQ Chicken Pizza 142
269. Orange Chicken Rice Bowl 142
270. PHILLY Chicken Pot Pie Minis 143
271. PLANTERS Chicken Piccata Skillet Simmer 143
272. Parmesan, Chicken And Pasta Toss 144
273. Parmesan, Chicken And Tomato Salad ... 144
274. Pecan Crusted Chicken With Citrus Tomato Topping 145
275. Pepper Chicken Macaroni And Cheese ... 145
276. Pesto Chicken Spirals 146
277. Pesto Chicken Pasta 146
278. Poppyseed & Pine Nut Chicken Salad 147
279. Pork Medallions With Cranberry Stuffing 147
280. Potato Chicken Pie 148
281. Pretzel Chicken Dippers 148
282. Quick & Easy Lemon Chicken & Rice ... 149
283. Quick 'n' Easy Italian Chicken & Pasta For Two 149

284. Quick Chicken & Peppers BBQ Fajitas . 150
285. Quick Indian Karhai Chicken 150
286. Quick Salsa Chicken Skillet.................... 151
287. Quick Thai Style Chicken Kabobs 151
288. Ranch Chicken & Rice Skillet.................. 152
289. Ranch Honey Chicken For Two............... 152
290. Recipe For Chicken Enchiladas 153
291. Roasted Sweet Potato And Chicken Salad 153
292. Rosemary Garlic Pasta Primavera........... 154
293. SHAKE 'N BAKE Chicken Nugget Kabobs... 154
294. STOVE TOP Easy Chicken Bake............ 155
295. STOVE TOP Spicy Chicken Sausage Stuffing 155
296. Salsa Chicken Wrap With Pineapple Pico De Gallo 156
297. Salsa Chicken Tostadas............................. 156
298. Sarah's Super Baked Chicken & Carrots 157
299. Saucy Chicken Stir Fry............................. 157
300. Savory Chicken Pie Recipe 157
301. Senorita Fajita Sandwich 158
302. Shortcut Salsa Chicken 158
303. Simple Chicken Enchiladas..................... 159
304. Simply Amazing Greek Chicken Recipe. 159
305. Sizzlin' Marinated Chicken Kabobs 160
306. Skillet Chicken & Dumplings 160
307. Skillet Chicken Breasts With Corn Sauce 161
308. Skillet Chicken Chili 162
309. Slow Cooker 'Osso Buco' With Chicken . 162
310. Slow Cooker BBQ Chicken Stir Fry 163
311. Slow Cooker Mini Chicken Pot Pies 163
312. Slow Cooker Pineapple BBQ Chicken ... 164
313. Smart Choice Swiss 'n Chicken Casserole 164
314. Smothered Chicken With Brown Rice.... 165
315. Soba Noodles Recipe 165
316. Southwest Chicken Panini 166
317. Southwest Chicken Skewers 166
318. Southwest Chicken With Corn & Rice ... 167
319. Southwestern Chicken With Black Beans & Rice 167
320. Southwestern Corn Bread Chicken 168
321. Southwestern Ranch Chicken Salad 168
322. Spatchcock BBQ Chicken With Grilled Green Bean Salad... 169
323. Speedy Sweet & Spicy Chicken Stir Fry . 169

324. Spicy BBQ Chicken Wings Recipe 170
325. Spicy Bacon Pizza 170
326. Spicy Buffalo Style Chicken Salad 171
327. Spicy Chicken Mac And Cheese Skillet ... 171
328. Spicy Chicken Skillet Stew 172
329. Spicy Chicken Stir Fry 172
330. Spicy Hot Wing Recipe 173
331. Spicy Island Chicken 173
332. Spicy Noodles In Peanut Sauce 174
333. Spicy Stir Fry Chicken 174
334. Spicy Stuffed Grilled Chicken Breasts 175
335. Spicy Vampire Bat Wings 175
336. Spicy Winter Chicken Soup 176
337. Spinach Alfredo Lasagna 177
338. Stir Fry Salad With Rice 177
339. Stuffed Chicken Breasts With Parmesan 178
340. Stuffing Topped Creamy Chicken Casserole 178
341. Summer Chicken Salad 179
342. Sun Dried Tomato Grilled Chicken & Vegetables 179
343. Sun Dried Tomato Drumsticks 179
344. Sunday Roasted Chicken 180
345. Sweet And Spicy BBQ Chicken Wraps ... 180
346. Tasty Bacon Two Cheese Pizza 181
347. The New Chicken Skillet 181
348. Three Cheese Chicken With Pasta 182
349. Three Cheese Pasta Bake 183
350. Thyme Roasted Chicken 183
351. Tomato, Spinach And Chicken Pasta Bake 184
352. Tuscan Garlic Chicken Skillet 184
353. Ultimate Chicken Stroganoff 185
354. Updated Chicken Parmesan 185
355. VELVEETA Chicken Curry Pot Pie 186
356. VELVEETA® Cheesy BBQ Chicken With A Kick 186
357. VELVEETA® Chicken And Vegetable Skillet 187
358. VELVEETA® Spicy Buffalo Chicken Dip 187
359. Waldorf Salad With A Twist 188
360. Warm Chicken Salad 188
361. Weeknight Cheddar Chicken Soup 189
362. West Coast Chicken Wings 189
363. Zesty Chicken Chili 190
364. Zesty One Pan Chicken And Potato Bake 190
365. Zucchini Chicken Salad 191

INDEX 192

CONCLUSION 196

365 Awesome Chicken Recipes

***

1. 'Oven Fried' Four Cheese Chicken

Serving: 8 | Prep: 10mins | Cook: 40mins | Ready in: 50mins

Ingredients

- 1 pkt. SHAKE 'N BAKE Seasoned Panko Seasoned Coating Mix
- 1/2 tsp. garlic powder
- 1/4 tsp. onion powder
- 1 cup KRAFT Mexican Style Finely Shredded Four Cheese
- 1 broiler-fryer chicken (4 lb.), cut up

Direction

- Heat oven to 375ºF.
- Combine coating mix and seasonings in medium bowl; stir in cheese.
- Moisten chicken with water. Coat with cheese mixture, 1 piece at a time. Lightly press cheese mixture onto both sides of chicken. (Chicken will not be completely coated.)
- Place on baking sheet sprayed with cooking spray; top with any remaining cheese mixture.
- Bake 38 to 40 min. or until chicken is done (165ºF).

Nutrition Information

- Calories: 370
- Total Fat: 16 g
- Saturated Fat: 6 g
- Sodium: 390 mg
- Protein: 50 g
- Fiber: 0.5302 g
- Total Carbohydrate: 6 g
- Cholesterol: 150 mg
- Sugar: 0 g

2. 30 Minute Chicken Manicotti Skillet

Serving: 8 | Prep: 30mins | Cook: | Ready in: 30mins

Ingredients

- 1-1/2 cups CLASSICO Tomato and Basil Pasta Sauce
- 1 can (14-1/2 oz.) diced tomatoes, undrained
- 1/2 cup water
- 2 cups chopped cooked chicken
- 1/4 cup KRAFT Tuscan House Italian Dressing
- 1/4 tsp. dried basil leaves
- 1 cup KRAFT Shredded Italian* Five Cheese with a TOUCH OF PHILADELPHIA, divided
- 8 manicotti shells, uncooked

Direction

- Mix pasta sauce, tomatoes and water until blended.
- Combine 3/4 cup of the sauce with chicken, dressing, basil and 1/2 cup cheese; spoon into manicotti shells. Place in nonstick skillet; top with remaining sauce. Turn to evenly coat manicotti with sauce. Bring to boil; cover. Simmer on medium heat 15 min. or until manicotti is tender, turning after 8 min.
- Remove from heat. Sprinkle with remaining cheese; let stand 5 min. or until melted.

Nutrition Information

- Calories: 350

- Sodium: 380 mg
- Protein: 19 g
- Saturated Fat: 3.5 g
- Fiber: 3 g
- Total Carbohydrate: 0 g
- Cholesterol: 35 mg
- Sugar: 0 g
- Total Fat: 10 g

- Cholesterol: 75 mg
- Total Carbohydrate: 0 g
- Sugar: 0 g
- Total Fat: 10 g
- Sodium: 990 mg
- Fiber: 3 g

3. 5 Cheese Italian Crispy Chicken Sandwiches

Serving: 4 | Prep: 10mins | Cook: 20mins | Ready in: 30mins

Ingredients

- 1 tsp. dried Italian seasoning
- 1 pkt. SHAKE 'N BAKE Chicken Coating Mix
- 4 small boneless skinless chicken breasts (1 lb.)
- 1/2 cup KRAFT Shredded Italian* Five Cheese Blend
- 4 French bread rolls, partially split
- 2 Tbsp. GREY POUPON Dijon Mustard
- 4 lettuce leaves
- 1 large tomato, cut into 4 slices

Direction

- Heat oven to 400°F.
- Add Italian seasoning to coating mix in shaker bag; shake gently to combine. Use to coat chicken as directed on package; place on foil-covered rimmed baking sheet.
- Bake 20 min. or until done (165°F). Top with cheese; bake 2 min. or until melted.
- Spread cut sides of rolls with mustard; fill with chicken, lettuce and tomatoes.

Nutrition Information

- Calories: 380
- Protein: 34 g
- Saturated Fat: 3.5 g

4. A.1. Fried Chicken Wings

Serving: 12 | Prep: 30mins | Cook: | Ready in: 30mins

Ingredients

- 1/2 cup A.1. Original Sauce
- 2 lb. chicken wings, separated at joints, tips removed
- 1 cup flour
- 1 Tbsp. pepper
- 1 tsp. Creole seasoning
- 1 cup canola oil

Direction

- Pour steak sauce over chicken in shallow glass dish. Refrigerate 1 hour to marinate, turning after 30 min. Remove chicken from marinade; discard marinade.
- Mix flour, pepper and seasoning in resealable plastic bag. Add chicken, in batches; toss to coat.
- Heat oil in skillet on medium-high heat. Add chicken, in batches; cook 10 to 12 min. or until done and golden brown. Drain on paper towels.

Nutrition Information

- Calories: 180
- Sodium: 170 mg
- Total Carbohydrate: 9 g
- Fiber: 0 g
- Protein: 10 g
- Total Fat: 11 g
- Saturated Fat: 2 g

- Cholesterol: 25 mg
- Sugar: 1 g

5. Achiote Chicken & Rice

Serving: 6 | Prep: 30mins | Cook: 25mins | Ready in: 55mins

Ingredients

- 1/2 cup KRAFT Real Mayo Mayonnaise
- 2 Tbsp. annatto paste
- 1 broiler-fryer chicken (3 lb.), cut up, skin removed
- 1 cup long-grain white rice, uncooked
- 1 cup chopped onions
- 1 red pepper, cut into strips
- 2 cloves garlic, minced
- 2 cups water
- 1 chicken bouillon cube
- 1/3 cup manzanilla olives, halved
- 1 Tbsp. chopped fresh cilantro

Direction

- Mix mayo and annatto paste. Add half to chicken in large bowl; toss to coat.
- Cook chicken in large deep skillet or Dutch oven on medium-high heat 5 min. or until evenly browned, turning occasionally. Remove chicken from skillet; discard drippings. Cover chicken to keep warm.
- Add rice, onions, peppers, garlic and remaining mayo mixture to skillet; cook on medium-low heat 3 min., stirring constantly. Add water and bouillon; stir. Top with chicken. Bring to boil; cover. Simmer on low heat 22 to 25 min. or until chicken is done (165°F) and liquid is absorbed.
- Top with olives and cilantro.

Nutrition Information

- Calories: 420
- Saturated Fat: 3.5 g
- Protein: 24 g
- Total Fat: 22 g
- Fiber: 2 g
- Sugar: 3 g
- Cholesterol: 70 mg
- Sodium: 470 mg
- Total Carbohydrate: 30 g

6. Air Fryer Chicken Nuggets

Serving: 4 | Prep: 15mins | Cook: 12mins | Ready in: 27mins

Ingredients

- 1 egg
- 2 cups panko bread crumbs
- 1/4 cup KRAFT Grated Parmesan Cheese
- 3 Tbsp. KRAFT Zesty Italian Dressing
- 1 lb. boneless skinless chicken breasts, cut into 1-inch pieces

Direction

- Heat air fryer to 390°F.
- Beat egg in pie plate until blended. Combine bread crumbs, cheese and dressing in separate pie plate.
- Dip chicken, 1 piece at a time, into egg, then crumb mixture, turning to evenly coat both sides of each piece with each ingredient.
- Spray air fryer basket with cooking spray. Place up to 5 chicken pieces in single layer in prepared basket; add to air fryer. Cook 10 to 12 min. or until chicken nuggets are crisp and done (165°F). Transfer chicken nuggets to plate. Repeat with remaining chicken pieces.

Nutrition Information

- Calories: 300
- Saturated Fat: 2.5 g
- Fiber: 1 g

- Sodium: 330 mg
- Total Carbohydrate: 0 g
- Total Fat: 7 g
- Protein: 26 g
- Sugar: 0 g
- Cholesterol: 90 mg

7. Amazing VELVEETA® And Chicken Nachos

Serving: 8 | Prep: 20mins | Cook: | Ready in: 20mins

Ingredients

- 8 cups tortilla chips (8 oz.)
- 8 oz. VELVEETA, cut into 1/2-inch cubes
- 1/2 lb. boneless skinless chicken breasts, cooked, shredded
- 1 cup shredded lettuce
- 1 tomato, chopped
- 1/2 cup guacamole

Direction

- Spread tortilla chips onto microwaveable platter; top with VELVEETA.
- Microwave on HIGH 2 min. or until VELVEETA is melted.
- Top with chicken and remaining ingredients.

Nutrition Information

- Calories: 270
- Protein: 13 g
- Total Fat: 14 g
- Total Carbohydrate: 24 g
- Cholesterol: 35 mg
- Fiber: 3 g
- Sodium: 560 mg
- Saturated Fat: 5 g
- Sugar: 3 g

8. Andouille Sausage Jambalaya

Serving: 8 | Prep: 15mins | Cook: 55mins | Ready in: 1hours10mins

Ingredients

- 3 Tbsp. flour
- 2 tsp. dried thyme leaves
- 1/4 tsp. each ground red pepper (cayenne) and black pepper
- 8 bone-in chicken thighs (2-1/2 lb.), skinned
- 1 Tbsp. oil
- 1 large onion, chopped
- 1 large green pepper, chopped
- 4 cloves garlic, minced
- 1 can (28 oz.) fire-roasted diced tomatoes, undrained
- 1/2 cup BULL'S-EYE Texas Style Barbecue Sauce
- 1 pkg. (9 oz.) fully cooked andouille sausage, sliced
- 3 cups fat-free reduced-sodium chicken broth
- 1-1/2 cups long-grain white rice, uncooked
- 1/2 lb. uncooked deveined peeled large shrimp
- 1/4 cup minced fresh parsley

Direction

- Mix flour and seasonings in shallow dish. Add chicken; turn to coat both sides of each thigh. Heat oil in Dutch oven or large deep skillet on medium heat. Add 4 chicken thighs; cook 4 min. on each side or until each is golden brown on both sides. Transfer to plate, reserving drippings in pan. Repeat with remaining chicken.
- Add onions, green peppers and garlic to drippings in pan; cook and stir 5 min. Stir in tomatoes, barbecue sauce and sausage. Return chicken and any juices from plate to tomato mixture; simmer 25 min. or until chicken is done (165°F), stirring occasionally. Meanwhile, bring broth to boil in medium saucepan. Stir in rice; cover. Simmer on medium-low heat 20 min. or until broth is absorbed and rice is tender.

- Add shrimp to tomato mixture; simmer 8 min. or until shrimp turn pink.
- Spoon rice into shallow bowls; top with chicken mixture and parsley.

Nutrition Information

- Calories: 410
- Saturated Fat: 4 g
- Total Carbohydrate: 45 g
- Sodium: 910 mg
- Total Fat: 14 g
- Fiber: 3 g
- Protein: 26 g
- Sugar: 9 g
- Cholesterol: 120 mg

9. Angel Chicken

Serving: 0 | Prep: 10mins | Cook: 4hours | Ready in: 4hours10mins

Ingredients

- 4 oz. (1/2 of 8-oz. pkg.) PHILADELPHIA Cream Cheese, softened
- 1 can (10-3/4 oz.) reduced-sodium condensed cream of mushroom soup
- 1/4 cup KRAFT Tuscan House Italian Dressing
- 1/4 cup dry white wine
- 1-1/2 lb. boneless skinless chicken thighs, cut into bite-size pieces
- 1/2 lb. angel hair pasta, uncooked
- 2 Tbsp. chopped fresh parsley

Direction

- Whisk first 4 ingredients until blended; pour over chicken in slow cooker. Cook on LOW 4 to 5 hours (or on HIGH 2 to 3 hours).
- Cook pasta as directed on package, omitting salt; drain. Serve topped with chicken mixture; sprinkle with parsley.

Nutrition Information

- Calories: 380
- Fiber: 2 g
- Protein: 21 g
- Total Fat: 14 g
- Sodium: 560 mg
- Sugar: 4 g
- Total Carbohydrate: 40 g
- Cholesterol: 75 mg
- Saturated Fat: 6 g

10. Angel Hair Pasta Chicken In Roasted Poblano Chile Sauce

Serving: 4 | Prep: 30mins | Cook: | Ready in: 30mins

Ingredients

- 4 small boneless skinless chicken breasts (1 lb.)
- 1/4 cup flour
- 1/4 cup KRAFT Italian Vinaigrette Dressing made with Extra Virgin Olive Oil
- 1/2 cup slivered onions
- 1/2 lb. angel hair pasta, uncooked
- 1/2 cup fat-free reduced-sodium chicken broth
- 4 oz. (1/2 of 8-oz. pkg.) PHILADELPHIA Cream Cheese, cubed
- 1/2 cup roasted poblano chiles
- 2 cloves garlic, peeled
- 1/4 cup chopped fresh cilantro

Direction

- Coat both sides of chicken with flour. Heat dressing in large skillet on medium-high heat. Add onions; cook and stir 5 min. or until crisp-tender. Add chicken; cook 6 to 8 min. on each side or until done (165°F).
- Meanwhile, cook pasta in large saucepan as directed on package, omitting salt. While pasta is cooking, blend broth, cream cheese, chiles and garlic in blender until smooth. Pour into

medium saucepan. Bring to boil on medium heat, stirring frequently; simmer on low heat 5 min., stirring occasionally.

- Drain pasta; return to pan. Add cream cheese mixture; mix lightly. Place on platter; top with chicken. Sprinkle with cilantro.

Nutrition Information

- Calories: 500
- Cholesterol: 105 mg
- Total Carbohydrate: 0 g
- Saturated Fat: 7 g
- Sugar: 0 g
- Protein: 35 g
- Sodium: 440 mg
- Total Fat: 15 g
- Fiber: 3 g

11. Angel Hair Puttanesca With Chicken

Serving: 0 | Prep: 10mins | Cook: 15mins | Ready in: 25mins

Ingredients

- 1/2 lb. (8 oz.) angel hair pasta, uncooked
- 2 Tbsp. KRAFT Lite Zesty Italian Dressing
- 1 lb. boneless skinless chicken breasts, cut into strips
- 3 cloves garlic, minced
- 1/2 tsp. crushed red pepper
- 2 cups CLASSICO Tomato and Basil Pasta Sauce
- 1/4 cup chopped pitted Kalamata olives
- 2 Tbsp. capers
- 2 Tbsp. KRAFT Grated Parmesan Cheese

Direction

- Cook pasta as directed on package.
- Meanwhile, heat dressing in large nonstick skillet on medium-high heat. Add chicken,

garlic and red pepper; cook 3 min., stirring frequently. Stir in pasta sauce, olives and capers; cook on medium heat 10 min. or until chicken is done, stirring occasionally.

- Drain pasta; transfer to serving plates. Top with sauce mixture and Parmesan.

Nutrition Information

- Calories: 460
- Protein: 35 g
- Total Fat: 9 g
- Sodium: 1080 mg
- Sugar: 0 g
- Fiber: 5 g
- Saturated Fat: 1.5 g
- Cholesterol: 70 mg
- Total Carbohydrate: 0 g

12. Apricot Pesto Glazed Chicken

Serving: 6 | Prep: 25mins | Cook: 20mins | Ready in: 45mins

Ingredients

- 6 small boneless skinless chicken breasts (1-1/2 lb.), pounded to 1/4-inch thickness
- 1 tsp. dried Italian seasoning
- 3/4 cup loosely packed fresh basil leaves
- 1/4 cup loosely packed fresh parsley
- 1/3 cup dried apricots
- 1/4 cup PLANTERS Slivered Almonds
- 2 cloves garlic, quartered
- 2 Tbsp. KRAFT 100% Grated Parmesan and Romano Cheese
- 2 Tbsp. oil
- 1/4 cup apricot preserves, melted

Direction

- Heat greased grill to medium heat.
- Place chicken, top sides down, on cutting board; sprinkle with Italian seasoning.

- Blend all remaining ingredients except preserves in blender until smooth; spread onto chicken to within 1/2 inch of sides. Fold in both long sides of each chicken breast, then roll up starting at one short end. Secure with wooden toothpicks.
- Grill, seam sides down, 18 to 20 min. or until done, turning after 10 min. and brushing with preserves for the last 5 min. Remove and discard toothpicks before serving chicken.

Nutrition Information

- Calories: 260
- Fiber: 2 g
- Protein: 27 g
- Total Fat: 10 g
- Cholesterol: 70 mg
- Sodium: 105 mg
- Saturated Fat: 2 g
- Total Carbohydrate: 0 g
- Sugar: 0 g

13. Asian Chicken With Broccoli & Chickpeas

Serving: 8 | Prep: 10mins | Cook: 50mins | Ready in: 1hours

Ingredients

- 8 bone-in chicken thighs (3 lb.)
- 1 can (14 oz.) chickpeas (garbanzo beans), rinsed
- 1 onion, thinly sliced
- 4 cups small broccoli florets
- 1/4 cup KRAFT Asian Toasted Sesame Dressing
- 2 Tbsp. KRAFT Original Barbecue Sauce
- 1/2 tsp. ground ginger
- 1 tsp. lite soy sauce

Direction

- Heat oven to 450°F.
- Place chicken on rimmed baking sheet sprayed with cooking spray. Bake on upper rack in oven 20 min.
- Place chickpeas, onions and broccoli on separate rimmed baking sheet sprayed with cooking spray; add to oven after 20 min. Meanwhile, mix remaining ingredients in small bowl.
- Bake chicken and vegetables 30 min. or until chicken is done (165°F) and vegetables are tender, brushing 3 Tbsp. dressing mixture on chicken for last 10 min. of baking time. Just before serving, drizzle remaining dressing mixture on vegetables; toss lightly.

Nutrition Information

- Calories: 330
- Saturated Fat: 4.5 g
- Sodium: 310 mg
- Protein: 28 g
- Sugar: 0 g
- Total Fat: 17 g
- Fiber: 4 g
- Cholesterol: 135 mg
- Total Carbohydrate: 0 g

14. BBQ Cherry Cola Chicken Legs

Serving: 0 | Prep: | Cook: |Ready in:

Ingredients

- 2 cups cherry-flavored cola
- 1 cup HEINZ BBQ Sauce Texas Bold & Spicy
- 2 lb. bone-in skinless drumsticks and thighs

Direction

- Mix cola and barbecue sauce until blended. Pour 1 cup cola mixture over chicken in medium bowl; toss to evenly coat chicken with cola mixture.

- Refrigerate 1 hour to marinate.
- Heat grill to medium-low heat. Remove chicken from marinade; discard marinade. Reserve 1-1/4 cups of the remaining cola mixture for serving with the cooked chicken. Grill chicken 30 min. or until done (165°F), turning and brushing occasionally with remaining cola mixture.
- Serve chicken topped with the reserved cola mixture.

Nutrition Information

- Calories: 0 g
- Saturated Fat: 0 g
- Cholesterol: 0 g
- Total Carbohydrate: 0 g
- Sugar: 0 g
- Protein: 0 g
- Fiber: 0 g
- Sodium: 0 g
- Total Fat: 0 g

15. BBQ Chicken & Rice Dinner

Serving: 4 | Prep: 25mins | Cook: | Ready in: 25mins

Ingredients

- 2 Tbsp. oil
- 4 small boneless skinless chicken breasts (1 lb.)
- 2 cups water
- 1 cup frozen corn
- 3/4 cup KRAFT Original Barbecue Sauce
- 2 cups instant brown rice, uncooked

Direction

- Heat oil in large nonstick skillet on medium-high heat. Add chicken; cook 6 to 7 min. on each side or until done (165°F). Remove chicken from skillet; cover to keep warm.
- Add water, corn and barbecue sauce to same skillet; stir. Bring to boil, stirring occasionally. Stir in rice.
- Top with chicken; cover. Cook on low heat 5 min.

Nutrition Information

- Calories: 480
- Fiber: 3 g
- Total Fat: 11 g
- Total Carbohydrate: 0 g
- Protein: 30 g
- Sugar: 0 g
- Cholesterol: 65 mg
- Saturated Fat: 2 g
- Sodium: 590 mg

16. BBQ Chicken & VELVEETA Casserole

Serving: 0 | Prep: 20mins | Cook: 10mins | Ready in: 30mins

Ingredients

- 1 pkg. (12 oz.) VELVEETA Shells & Cheese Dinner
- 1 can (15 oz.) kidney beans, rinsed
- 1 can (12.5 oz.) chunk white chicken breast, drained
- 1/3 cup milk
- 1/3 cup KRAFT Original Barbecue Sauce
- 3 slices OSCAR MAYER Fully Cooked Bacon, chopped

Direction

- Heat oven to 400°F.
- Prepare Dinner in large saucepan as directed on package. Stir in beans, chicken and milk.
- Spoon mixture into 8-inch square baking dish spayed with cooking spray. Top with barbecue sauce and bacon. Cover.

- Bake 10 min. or until heated through.

Nutrition Information

- Calories: 310
- Protein: 19 g
- Cholesterol: 35 mg
- Sugar: 8 g
- Total Carbohydrate: 37 g
- Fiber: 3 g
- Total Fat: 10 g
- Saturated Fat: 2.5 g
- Sodium: 850 mg

17. BBQ Chicken Fingers

Serving: 0 | Prep: 10mins | Cook: 20mins | Ready in: 30mins

Ingredients

- 1/4 cup KRAFT Grated Parmesan Cheese
- 1/4 tsp. ground black pepper
- 1/8 tsp. ground red pepper (cayenne)
- 1 lb. boneless skinless chicken breasts, cut into strips
- 1/2 cup sugar-free barbecue sauce
- 1/2 cup KRAFT 2% Milk Shredded Colby & Monterey Jack Cheeses
- 1 pkg. (6 oz.) baby spinach leaves (about 7 cups)

Direction

- Heat oven to 400°F.
- Mix Parmesan and seasonings. Add to chicken; toss to coat. Place in shallow pan.
- Bake 10 to 15 min. or until chicken is done; top with barbecue sauce and cheese. Bake 5 min. or until cheese is melted.
- Serve over spinach.

Nutrition Information

- Calories: 150
- Cholesterol: 55 mg
- Sodium: 490 mg
- Sugar: 0 g
- Total Fat: 5 g
- Saturated Fat: 2.5 g
- Total Carbohydrate: 0 g
- Fiber: 1 g
- Protein: 21 g

18. BBQ Chicken Soft Taco

Serving: 4 | Prep: 15mins | Cook: | Ready in: 15mins

Ingredients

- 1 tsp. oil
- 1 pkg. (6 oz.) OSCAR MAYER CARVING BOARD Hickory Smoked BBQ Chicken Breast Strips
- 1/2 cup chopped onions
- 4 flour tortillas (8 inch), warmed
- 1 fully ripe avocado, mashed
- 1 cup shredded lettuce
- 1 cup chopped tomatoes
- 1/4 cup drained pickled jalapeño slices
- 1/4 cup fresh cilantro leaves

Direction

- Heat oil in medium skillet on medium heat.
- Add chicken and onions; cook 2 to 3 min. or until heated through, stirring occasionally.
- Spread tortillas with avocado; top with chicken mixture and remaining ingredients.

Nutrition Information

- Calories: 310
- Cholesterol: 35 mg
- Sugar: 0 g
- Saturated Fat: 2 g
- Sodium: 740 mg
- Total Carbohydrate: 0 g

- Total Fat: 11 g
- Fiber: 5 g
- Protein: 17 g

19. BBQ Chicken Stir Fry

Serving: 4 | Prep: 25mins | Cook: | Ready in: 25mins

Ingredients

- 1 Tbsp. oil
- 1 lb. boneless skinless chicken breasts, cut into bite-size pieces
- 1/2 cup KRAFT Original Barbecue Sauce
- 2 Tbsp. lite soy sauce
- 1/2 tsp. garlic powder
- 1 pkg. (16 oz.) frozen mixed vegetables (broccoli, carrots, cauliflower), thawed, drained
- 2 cups hot cooked long-grain brown rice

Direction

- Heat oil in large skillet on medium-high heat. Add chicken; cook and stir 8 to 10 min. or until chicken is done.
- Stir in barbecue sauce, soy sauce and garlic powder. Add vegetables; cook 3 to 4 min. or until heated through, stirring occasionally.
- Serve over rice.

Nutrition Information

- Calories: 370
- Cholesterol: 65 mg
- Sodium: 830 mg
- Sugar: 0 g
- Total Fat: 7 g
- Saturated Fat: 1.5 g
- Fiber: 5 g
- Protein: 30 g
- Total Carbohydrate: 0 g

20. BBQ Chicken Strip Sandwich

Serving: 0 | Prep: 5mins | Cook: | Ready in: 5mins

Ingredients

- 2 tsp. GREY POUPON Savory Honey Mustard
- 1 kaiser roll, split
- 2 oz. OSCAR MAYER CARVING BOARD Hickory Smoked BBQ Chicken Breast Strips
- 1 slice cooked OSCAR MAYER Bacon
- 1 slice KRAFT Provolone Cheese
- 2 lettuce leaves
- 5 cucumber slices

Direction

- Spread mustard onto cut sides of roll.
- Fill with remaining ingredients.

Nutrition Information

- Calories: 440
- Total Carbohydrate: 47 g
- Protein: 34 g
- Sugar: 11 g
- Saturated Fat: 6 g
- Fiber: 5 g
- Cholesterol: 70 mg
- Sodium: 1120 mg
- Total Fat: 13 g

21. BBQ Chicken And Blue Cheese Pizza

Serving: 2 | Prep: 10mins | Cook: 10mins | Ready in: 20mins

Ingredients

- 1 ready-to-use baked pizza crust (8 inch)
- 2 Tbsp. KRAFT Hickory Smoke Barbecue Sauce

- 1/2 cup shredded rotisserie chicken
- 2 Tbsp. chopped red onions
- 2 Tbsp. ATHENOS Crumbled Blue Cheese
- 2 Tbsp. chopped fresh cilantro

Direction

- Heat oven to 425°F.
- Spread pizza crust with barbecue sauce; top with remaining ingredients.
- Place pizza directly on middle rack of oven.
- Bake 8 to 10 min. or until cheese is melted.

Nutrition Information

- Calories: 350
- Sugar: 0 g
- Sodium: 900 mg
- Fiber: 1 g
- Saturated Fat: 4.5 g
- Protein: 16 g
- Total Carbohydrate: 0 g
- Total Fat: 12 g
- Cholesterol: 50 mg

22. BBQ Chicken And Rice Skillet

Serving: 0 | Prep: 25mins | Cook: | Ready in: 25mins

Ingredients

- 1 tsp. oil
- 8 boneless skinless chicken thighs (1 lb.), cut into bite-size pieces
- 1-1/4 cups water
- 1/2 cup KRAFT Original Barbecue Sauce
- 1-1/2 cups instant white rice, uncooked
- 1 large red pepper, chopped
- 1 zucchini, chopped

Direction

- Heat oil in large nonstick skillet on medium-high heat. Add chicken; cook 3 min., stirring occasionally.
- Add water, barbecue sauce and rice. Bring to boil.
- Reduce heat to medium-low; sprinkle with pepper and zucchini. Cover. Simmer 10 min.

Nutrition Information

- Calories: 350
- Protein: 24 g
- Fiber: 2 g
- Total Fat: 10 g
- Cholesterol: 75 mg
- Sodium: 490 mg
- Saturated Fat: 2.5 g
- Total Carbohydrate: 0 g
- Sugar: 0 g

23. BBQ Grilled Chicken Pizza With Feta

Serving: 6 | Prep: 10mins | Cook: 12mins | Ready in: 22mins

Ingredients

- 1 ready-to-use baked pizza crust (12 inch)
- 1 cup KRAFT Shredded Mozzarella Cheese, divided
- 1 pkg. (6 oz.) OSCAR MAYER CARVING BOARD Flame Grilled Chicken Breast Strips, coarsely chopped
- 1/4 cup BULL'S-EYE Original Barbecue Sauce
- 1 pkg. (4 oz.) ATHENOS Traditional Crumbled Feta Cheese
- 1 small red onion, halved, sliced and separated into rings

Direction

- Heat oven to 450°F.
- Place pizza crust on baking sheet; sprinkle with 1/2 cup shredded cheese.

- Toss chicken with barbecue sauce; spoon onto crust. Top with feta, onions and remaining shredded cheese.
- Bake 10 to 12 min. or until shredded cheese is melted and crust is golden brown. Let stand 5 min. before cutting to serve.

Nutrition Information

- Calories: 300
- Fiber: 2 g
- Sugar: 5 g
- Total Carbohydrate: 32 g
- Total Fat: 11 g
- Protein: 20 g
- Saturated Fat: 6 g
- Cholesterol: 45 mg
- Sodium: 860 mg

24. BBQ Oven Baked Chicken Wings

Serving: 18 | Prep: 15mins | Cook: 20mins | Ready in: 35mins

Ingredients

- 3 lb. chicken wings, split at joints, tips removed
- 1 cup BULL'S-EYE Memphis Style Barbecue Sauce
- 1/2 cup KRAFT Classic Ranch Dressing
- 1/2 cup ATHENOS Crumbled Blue Cheese

Direction

- Heat oven to 450°F.
- Place wings in single layer in shallow foil-lined pan. Bake 20 min. or until done.
- Meanwhile, cook barbecue sauce and dressing in saucepan on medium heat 15 min., stirring occasionally.
- Place wings on large plate; sprinkle with cheese. Serve with sauce.

Nutrition Information

- Calories: 160
- Total Fat: 10 g
- Cholesterol: 35 mg
- Fiber: 0 g
- Sodium: 290 mg
- Saturated Fat: 3 g
- Protein: 10 g
- Total Carbohydrate: 6 g
- Sugar: 5 g

25. Bacon & Cheese Stuffed Chicken Breast

Serving: 4 | Prep: 20mins | Cook: 25mins | Ready in: 45mins

Ingredients

- 4 small boneless skinless chicken breasts (1 lb.)
- 1/4 cup KRAFT Shredded American & Cheddar Cheeses
- 2 Tbsp. OSCAR MAYER Real Bacon Bits
- 1 egg
- 1/4 cup chopped fresh cilantro
- 2 Tbsp. KRAFT Shredded Parmesan Cheese

Direction

- Heat oven to 350°F.
- Make 2-inch-long cut in one long side of each chicken breast to form pocket; fill with combined American cheese blend and bacon. Press cut edges of pockets together to seal.
- Whisk egg in pie plate. Combine cilantro and Parmesan in separate pie plate. Dip chicken, 1 breast at a time, in egg, then in cilantro mixture, turning to evenly coat both sides of each breast. Place in 8-inch square baking dish sprayed with cooking spray.
- Bake 20 to 25 min. or until chicken is done (165°F).

Nutrition Information

- Calories: 220
- Total Fat: 9 g
- Fiber: 0 g
- Saturated Fat: 4 g
- Total Carbohydrate: 0 g
- Protein: 31 g
- Sugar: 0 g
- Cholesterol: 140 mg
- Sodium: 250 mg

26. Bacon, Corn, Salsa And Chicken Roll Up

Serving: 0 | Prep: 30mins | Cook: | Ready in: 30mins

Ingredients

- 4 slices OSCAR MAYER Center Cut Bacon, cut into 1/2-inch pieces
- 2 green onions, finely chopped
- 1/4 cup finely chopped red peppers
- 1 pkg. (6 oz.) OSCAR MAYER CARVING BOARD Southwestern Seasoned Chicken Breast Strips
- 1/2 cup frozen corn
- 4 whole wheat tortillas (6 inch)
- 1/4 cup TACO BELL® Thick & Chunky Mild Salsa
- 1/4 cup KRAFT 2% Milk Shredded Colby & Monterey Jack Cheeses

Direction

- Cook bacon in medium skillet on medium heat 10 min. or until crisp, stirring occasionally. Use slotted spoon to transfer bacon to paper towels to drain. Discard all but 1 tsp. drippings from skillet.
- Add onions and peppers to skillet; cook and stir 5 min. or until crisp-tender. Add chicken and corn; cook 5 min. or until heated through, stirring occasionally. Stir in bacon.
- Spread tortillas with salsa; top with chicken mixture and cheese. Roll up.

Nutrition Information

- Calories: 290
- Sodium: 830 mg
- Total Carbohydrate: 25 g
- Cholesterol: 45 mg
- Protein: 21 g
- Total Fat: 13 g
- Saturated Fat: 5 g
- Sugar: 3 g
- Fiber: 4 g

27. Bacon Wrapped Chicken Appetizers

Serving: 5 | Prep: 15mins | Cook: 18mins | Ready in: 33mins

Ingredients

- 5 slices OSCAR MAYER Bacon
- 1/2 lb. boneless skinless chicken breasts, cut into 15 bite-size pieces
- 1/4 cup KRAFT Zesty Lime Vinaigrette Dressing
- 2 Tbsp. seedless raspberry jam

Direction

- Heat oven to 400°F.
- Place bacon in single layer on paper towel-covered microwaveable plate; cover with second paper towel. Microwave on HIGH 1-1/2 min. (Bacon will not be done.) Meanwhile, toss chicken with dressing.
- Cut bacon slices into thirds. Wrap 1 bacon piece around each chicken piece; secure with wooden toothpick. Place on baking sheet

sprayed with cooking spray. Drizzle with any remaining dressing.
- Bake 17 to 18 min. or until chicken is done (165°F) and bacon is crisp. Meanwhile, warm jam.
- Drizzle chicken with jam.

Nutrition Information

- Calories: 110
- Total Fat: 5 g
- Total Carbohydrate: 6 g
- Saturated Fat: 1 g
- Sodium: 240 mg
- Sugar: 6 g
- Fiber: 0 g
- Cholesterol: 30 mg
- Protein: 10 g

28. Baja Grilled Chicken Quesadillas

Serving: 4 | Prep: 45mins | Cook: | Ready in: 45mins

Ingredients

- 1/4 cup KRAFT Zesty Lime Vinaigrette Dressing
- 1/2 tsp. ground cumin
- 2 small boneless skinless chicken breasts (1/2 lb.), pounded to 1/2-inch thickness
- 1 ear corn on the cob, husks and silk removed
- 1/4 cup pico de gallo
- 4 flour tortillas (6 inch)
- 1 cup KRAFT Shredded Colby & Monterey Jack Cheeses

Direction

- Heat grill to medium heat.
- Mix dressing and cumin until blended; pour over chicken in shallow dish. Turn to evenly coat both sides of each breast. Refrigerate 15 min. to marinate. Meanwhile, grill corn 15 min. or until tender, turning occasionally.
- Remove corn from grill; set aside to cool. Remove chicken from marinade; discard marinade. Grill chicken 5 min. on each side or until done (165°F).
- Cut chicken into thin strips, then cut kernels off corn. Combine corn and pico de gallo.
- Top tortillas with corn mixture, cheese and chicken; fold in half. Grill 1 to 2 min. on each side or until cheese is melted and quesadillas are lightly browned on both sides.

Nutrition Information

- Calories: 300
- Total Fat: 14 g
- Sodium: 520 mg
- Total Carbohydrate: 0 g
- Fiber: 1 g
- Cholesterol: 60 mg
- Sugar: 0 g
- Saturated Fat: 6 g
- Protein: 21 g

29. Baked Chicken Tenderloin Recipe

Serving: 16 | Prep: 20mins | Cook: 20mins | Ready in: 40mins

Ingredients

- 3 Tbsp. low-fat buttermilk
- 3 Tbsp. hot pepper sauce, divided
- 3 Tbsp. HEINZ Distilled White Vinegar, divided
- 2 lb. chicken tenders
- 1-1/2 cups panko bread crumbs
- 2/3 cup BREAKSTONE'S Reduced Fat or KNUDSEN Light Sour Cream
- 2/3 cup ATHENOS Crumbled Blue Cheese
- 1/2 tsp. ground red pepper (cayenne)
- 2 cups carrot sticks

- 2 cups celery sticks

Direction

- Heat oven to 400°F.
- Whisk buttermilk and 2 Tbsp. each hot sauce and vinegar in large bowl until blended. Add chicken; toss to coat. Refrigerate 10 min., stirring occasionally.
- Meanwhile, place bread crumbs in shallow dish. Mix remaining hot sauce and vinegar in small bowl. Mix sour cream and blue cheese; refrigerate until ready to serve.
- Remove chicken from buttermilk mixture. Dip chicken, 1 piece at a time, in crumb mixture, turning to evenly coat. Place in single layer on baking sheet sprayed with cooking spray. (Discard any remaining buttermilk mixture and crumbs.) Sprinkle both sides of chicken evenly with red pepper.
- Bake 20 min.; transfer to platter. Drizzle with hot sauce mixture. Serve with carrots, celery and blue cheese dip.

Nutrition Information

- Calories: 140
- Sugar: 0 g
- Total Carbohydrate: 0 g
- Total Fat: 4.5 g
- Fiber: 0.9008 g
- Sodium: 180 mg
- Saturated Fat: 2 g
- Protein: 15 g
- Cholesterol: 40 mg

30. Baked Chicken Thigh Dinner

Serving: 8 | Prep: 50mins | Cook: | Ready in: 50mins

Ingredients

- 8 bone-in skinless chicken thighs (3-1/2 lb.)
- 1 tsp. black pepper
- 1/4 cup margarine, divided
- 1/2 tsp. smoked paprika
- 3 Tbsp. flour
- 1-1/2 cups fat-free milk
- 1 can (12 oz.) fat-free evaporated milk
- 1 pkg. (7 oz.) MAYBUD Smoked Gouda Cheese, shredded
- 3 oz. PHILADELPHIA Neufchatel Cheese, cubed
- 1 lb. rotini pasta, cooked
- 1-1/2 cups corn flakes, crushed
- 1/2 cup KRAFT Original Barbecue Sauce

Direction

- Heat oven to 350°F.
- Season chicken with pepper; place on rimmed baking sheet sprayed with cooking spray. Bake 15 min.
- Meanwhile, melt 2 Tbsp. margarine in medium saucepan. Whisk in paprika, then flour; cook 2 min., stirring constantly. Gradually stir in 2% milk, then evaporated milk; cook 2 to 3 min. or until thickened, stirring constantly. Add Gouda and Neufchatel; cook and stir 2 to 3 min. or until cheeses are completely melted and mixture is well blended. Pour over pasta in large bowl; toss until evenly coated.
- Spoon pasta mixture into 3-qt. casserole sprayed with cooking spray. Melt remaining margarine; mix with corn flake crumbs. Sprinkle over pasta mixture.
- Add pasta casserole to oven with chicken. Bake 30 min. or until pasta mixture is heated through and chicken is done (165°F).
- Microwave barbecue sauce in microwaveable bowl on HIGH 15 to 30 sec. or just until warmed; stir. Place chicken on platter; drizzle with barbecue sauce. Serve with pasta casserole.

Nutrition Information

- Calories: 730
- Sodium: 770 mg
- Total Carbohydrate: 73 g

- Fiber: 3 g
- Saturated Fat: 10 g
- Sugar: 17 g
- Protein: 50 g
- Total Fat: 26 g
- Cholesterol: 185 mg

31. Baked Garden Ratatouille

Serving: 6 | Prep: 30mins | Cook: 15mins | Ready in: 45mins

Ingredients

- 6 small boneless skinless chicken breasts (1-1/2 lb.)
- 1 Tbsp. olive oil
- 1/2 cup sliced onions
- 2 cloves garlic, minced
- 1 small eggplant, trimmed, cut lengthwise in half, then crosswise into 1/4-inch-thick slices
- 1 zucchini, trimmed, cut lengthwise in half, then crosswise into 1/4-inch-thick slices
- 1 cup cremini mushrooms, quartered
- 6 plum tomatoes, coarsely chopped
- 2 Tbsp. chopped fresh parsley, divided
- 2 tsp. each chopped fresh rosemary and thyme
- 1-1/2 cups KRAFT Shredded Mozzarella Cheese with a TOUCH OF PHILADELPHIA
- 1 loaf rustic white bread (12 oz.), sliced

Direction

- Heat oven to 375°F.
- Cook chicken in large nonstick ovenproof skillet on medium heat 4 min. on each side or until each breast is lightly browned on both sides. Remove from skillet; set aside.
- Add oil, onions and garlic to skillet; cook and stir 2 min. Stir in remaining vegetables, 1 Tbsp. parsley, rosemary and thyme; cook and stir 4 min. Top with chicken.
- Bake 15 min. or until chicken is done (165°F). Top with cheese; bake 5 min. or until melted. Serve with bread.

Nutrition Information

- Calories: 420
- Fiber: 4 g
- Total Fat: 13 g
- Saturated Fat: 5 g
- Total Carbohydrate: 38 g
- Sugar: 7 g
- Protein: 33 g
- Sodium: 520 mg
- Cholesterol: 85 mg

32. Balsamic Chicken Wrap With Mozzarella

Serving: 4 | Prep: 15mins | Cook: | Ready in: 15mins

Ingredients

- 1 cup each sliced plum and yellow tomatoes
- 1/2 cup KRAFT 2% Milk Shredded Mozzarella Cheese
- 1/4 cup chopped fresh basil
- 2 Tbsp. KRAFT Lite Balsamic Vinaigrette Dressing
- 4 whole wheat tortillas (8 inch)
- 2 Tbsp. MIRACLE WHIP Light Dressing
- 1 pkg. (6 oz.) OSCAR MAYER CARVING BOARD Flame Grilled Chicken Breast Strips

Direction

- Combine tomatoes, cheese, basil and vinaigrette dressing.
- Spread tortillas with MIRACLE WHIP; top with chicken and tomato mixture.
- Fold in opposite sides of each tortilla, then roll up burrito style.

Nutrition Information

- Calories: 270
- Cholesterol: 40 mg

- Saturated Fat: 1.5 g
- Fiber: 2 g
- Total Fat: 8 g
- Sugar: 0 g
- Protein: 21 g
- Total Carbohydrate: 0 g
- Sodium: 740 mg

- Saturated Fat: 4 g
- Sodium: 630 mg

33. Barbecue Chicken Nachos

Serving: 6 | Prep: 15mins | Cook: | Ready in: 15mins

Ingredients

- 6 cups tortilla chips (6 oz.)
- 1 cup shredded rotisserie chicken
- 1/4 cup BULL'S-EYE Original Barbecue Sauce
- 6 oz. VELVEETA, cut into 1/2-inch cubes
- 2 Tbsp. milk
- 1/2 cup chopped tomatoes
- 1 jalapeño pepper, sliced

Direction

- Spread chips onto platter.
- Combine chicken and barbecue sauce in small microwaveable bowl. Microwave on HIGH 45 sec. to 1 min. or until heated through; stir.
- Microwave VELVEETA and milk in separate small microwaveable bowl 1-1/2 min. or until VELVEETA is completely melted and sauce is well blended, stirring every 45 sec.
- Spoon chicken mixture over chips; top with VELVEETA sauce, tomatoes and peppers.

Nutrition Information

- Calories: 270
- Sugar: 7 g
- Total Carbohydrate: 28 g
- Fiber: 2 g
- Cholesterol: 35 mg
- Total Fat: 12 g
- Protein: 13 g

34. Basil Chicken Breasts

Serving: 4 | Prep: 15mins | Cook: 55mins | Ready in: 1hours10mins

Ingredients

- 4 small boneless skinless chicken breasts (1 lb.)
- 1/2 cup KRAFT Tuscan House Italian Dressing, divided
- 20 round buttery crackers, crushed
- 2 cloves garlic, minced
- 1/3 cup chopped fresh basil leaves, divided
- 4 tsp. KRAFT Grated Parmesan Cheese
- 1 can (14-1/2 oz.) Italian-style diced tomatoes, undrained

Direction

- Make 3-inch-long cut in one long side of each chicken breast to form pocket, being careful to not cut all the way through to opposite side of chicken. Place chicken in shallow dish; drizzle with 1/4 cup dressing. Refrigerate 30 min. to marinate.
- Heat oven to 375°F. Combine cracker crumbs, garlic, 1/4 cup basil and remaining dressing. Remove chicken from marinade; discard marinade. Spoon about 3 Tbsp. crumb mixture into pocket in each chicken breast; place on rimmed baking sheet sprayed with cooking spray.
- Bake 25 min. or until chicken is done (165°F). Meanwhile, combine cheese and remaining basil. About 5 min. before chicken is done, cook tomatoes in saucepan on medium heat until heated through, stirring occasionally.
- Drain tomatoes. Serve chicken topped with tomatoes and cheese mixture.

Nutrition Information

- Calories: 340
- Protein: 28 g
- Cholesterol: 70 mg
- Sodium: 970 mg
- Total Fat: 16 g
- Saturated Fat: 3.5 g
- Total Carbohydrate: 0 g
- Fiber: 1 g
- Sugar: 0 g

35. Basil Chicken With Roasted Tomatoes

Serving: 4 | Prep: 15mins | Cook: 30mins | Ready in: 45mins

Ingredients

- 4 small boneless skinless chicken breasts (1 lb.)
- 12 large fresh basil leaves, divided
- 2 oz. KRAFT Mozzarella Cheese, cut into 4 slices
- 4 large oil-packed sun-dried tomatoes, drained
- 1/4 cup KRAFT Balsamic Vinaigrette Dressing, divided
- 2-1/4 cups grape tomatoes, halved

Direction

- Heat oven to 400°F.
- Make cut in one long side of each chicken breast, being careful to not cut through to opposite side. Fill each pocket with 2 basil leaves and 1 each cheese slice and sun-dried tomato.
- Place chicken on one side of rimmed baking sheet sprayed with cooking spray; add tomatoes to other side of baking sheet. Brush chicken evenly with 1 Tbsp. dressing.
- Bake 30 min. or until chicken is done (165°F).
- Cut remaining basil leaves into thin slices. Top tomatoes with basil and remaining dressing; toss lightly. Serve chicken topped with tomato mixture.

Nutrition Information

- Calories: 260
- Cholesterol: 75 mg
- Sugar: 0 g
- Total Fat: 12 g
- Sodium: 360 mg
- Saturated Fat: 3 g
- Total Carbohydrate: 0 g
- Protein: 29 g
- Fiber: 2 g

36. Beer & BBQ Marinated Grilled Chicken Wings

Serving: 32 | Prep: 25mins | Cook: 40mins | Ready in: 1hours5mins

Ingredients

- 1 bottle (18 oz.) BULL'S-EYE Original Barbecue Sauce, divided
- 1 bottle (12 oz.) beer
- 1/4 cup olive oil
- 2 Tbsp. LEA & PERRINS Worcestershire Sauce
- 1 Tbsp. minced garlic
- 1-1/2 tsp. onion powder
- 5 lb. chicken wings, split at joints, tips removed

Direction

- Mix 1 cup barbecue sauce with next 5 ingredients until blended; pour over chicken in large bowl; toss to evenly coat chicken. Refrigerate 30 min. to marinate.
- Heat grill to medium-high heat. Remove chicken from marinade; discard marinade.
- Grill chicken 20 min. or until done, turning occasionally and brushing with remaining barbecue sauce for the last 10 min.

Nutrition Information

- Calories: 120

- Sodium: 150 mg
- Cholesterol: 25 mg
- Saturated Fat: 2 g
- Protein: 8 g
- Sugar: 4 g
- Fiber: 0 g
- Total Fat: 7 g
- Total Carbohydrate: 5 g

37. Berry Sweet Chicken Salad Sandwich

Serving: 0 | Prep: 10mins | Cook: | Ready in: 10mins

Ingredients

- 1/3 cup chopped grilled chicken breast
- 10 fresh sweet cherries, cut in half, pitted
- 2 Tbsp. finely chopped red onions
- 1 Tbsp. finely shredded fresh basil
- 1 Tbsp. KRAFT Light Mayo Reduced Fat Mayonnaise
- 1 ciabatta sandwich roll, split
- 1 cup torn salad greens
- 1 KRAFT Slim Cut Sharp Cheddar Cheese Slice

Direction

- Combine first 5 ingredients.
- Fill roll with salad greens, chicken mixture and cheese.

Nutrition Information

- Calories: 320
- Sugar: 0 g
- Saturated Fat: 2.5 g
- Total Fat: 10 g
- Sodium: 470 mg
- Protein: 23 g
- Cholesterol: 50 mg
- Total Carbohydrate: 0 g
- Fiber: 4 g

38. Better Than Ever Slow Cooker Cacciatore

Serving: 8 | Prep: 15mins | Cook: 7hours | Ready in: 7hours15mins

Ingredients

- 1 large onion, halved, thinly sliced
- 2 lb. boneless skinless chicken thighs
- 1 bay leaf
- 2 cans (6 oz. each) tomato paste
- 1/4 cup fat-free reduced-sodium chicken broth
- 3 cloves garlic, minced
- 1 tsp. dried basil leaves
- 1 tsp. dried oregano leaves
- 1/4 tsp. black pepper
- 1 pkg. (8 oz.) sliced fresh mushrooms
- 4 cups rotini pasta, uncooked
- 1 cup KRAFT Shredded Low-Moisture Part-Skim Mozzarella Cheese
- 1/3 cup chopped fresh parsley

Direction

- Place onions in slow cooker; top with chicken and bay leaf. Mix next 6 ingredients in medium bowl. Add mushrooms; stir to evenly coat. Spoon over chicken; cover with lid.
- Cook on LOW 7 to 9 hours (or on HIGH 4 to 5 hours). About 15 min. before ready to serve, cook pasta as directed on package, omitting salt.
- Drain pasta. Remove bay leaf from chicken mixture; discard. Spoon chicken mixture over pasta; top with cheese and parsley.

Nutrition Information

- Calories: 410
- Cholesterol: 80 mg
- Sodium: 530 mg
- Saturated Fat: 4 g

- Total Carbohydrate: 0 g
- Sugar: 0 g
- Protein: 32 g
- Total Fat: 12 g
- Fiber: 4 g

39. Bistro Chicken And Pasta

Serving: 4 | Prep: 30mins | Cook: | Ready in: 30mins

Ingredients

- 2 tsp. oil
- 3 cups sliced fresh mushrooms
- 1 onion, chopped
- 1 can (14-1/2 oz.) Italian-style diced tomatoes, undrained
- 1/4 cup KRAFT Lite Zesty Italian Dressing
- 4 small boneless skinless chicken breasts (1 lb.)
- 1/2 lb. spaghetti, uncooked
- 1 cup KRAFT 2% Milk Shredded Mozzarella Cheese
- 4 slices OSCAR MAYER Bacon, cooked, crumbled

Direction

- Heat oil in large nonstick skillet on medium-high heat. Add mushrooms and onions; cook 5 min., stirring occasionally. Stir in tomatoes and dressing.
- Add chicken; cover. Simmer on medium-low heat 12 min. or until chicken is done (165°F). Meanwhile, cook spaghetti as directed on package, omitting salt.
- Top chicken with cheese and bacon; simmer, covered, 5 min. or until cheese is melted. Drain spaghetti; place on platter. Top with chicken mixture.

Nutrition Information

- Calories: 520
- Fiber: 4 g

- Total Fat: 13 g
- Protein: 44 g
- Sugar: 0 g
- Saturated Fat: 4.5 g
- Cholesterol: 85 mg
- Total Carbohydrate: 0 g
- Sodium: 890 mg

40. Bistro Chicken Pasta Salad

Serving: 0 | Prep: 25mins | Cook: | Ready in: 25mins

Ingredients

- 1-1/3 cups penne pasta, cooked
- 1 cup quartered cherry tomatoes
- 1 pkg. (4 oz.) ATHENOS Traditional Crumbled Feta Cheese
- 1/2 cup prepared with less oil GOOD SEASONS Italian, Mild Italian or Zesty Italian Dressing Mix (see Tip)
- 1/3 cup loosely packed fresh basil leaves, cut into strips
- 1/4 cup chopped red onions
- 1/4 cup chopped sun-dried tomatoes
- 1/2 lb. boneless skinless chicken breasts, grilled, cut into 1/4-inch-thick slices

Direction

- Combine all ingredients except chicken.
- Top with chicken.

Nutrition Information

- Calories: 380
- Cholesterol: 55 mg
- Sodium: 690 mg
- Fiber: 3 g
- Sugar: 0 g
- Saturated Fat: 5 g
- Total Carbohydrate: 0 g
- Protein: 24 g
- Total Fat: 15 g

41. Blue Cheese, Chicken And Spinach Pizza

Serving: 8 | Prep: 20mins | Cook: | Ready in: 20mins

Ingredients

- 1 ready-to-use thin baked pizza crust (12 inch)
- 1 cup POLLY-O Natural Part Skim Ricotta Cheese
- 1/4 cup KRAFT ROKA Blue Cheese Dressing
- 1/2 cup KRAFT Grated Parmesan Cheese
- 1/4 tsp. ground red pepper (cayenne)
- 1 pkg. (10 oz.) frozen chopped spinach, thawed, drained and squeezed dry
- 1 pkg. (6 oz.) OSCAR MAYER CARVING BOARD Flame Grilled Chicken Breast Strips
- 1/2 cup coarsely chopped red bell peppers
- 2 tsp. lemon zest
- 2 tsp. dried tarragon leaves
- 1 clove garlic, minced
- 1/4 cup ATHENOS Crumbled Blue Cheese
- 1/4 cup sliced black olives
- 1/4 cup chopped fresh parsley

Direction

- Heat oven to 450°F.
- Place pizza crust on baking sheet. Combine ricotta, dressing, Parmesan and ground red pepper; spread onto pizza crust to within 1/2 inch of edge. Bake 5 min.
- Meanwhile, microwave spinach in microwaveable bowl on HIGH 3 min. Add chicken, bell peppers, lemon zest, tarragon and garlic; mix well. Microwave 1 min.; stir.
- Spread spinach mixture over pizza; top with blue cheese and olives.
- Bake 5 min. or until pizza is heated through and edge of crust is lightly browned. Sprinkle with parsley.

Nutrition Information

- Calories: 310
- Fiber: 3 g
- Sugar: 0 g
- Saturated Fat: 6 g
- Total Fat: 13 g
- Cholesterol: 35 mg
- Protein: 20 g
- Sodium: 750 mg
- Total Carbohydrate: 0 g

42. Breaded Chicken Salad With Berries

Serving: 8 | Prep: 30mins | Cook: | Ready in: 30mins

Ingredients

- 1 lemon
- 1/2 cup white whole wheat flour
- 1/4 cup finely chopped fresh basil, divided
- 2 Tbsp. KRAFT Grated Parmesan Cheese, divided
- 2 eggs
- 6 boneless skinless chicken thighs (1-1/2 lb.), cut into thin strips
- 2 Tbsp. oil
- 4 cups tightly packed mixed Italian greens
- 1 head radicchio, torn into bite-size pieces
- 1 cup sliced strawberries
- 1 cup raspberries
- 1/2 cup KRAFT Lite Balsamic Vinaigrette Dressing
- 1/4 cup PLANTERS Sliced Almonds, toasted

Direction

- Grate enough lemon peel to measure 1 Tbsp. Reserve 1 Tbsp. lemon juice for later use. Mix zest with flour, and half each of the basil and cheese in shallow dish. Whisk eggs in separate shallow dish until blended. Dip chicken, 1 strip at a time, in flour mixture, then in eggs; shake chicken gently to remove excess egg, then dip in flour again.

- Heat oil in large skillet on medium-high heat. Add chicken; cover. Cook on medium heat 6 to 8 min. or until done. Cool slightly.
- Meanwhile, toss salad greens with radicchio, berries, and remaining basil and cheese. Add dressing and reserved lemon juice; mix lightly.
- Spoon chicken over salad; sprinkle with nuts.

Nutrition Information

- Calories: 260
- Sugar: 0 g
- Fiber: 4 g
- Total Fat: 12 g
- Sodium: 270 mg
- Saturated Fat: 2.5 g
- Total Carbohydrate: 0 g
- Protein: 20 g
- Cholesterol: 125 mg

43. Brined BBQ Chicken Legs

Serving: 4 | Prep: 20mins | Cook: 2hours55mins | Ready in: 3hours15mins

Ingredients

- 2 cups water
- 1 small onion, quartered
- 2 Tbsp. kosher salt
- 2 WYLER'S Instant Bouillon Beef Flavored Cubes
- 1 Tbsp. peppercorns
- 1 tsp. herbes de Provence
- 1 large clove garlic, quartered
- 2 cups ice water
- 2 lb. bone-in chicken leg quarters
- 1/2 cup HEINZ BBQ Sauce Memphis Sweet & Spicy

Direction

- Bring first 7 ingredients to boil in large saucepan on high heat, stirring occasionally. Remove from heat. Add ice water; stir until ice is melted.
- Place chicken in plastic brining bag. Slowly pour seasoned brining mixture over chicken in bag; tightly close bag. Refrigerate 2 hours.
- Heat grill to medium heat. Remove chicken from bag; discard bag and brine. Pat chicken dry with paper towels. Place chicken in single layer on center of large sheet heavy-duty foil; fold to make packet. Grill 40 min. Remove chicken from foil; discard foil.
- Return chicken to grill; brush with half the barbecue sauce. Grill 10 to 15 min. or until chicken is done (165ºF), turning and brushing occasionally with remaining barbecue sauce.

Nutrition Information

- Calories: 400
- Total Fat: 19 g
- Total Carbohydrate: 13 g
- Protein: 42 g
- Sodium: 940 mg
- Sugar: 12 g
- Saturated Fat: 5 g
- Cholesterol: 225 mg
- Fiber: 0 g

44. Broccoli, Cauliflower & Chicken Salad

Serving: 0 | Prep: 15mins | Cook: 3hours | Ready in: 3hours15mins

Ingredients

- 2 cups each broccoli and cauliflower florets
- 1 red pepper, cut into strips
- 1-1/2 cups chopped cooked boneless skinless chicken breast s
- 1 cup cherry tomatoes, halved
- 1/2 cup KRAFT Lite Ranch Dressing
- 1 cup KRAFT Natural 2% Milk Colby & Monterey Jack Cheese Crumbles

- 4 slices OSCAR MAYER Bacon, cooked, crumbled

Direction

- Combine vegetables, chicken and tomatoes in large bowl. Add dressing; toss to coat.
- Add cheese and bacon; mix lightly.
- Refrigerate several hours or until chilled.

Nutrition Information

- Calories: 310
- Total Carbohydrate: 15 g
- Saturated Fat: 6 g
- Fiber: 3 g
- Cholesterol: 75 mg
- Sodium: 820 mg
- Total Fat: 15 g
- Protein: 28 g
- Sugar: 5 g

45. Buffalo Chicken Party Sandwiches

Serving: 12 | Prep: 20mins | Cook: | Ready in: 20mins

Ingredients

- 4 cups shredded cooked chicken
- 1/2 cup Buffalo wing sauce
- 1/4 cup water
- 1/4 cup KRAFT Real Mayo Mayonnaise
- 1/4 cup KRAFT Classic Ranch Dressing
- 6 stalks celery, finely chopped
- 1/4 cup KRAFT Natural Blue Cheese Crumbles
- 12 small sandwich buns (3 inch), split
- 1-1/2 cups KRAFT Shredded Cheddar Cheese

Direction

- Cook chicken, sauce and water in saucepan on medium heat 5 min. or until heated through, stirring occasionally.
- Meanwhile, mix mayo, dressing, celery and blue cheese.
- Fill buns with chicken mixture, cheddar and mayo mixture.

Nutrition Information

- Calories: 300
- Fiber: 1 g
- Saturated Fat: 5 g
- Protein: 21 g
- Sodium: 650 mg
- Total Carbohydrate: 19 g
- Sugar: 4 g
- Total Fat: 16 g
- Cholesterol: 60 mg

46. Buffalo Chicken Pinwheels

Serving: 0 | Prep: 10mins | Cook: | Ready in: 10mins

Ingredients

- 2 flour tortillas (6 inch)
- 1/4 cup PHILADELPHIA Whipped Cream Cheese Spread
- 4 tsp. Buffalo wing sauce
- 1/4 cup shredded carrots
- 1/4 cup finely chopped celery
- 6 slices OSCAR MAYER Natural Slow Roasted Chicken Breast

Direction

- Spread tortillas with cream cheese spread; drizzle with wing sauce.
- Top with vegetables and chicken; roll up tightly.
- Cut each roll-up into 6 slices to serve.

Nutrition Information

- Calories: 130
- Total Carbohydrate: 0 g

- Fiber: 2 g
- Total Fat: 6 g
- Protein: 6 g
- Sugar: 0 g
- Cholesterol: 20 mg
- Saturated Fat: 3 g
- Sodium: 550 mg

47. Buffalo Chicken Salad

Serving: 0 | Prep: 15mins | Cook: | Ready in: 15mins

Ingredients

- 1 lb. boneless skinless chicken breasts, cut into strips
- 1 Tbsp. plus 1 tsp. hot pepper sauce, divided
- 1 pkg. (10 oz.) torn salad greens
- 2 stalks celery, sliced
- 2 carrots, peeled, sliced
- 1/2 cup KRAFT Lite Ranch Dressing
- 1/4 cup ATHENOS Crumbled Blue Cheese

Direction

- Heat large nonstick skillet on medium-high heat. Add chicken; cook and stir 4 to 5 min. or until done. Stir in 1 Tbsp. hot sauce.
- Cover platter with salad greens; top with celery and carrots. Drizzle with dressing.
- Top with chicken, cheese and remaining hot sauce.

Nutrition Information

- Calories: 170
- Saturated Fat: 2 g
- Total Fat: 7 g
- Sodium: 440 mg
- Fiber: 2 g
- Cholesterol: 55 mg
- Total Carbohydrate: 0 g
- Sugar: 0 g
- Protein: 18 g

48. Buffalo Chicken Tostada

Serving: 8 | Prep: 20mins | Cook: | Ready in: 20mins

Ingredients

- 1/4 cup KRAFT Zesty CATALINA Dressing
- 1/4 cup Buffalo wing sauce
- 2 cups shredded cooked chicken
- 8 tostada shells
- 1 can (16 oz.) TACO BELL® 99% Fat Free Refried Beans
- 2 cups loosely packed torn mixed salad greens
- 1 avocado, cut into 8 wedges
- 8 radishes, sliced
- 1 pkg. (4 oz.) ATHENOS Traditional Crumbled Feta Cheese
- 1/2 cup BREAKSTONE'S or KNUDSEN Sour Cream

Direction

- Mix dressing and wing sauce in medium bowl. Add chicken; toss to evenly coat.
- Spread tostada shells with beans; cover with salad greens and chicken mixture.
- Top with remaining ingredients.

Nutrition Information

- Calories: 350
- Sodium: 640 mg
- Saturated Fat: 6 g
- Cholesterol: 50 mg
- Sugar: 0 g
- Total Fat: 18 g
- Fiber: 4 g
- Total Carbohydrate: 0 g
- Protein: 18 g

49. Butternut Squash And Chicken Pot Pie

Serving: 6 | Prep: 45mins | Cook: 30mins | Ready in: 1hours15mins

Ingredients

- 1 Tbsp. oil
- 1-1/2 cups chopped peeled butternut squash
- 1 onion, chopped
- 2 stalks celery, chopped
- 2 Tbsp. chopped fresh sage
- 1/2 tsp. pepper
- 1 lb. boneless skinless chicken breasts, cut into bite-size pieces
- 1 pkg. (8 oz.) fresh mushrooms, quartered
- 2 Tbsp. butter
- 1/4 cup flour
- 2 cups fat-free reduced-sodium chicken broth
- 1/2 cup KRAFT Sweet Brown Sugar Barbecue Sauce
- 1 Tbsp. Dijon mustard
- 1/2 cup frozen peas
- 1/2 cup BREAKSTONE'S or KNUDSEN Sour Cream
- 1 frozen puff pastry sheet (1/2 of 17.3-oz. pkg.), thawed
- 1 egg, beaten

Direction

- Heat oil in large skillet on medium-high heat. Add squash, onions, celery, sage and pepper; stir. Cook 5 min. or until vegetables begin to soften, stirring occasionally. Add chicken and mushrooms; cook 8 to 10 min. or until chicken is done, stirring frequently. Spoon chicken mixture into bowl.
- Melt butter in same skillet on low heat. Add flour; mix well. Cook 2 min. or until hot and bubbly, stirring constantly. Gradually stir in broth, barbecue sauce and mustard. Bring to boil on medium heat, stirring constantly; cook 2 min. or until thickened, stirring occasionally. Remove from heat; stir in peas, sour cream and chicken mixture.
- Spoon into 11x7-inch baking dish sprayed with cooking spray.
- Heat oven to 425°F. Roll pastry on lightly floured surface to 12x8-inch rectangle. Brush rim of baking dish with some of the beaten egg; place pastry over filling. Press edges of pastry to rim of dish to secure. Brush top of pastry with remaining egg; cut several slits in pastry to vent. Place on foil-covered rimmed baking sheet.
- Bake 30 min. or until pastry is golden brown and filling begins to bubble through slits.

Nutrition Information

- Calories: 530
- Total Fat: 29 g
- Sodium: 650 mg
- Sugar: 0 g
- Total Carbohydrate: 0 g
- Cholesterol: 100 mg
- Fiber: 3 g
- Saturated Fat: 10 g
- Protein: 25 g

50. CATALINA® Asian Chicken Salad

Serving: 0 | Prep: 20mins | Cook: 8mins | Ready in: 28mins

Ingredients

- 3/4 cup KRAFT Fat Free CATALINA Dressing
- 1/4 cup soy sauce
- 1/2 tsp. crushed red pepper
- 1 lb. boneless skinless chicken breasts, cut into strips
- 1 pkg. (10 oz.) salad greens
- 1 can (8 oz.) sliced water chestnuts, drained
- 1/2 cup pea pods, blanched
- 1/2 cup shredded carrots
- 1/2 cup bean sprouts

Direction

- Mix dressing, soy sauce and crushed red pepper in large skillet.
- Add chicken; cook and stir over medium heat until chicken is cooked through. Cool completely.
- Toss chicken mixture with remaining ingredients. Serve immediately.

Nutrition Information

- Calories: 170
- Total Carbohydrate: 0 g
- Sugar: 0 g
- Protein: 19 g
- Fiber: 3 g
- Total Fat: 2.5 g
- Cholesterol: 45 mg
- Sodium: 1060 mg
- Saturated Fat: 0.5 g

51. Cacciatore Style Chicken Bake

Serving: 6 | Prep: 15mins | Cook: 30mins | Ready in: 45mins

Ingredients

- 1-2/3 cups hot water
- 1 pkg. (6 oz.) STOVE TOP Stuffing Mix for Chicken
- 1-1/2 lb. boneless skinless chicken breasts, cut into bite-size pieces
- 1 small each green and red pepper, chopped
- 1 small onion, chopped
- 1-1/2 cups CLASSICO Tomato and Basil Pasta Sauce

Direction

- Heat oven to 425°F.
- Add hot water to stuffing mix; stir just until moistened.
- Combine chicken and vegetables in 13x9-inch baking dish sprayed with cooking spray. Cover with pasta sauce; top with stuffing.
- Bake 30 min. or until casserole is heated through and chicken is done.

Nutrition Information

- Calories: 280
- Protein: 29 g
- Total Carbohydrate: 0 g
- Saturated Fat: 1 g
- Sugar: 0 g
- Cholesterol: 70 mg
- Sodium: 740 mg
- Fiber: 3 g
- Total Fat: 5 g

52. Cajun Chicken Lasagna With Andouille Sausage

Serving: 16 | Prep: 45mins | Cook: 1hours | Ready in: 1hours45mins

Ingredients

- 16 whole wheat lasagna noodles, uncooked
- 1 lb. andouille sausage links, quartered lengthwise, then sliced crosswise
- 1 lb. boneless skinless chicken thighs, cut into bite-size pieces
- 2 tsp. Cajun seasoning
- 1 small onion, chopped
- 1 stalk celery, chopped
- 1/2 cup chopped green peppers
- 2 cloves garlic, finely chopped
- 2 jars (15 oz. each) CLASSICO Mushroom Alfredo Pasta Sauce, divided
- 1/4 cup KRAFT Grated Parmesan Cheese, divided
- 1 pkg. (7 oz.) KRAFT 2% Milk Shredded Mozzarella Cheese, divided

Direction

- Heat oven to 350°F.
- Cook noodles as directed on package, omitting salt. Meanwhile, cook sausage, chicken and Cajun seasoning in large skillet 8 min. or until chicken is no longer pink, stirring occasionally. Remove meat mixture from skillet with slotted spoon; set aside. Discard all but 1 Tbsp. drippings from skillet. Add vegetables and garlic to reserved drippings; cook and stir 4 to 5 min. or until vegetables are crisp-tender. Stir in meat mixture, 2 cups pasta sauce and 2 Tbsp. Parmesan.
- Drain noodles. Spread 1/2 cup of the remaining pasta sauce onto bottom of 13x9-inch baking dish sprayed with cooking spray; cover with layers of 4 noodles, 1/3 of the meat mixture and 1/2 cup mozzarella. Repeat all layers twice. Cover with remaining noodles, pasta sauce, mozzarella and Parmesan. Cover with foil sprayed with cooking spray.
- Bake 1 hour or until heated through. Let stand 15 min. before cutting to serve.

Nutrition Information

- Calories: 230
- Protein: 15 g
- Saturated Fat: 6 g
- Total Fat: 13 g
- Cholesterol: 75 mg
- Fiber: 2 g
- Sodium: 570 mg
- Sugar: 0 g
- Total Carbohydrate: 0 g

53. Caribbean Coconut Chicken Bites

Serving: 0 | Prep: 15mins | Cook: | Ready in: 15mins

Ingredients

- 1/4 cup vanilla low-fat yogurt
- 1/8 tsp. lime zest
- 1/2 tsp. fresh lime juice
- 1/8 tsp. Caribbean seasoning
- 36 RITZ Crackers
- 1/2 avocado, cut into 36 thin slices, then cut in half
- 1/2 lb. cooked boneless skinless chicken breasts, thinly sliced, cut into 36 pieces
- 2 Tbsp. BAKER'S ANGEL FLAKE Coconut, toasted
- 1 Tbsp. chopped cilantro

Direction

- Mix first 4 ingredients. Refrigerate 20 min. or until ready to serve.
- Top crackers with avocados, chicken, yogurt mixture, coconut and cilantro.

Nutrition Information

- Calories: 70
- Sodium: 70 mg
- Fiber: 1 g
- Sugar: 0 g
- Total Carbohydrate: 0 g
- Saturated Fat: 1 g
- Cholesterol: 10 mg
- Protein: 5 g
- Total Fat: 3 g

54. Champion Chicken Parmesan

Serving: 0 | Prep: 5mins | Cook: 20mins | Ready in: 25mins

Ingredients

- 1 pkg. (11.5 oz.) frozen breaded chicken patties
- 1-1/2 cups CLASSICO Tomato and Basil Pasta Sauce
- 1 cup KRAFT Shredded Mozzarella Cheese
- 1 Tbsp. KRAFT Grated Parmesan Cheese

Direction

- Place chicken in single layer in large skillet; top with sauce. Cover; cook on medium heat 15 min.
- Sprinkle with mozzarella; cover. Remove from heat; let stand 5 min.
- Top with Parmesan.

Nutrition Information

- Calories: 370
- Saturated Fat: 7 g
- Cholesterol: 60 mg
- Protein: 22 g
- Total Carbohydrate: 0 g
- Sugar: 0 g
- Total Fat: 22 g
- Sodium: 920 mg
- Fiber: 2 g

55. Cheddar Chicken And Potatoes

Serving: 4 | Prep: 5mins | Cook: 22mins | Ready in: 27mins

Ingredients

- 4 slices OSCAR MAYER Bacon
- 4 small boneless skinless chicken breasts (1 lb.)
- 4 cups (1 lb.) frozen diced potatoes with peppers and onions, thawed
- 4 oz. (1 cup) KRAFT 2% Milk Shredded Sharp Cheddar Cheese

Direction

- Cook bacon in large nonstick skillet on medium heat 5 min. or until crisp. Remove bacon from skillet to paper towel; discard drippings in skillet.
- Add chicken to skillet; cook 5 min. on each side or until done (165ºF). Remove chicken from skillet; cover to keep warm. Crumble bacon. Add to skillet with potatoes; cook and stir 5 min. or until heated through.
- Place chicken over potatoes; top with cheese. Cover; cook 2 min. or until cheese is melted.

Nutrition Information

- Calories: 310
- Protein: 35 g
- Total Fat: 11 g
- Saturated Fat: 5 g
- Sodium: 460 mg
- Cholesterol: 90 mg
- Fiber: 2 g
- Total Carbohydrate: 18 g
- Sugar: 0 g

56. Cheddar, Bacon And Vegetable Chopped Salad

Serving: 0 | Prep: 15mins | Cook: 3hours | Ready in: 3hours15mins

Ingredients

- 1-1/2 cups chopped cooked skinless chicken breasts
- 2 cups each broccoli and cauliflower florets
- 1 red pepper, cut into strips
- 1 cup cherry tomatoes, halved
- 1/2 cup KRAFT Balsamic Vinaigrette Dressing
- 1 cup KRAFT Natural Sharp Cheddar Cheese Crumbles
- 4 slices cooked OSCAR MAYER Bacon, crumbled

Direction

- Combine chicken and vegetables in large bowl. Add dressing; toss to coat.
- Add cheese and bacon; mix lightly.
- Refrigerate several hours or until chilled.

Nutrition Information

- Calories: 200

- Total Fat: 13 g
- Saturated Fat: 4.5 g
- Cholesterol: 45 mg
- Fiber: 2 g
- Protein: 15 g
- Sugar: 0 g
- Sodium: 400 mg
- Total Carbohydrate: 0 g

57. Cheese & Chicken Empanadas

Serving: 6 | Prep: 40mins | Cook: 35mins | Ready in: 1hours15mins

Ingredients

- 1 cup flour
- 1/2 tsp. CALUMET Baking Powder
- 1/2 tsp. salt
- 1/4 cup shortening
- 1/4 cup plus 1 Tbsp. cold water, divided
- 1/2 lb. boneless skinless chicken breast s, cut into 1/2-inch pieces
- 1/2 cup chopped onion s
- 1/2 cup chopped green pepper s
- 1/2 cup salsa
- 1 cup KRAFT Mexican Style Shredded Four Cheese with a TOUCH OF PHILADELPHIA
- 1 egg

Direction

- Mix flour, baking powder and salt in medium bowl. Cut in shortening with pastry blender or 2 knives until mixture resembles coarse crumbs. Gradually add 1/4 cup water, stirring until mixture forms ball. Knead dough on lightly floured surface 5 min. or until smooth and elastic. Wrap tightly in plastic wrap; refrigerate while preparing empanada filling.
- Cook chicken, onions and peppers in nonstick skillet on medium-high heat 5 min. or until chicken is no longer pink. Add salsa; cook and stir 2 min. Cool completely. Heat oven to 375ºF. Divide dough into 6 pieces. Roll out each piece on lightly floured surface to 7-inch round; place on parchment-covered baking sheet.
- Stir cheese into chicken mixture; spoon about 1/2 cup onto half of each dough round. Beat egg and remaining water; brush onto edges of dough rounds. Fold in half to enclose filling. Press tops lightly to remove excess air; seal edges with fork.
- Brush tops with remaining egg. Bake 18 to 20 min. or until golden brown.

Nutrition Information

- Calories: 290
- Fiber: 2 g
- Total Carbohydrate: 20 g
- Cholesterol: 70 mg
- Total Fat: 16 g
- Sodium: 530 mg
- Sugar: 2 g
- Protein: 16 g
- Saturated Fat: 6 g

58. Cheesy BBQ Chicken Salad Pizza

Serving: 6 | Prep: 10mins | Cook: 12mins | Ready in: 22mins

Ingredients

- 1 ready-to-use baked pizza crust (12 inch)
- 1/4 cup KRAFT Original Barbecue Sauce
- 1-1/2 cups KRAFT Shredded Cheddar Cheese
- 1 pkg. (10 oz.) mixed salad greens
- 1 cup chopped cooked chicken
- 1 small red onion, sliced
- 1/2 cup KRAFT Classic Ranch Dressing

Direction

- Heat oven to 400ºF.

- Spread pizza crust with barbecue sauce; top with cheese. Bake 12 min. or until cheese is melted.
- Toss salad greens with remaining ingredients.
- Serve pizza wedges topped with salad.

Nutrition Information

- Calories: 410
- Total Carbohydrate: 34 g
- Saturated Fat: 8 g
- Sodium: 840 mg
- Protein: 18 g
- Total Fat: 22 g
- Sugar: 6 g
- Cholesterol: 55 mg
- Fiber: 2 g

59. Cheesy BBQ Chicken Wraps

Serving: 4 | Prep: 30mins | Cook: | Ready in: 30mins

Ingredients

- 4 small boneless skinless chicken breasts (1 lb.)
- 2 green peppers, cut into wedges
- 1 onion, cut into 4 slices
- 1/2 cup KRAFT Original Barbecue Sauce
- 4 flour tortillas (8 inch)
- 1 cup KRAFT Mexican Style Finely Shredded Four Cheese

Direction

- Heat greased grill to medium heat.
- Grill chicken 6 to 7 min. on each side and grill vegetables 4 to 5 min. on each side or until chicken is done (165°F) and vegetables are crisp-tender, brushing frequently with barbecue sauce for the last few minutes.
- Cut chicken and vegetables into thin strips; place down centers of tortillas. Top with cheese; roll up.

Nutrition Information

- Calories: 460
- Cholesterol: 90 mg
- Total Carbohydrate: 0 g
- Protein: 35 g
- Fiber: 3 g
- Sugar: 0 g
- Sodium: 930 mg
- Total Fat: 14 g
- Saturated Fat: 6 g

60. Cheesy Bacon Orchard Chicken

Serving: 6 | Prep: 20mins | Cook: 45hours | Ready in: 45hours20mins

Ingredients

- 1 Tbsp. olive oil
- 1/2 cup flour
- 1/2 tsp. ground black pepper
- 1 broiler-fryer chicken (3-1/2 lb.), cut up
- 1 lb. sweet potatoes (about 2), cut into 1/2-inch-thick slices
- 2 cloves garlic, minced
- 1 Tbsp. chopped fresh thyme
- 1 pkt. SHAKE 'N BAKE Seasoned Panko Seasoned Coating Mix
- 2 Tbsp. OSCAR MAYER Real Bacon Bits
- 1/4 tsp. smoked paprika
- 1 cup KRAFT Finely Shredded Colby & Monterey Jack Cheeses
- 2 Fuji apples, cut into 1/2-inch-thick slices

Direction

- Heat oven to 375°F.
- Heat oil in large heavy ovenproof skillet on medium heat. Meanwhile, combine flour and pepper. Add chicken, 1 piece at a time, to flour mixture, turning to evenly coat both sides of each piece. Add to skillet; cook 4 min. on each side or until evenly browned on both sides.

- Remove chicken from skillet; set aside. Add potatoes, garlic and thyme to skillet; cook 2 min., stirring frequently. Return chicken to skillet; cover with foil.
- Bake 30 min. Meanwhile, combine coating mix, bacon and paprika in medium bowl. Stir in cheese.
- Top chicken with apples and cheese mixture. Bake, uncovered, 10 to 15 min. or until potatoes and apples are tender, and chicken is done (165°F).

Nutrition Information

- Calories: 480
- Saturated Fat: 8 g
- Total Fat: 23 g
- Sodium: 520 mg
- Total Carbohydrate: 0 g
- Protein: 36 g
- Fiber: 4 g
- Sugar: 0 g
- Cholesterol: 110 mg

61. Cheesy Chicken & Salsa Skillet

Serving: 0 | Prep: 30mins | Cook: | Ready in: 30mins

Ingredients

- 2 cups multi-grain penne pasta, uncooked
- 1 lb. boneless skinless chicken breasts, cut into bite-size pieces
- 1-1/4 cups TACO BELL® Thick & Chunky Salsa
- 1 cup frozen corn
- 1 large green pepper, cut into strips
- 1 cup KRAFT Mexican Style 2% Milk Finely Shredded Four Cheese

Direction

- Cook pasta as directed on package, omitting salt.
- Meanwhile, cook and stir chicken in large nonstick skillet sprayed with cooking spray on medium heat 2 min. Stir in salsa, corn and peppers. Bring to boil. Simmer on medium-low heat 10 min. or until chicken is done, stirring occasionally.
- Drain pasta. Add to chicken mixture; mix lightly. Top with cheese. Remove from heat; cover. Let stand 1 min. or until cheese is melted.

Nutrition Information

- Calories: 460
- Sugar: 6 g
- Total Carbohydrate: 52 g
- Protein: 43 g
- Sodium: 830 mg
- Total Fat: 10 g
- Saturated Fat: 4 g
- Cholesterol: 85 mg
- Fiber: 6 g

62. Cheesy Chicken & Stuffing Skillet

Serving: 6 | Prep: 20mins | Cook: | Ready in: 20mins

Ingredients

- 6 small boneless skinless chicken breasts (1-1/2 lb.)
- 3 cups frozen mixed vegetables (carrots, corn, green beans, peas)
- 1-1/3 cups water
- 1/2 tsp. dry mustard
- 1 pkg. (6 oz.) STOVE TOP Stuffing Mix for Chicken
- 1 cup KRAFT Shredded Sharp Cheddar Cheese

Direction

- Cook chicken in large skillet sprayed with cooking spray on medium-high heat 2 to 3 min. on each side or until evenly browned. Remove from skillet.
- Add vegetables, water and mustard to skillet; bring to boil. Add stuffing mix; stir just until moistened.
- Top with chicken and cheese; cover. Cook on low heat 5 min. or until chicken is done (165°F) and cheese is melted.

Nutrition Information

- Calories: 360
- Cholesterol: 85 mg
- Fiber: 3 g
- Protein: 33 g
- Saturated Fat: 5 g
- Sugar: 5 g
- Sodium: 590 mg
- Total Carbohydrate: 31 g
- Total Fat: 10 g

63. Cheesy Chicken BLT Club Sandwich

Serving: 4 | Prep: 15mins | Cook: | Ready in: 15mins

Ingredients

- 12 slices multi-grain bread, toasted
- 1/4 cup MIRACLE WHIP Dressing
- 4 KRAFT Big Slice Mild Cheddar Cheese Slices, cut in half
- 16 slices OSCAR MAYER Deli Fresh Rotisserie Seasoned Chicken Breast
- 4 lettuce leaves
- 1 tomato, cut into 4 slices
- 8 slices cooked OSCAR MAYER Bacon

Direction

- Spread 3 toast slices with dressing; top each with cheese piece. Cover with chicken, lettuce and second toast slice.
- Top with remaining cheese pieces, tomatoes and bacon. Cover with remaining toast slices.
- Cut into quarters. Secure with decorative picks, if desired.

Nutrition Information

- Calories: 450
- Sodium: 1210 mg
- Total Carbohydrate: 0 g
- Total Fat: 21 g
- Saturated Fat: 8 g
- Protein: 27 g
- Cholesterol: 60 mg
- Fiber: 6 g
- Sugar: 0 g

64. Cheesy Chicken Pot Pie

Serving: 8 | Prep: 10mins | Cook: 25mins | Ready in: 35mins

Ingredients

- 3 cups chopped cooked chicken
- 1 pkg. (16 oz.) frozen mixed vegetables (carrots, corn, green beans, peas), thawed, drained
- 1/2 lb. (8 oz.) VELVEETA, cut into 1/2-inch cubes
- 1 can (10-3/4 oz.) reduced-sodium condensed cream of chicken soup
- 1 can (8 oz.) refrigerated crescent dinner rolls

Direction

- Heat oven to 375°F.
- Combine first 4 ingredients in 13x9-inch baking dish.
- Unroll dough; place over chicken mixture.

- Bake 20 to 25 min. or until crust is golden brown.

Nutrition Information

- Calories: 350
- Cholesterol: 65 mg
- Fiber: 1 g
- Protein: 24 g
- Total Fat: 16 g
- Sodium: 790 mg
- Total Carbohydrate: 25 g
- Saturated Fat: 7 g
- Sugar: 7 g

65. Cheesy Chicken Taco Casserole

Serving: 6 | Prep: 35mins | Cook: 15mins | Ready in: 50mins

Ingredients

- 1 Tbsp. oil
- 1-1/2 lb. boneless skinless chicken breasts, cut into bite-size pieces
- 2 green onions, chopped
- 1 pkg. (1 oz.) TACO BELL® Reduced Sodium Taco Seasoning Mix
- 1 can (14.5 oz.) fire-roasted diced tomatoes with garlic, undrained
- 1/4 cup water
- 1/2 cup frozen roasted corn
- 1/2 cup BREAKSTONE'S Reduced Fat or KNUDSEN Light Sour Cream
- 1/4 cup chopped fresh cilantro, divided
- 10 whole wheat tortillas (6 inch)
- 1 pkg. (7 oz.) KRAFT 2% Milk Shredded Colby & Monterey Jack Cheeses, divided
- 1/2 cup TACO BELL® Verde Salsa

Direction

- Heat oven to 350°F.
- Heat oil in large nonstick skillet on medium heat. Add chicken and onions; cook and stir 8 to 10 min. or until chicken is done. Add seasoning mix, tomatoes and water; stir. Bring to boil; simmer on medium-low heat 10 min., stirring occasionally. Remove from heat; stir in corn, sour cream and 2 Tbsp. cilantro.
- Spray 13x9-inch baking dish with cooking spray; cover bottom of prepared dish with 5 tortillas. Top with 1 cup cheese, chicken mixture and remaining tortillas; drizzle with salsa.
- Bake 15 min. or until heated through. Sprinkle with remaining cheese and cilantro; bake 5 min. or until cheese is melted.

Nutrition Information

- Calories: 470
- Fiber: 4 g
- Total Fat: 18 g
- Total Carbohydrate: 0 g
- Cholesterol: 95 mg
- Protein: 40 g
- Saturated Fat: 6 g
- Sugar: 0 g
- Sodium: 1170 mg

66. Cheesy Chicken Tacos

Serving: 0 | Prep: 10mins | Cook: 10mins | Ready in: 20mins

Ingredients

- 1/2 lb. boneless skinless chicken breasts, cut into 1/2-inch-wide strips
- 1/2 tsp. chili powder
- 4 flour tortillas (8 inch)
- 1/2 cup chopped tomatoes
- 1/2 cup shredded lettuce
- 1 cup KRAFT 2% Milk Shredded Mild Cheddar Cheese
- 1/2 cup salsa

Direction

- Place chicken in large skillet sprayed with cooking spray. Sprinkle evenly with chili powder; mix well. Cook on medium heat 10 min. or until chicken is cooked through, stirring frequently.
- Spoon evenly onto tortillas; sprinkle with the tomatoes, lettuce and cheese. Fold each tortilla in half.
- Serve topped with the salsa.

Nutrition Information

- Calories: 320
- Sodium: 710 mg
- Sugar: 0 g
- Saturated Fat: 5 g
- Cholesterol: 50 mg
- Total Carbohydrate: 0 g
- Total Fat: 11 g
- Fiber: 2 g
- Protein: 24 g

67. Cheesy Chicken And Rice

Serving: 4 | Prep: 25mins | Cook: | Ready in: 25mins

Ingredients

- 1 Tbsp. oil
- 4 small boneless skinless chicken breasts (1 lb.)
- 1-1/4 cups fat-free reduced-sodium chicken broth
- 2 cups instant white rice, uncooked
- 2 cups small fresh broccoli florets
- 1/4 lb. (4 oz.) VELVEETA, cut into 1/2-inch cubes

Direction

- Heat oil in large nonstick skillet on medium heat. Add chicken; cook 6 to 7 min. on each side or until done (165°F). Remove chicken from skillet; cover to keep warm.
- Add broth to skillet. Bring to boil.
- Stir in rice, broccoli and VELVEETA. Top with chicken; cover. Cook on low heat 5 min. Remove chicken from skillet. Stir rice mixture until VELVEETA is completely melted and mixture is well blended.
- Serve chicken with the rice mixture.

Nutrition Information

- Calories: 410
- Sugar: 3 g
- Protein: 34 g
- Total Carbohydrate: 40 g
- Fiber: 2 g
- Saturated Fat: 5 g
- Sodium: 590 mg
- Cholesterol: 85 mg
- Total Fat: 12 g

68. Cheesy Chicken And Veggie Pasta Skillet

Serving: 4 | Prep: 30mins | Cook: | Ready in: 30mins

Ingredients

- 4 small boneless skinless chicken thighs (1 lb.)
- 2-1/2 cups water
- 1 pkg. (12 oz.) VELVEETA Shells & Cheese Dinner
- 1 pkg. (10 oz.) frozen peas and carrots, thawed
- 1/2 cup frozen bell pepper and onion strips

Direction

- Cook chicken in large nonstick skillet on medium-high heat 4 to 5 min. on each side or until browned on both sides. Remove from skillet; cover to keep warm.
- Add water and Shell Macaroni to skillet. Bring to boil; cover. Simmer on medium-low heat 15 min. or until Macaroni is tender, stirring occasionally and adding vegetables to the

boiling water for the last 5 min. Return chicken to skillet.
- Stir in Cheese Sauce; cook 3 to 5 min. or until chicken is done (165°F) and mixture is heated through, stirring occasionally.

Nutrition Information

- Calories: 450
- Total Fat: 16 g
- Total Carbohydrate: 46 g
- Fiber: 4 g
- Protein: 31 g
- Cholesterol: 115 mg
- Sodium: 810 mg
- Sugar: 6 g
- Saturated Fat: 4.5 g

69. Cheesy Chicken Pepper Quesadillas

Serving: 4 | Prep: 25mins | Cook: 25mins | Ready in: 50mins

Ingredients

- 1/4 cup KRAFT Zesty Italian Dressing
- 1 onion, chopped
- 2 cloves garlic, minced
- 2 red peppers, cut into thin strips
- 1 cup fresh mushrooms, sliced
- 2 cups chopped cooked chicken
- 4 flour tortillas (10 inch)
- 1 cup KRAFT Mexican Style Finely Shredded Four Cheese

Direction

- Heat oven to 325°F.
- Heat dressing in large skillet on medium-high heat. Add onions and garlic; cook and stir 2 to 3 min. or until onions are crisp-tender. Add peppers and mushrooms; cook 8 to 10 min or until peppers are crisp-tender, stirring occasionally. Stir in chicken.
- Place 2 tortillas on foil-covered baking sheet. Sprinkle tortillas with half the cheese. Top with chicken mixture and remaining cheese; cover with remaining tortillas.
- Bake 20 to 25 min. or until golden brown. Cut each quesadilla in half to serve.

Nutrition Information

- Calories: 520
- Sodium: 900 mg
- Total Carbohydrate: 0 g
- Fiber: 4 g
- Saturated Fat: 8 g
- Cholesterol: 85 mg
- Sugar: 0 g
- Protein: 33 g
- Total Fat: 21 g

70. Cheesy Mac And Chicken Taco Soup

Serving: 0 | Prep: 20mins | Cook: | Ready in: 20mins

Ingredients

- 1 pkg. (7-1/4 oz.) KRAFT Macaroni & Cheese Dinner
- 1/2 lb. lean ground chicken
- 1-1/2 tsp. chipotle chile pepper powder
- 1/4 tsp. garlic powder
- 2 cans (14.5 oz. each) fat-free reduced-sodium chicken broth
- 2 Tbsp. TACO BELL® Thick & Chunky Salsa

Direction

- Prepare Dinner in large saucepan as directed on package, reducing butter to 2 Tbsp.
- Meanwhile, cook chicken with chili pepper powder and garlic powder in nonstick skillet until done; drain.

- Stir chicken mixture, broth and salsa into Dinner; cook 5 min. or until heated through, stirring occasionally.

Nutrition Information

- Calories: 200
- Cholesterol: 25 mg
- Total Carbohydrate: 25 g
- Sugar: 4 g
- Saturated Fat: 2 g
- Sodium: 670 mg
- Protein: 12 g
- Total Fat: 6 g
- Fiber: 1 g

71. Cheesy Primavera Skillet

Serving: 0 | Prep: 35mins | Cook: | Ready in: 35mins

Ingredients

- 1 lb. boneless skinless chicken breasts, cut into bite-size pieces
- 1/2 cup chopped red peppers
- 1 pkg. (14.64 oz.) VELVEETA CHEESY SKILLETS Dinner Kit Chicken and Broccoli
- 2-1/2 cups water
- 1 Tbsp. KRAFT Grated Parmesan Cheese

Direction

- Cook and stir chicken and peppers in large skillet on medium heat 10 min. or until chicken is done. Add Orzo Pasta, Seasoning and water; stir.
- Bring to boil; simmer on medium-low heat 7 min. Add Broccoli; stir. Simmer 3 min.
- Stir in Cheese Sauce; top with Parmesan.

Nutrition Information

- Calories: 380
- Total Carbohydrate: 0 g
- Saturated Fat: 3 g
- Protein: 30 g
- Sugar: 0 g
- Cholesterol: 70 mg
- Fiber: 2 g
- Total Fat: 11 g
- Sodium: 710 mg

72. Chicken & Bacon Pot Pie

Serving: 8 | Prep: 35mins | Cook: 1hours40mins | Ready in: 2hours15mins

Ingredients

- 1 Foolproof PHILLY Pie Crust Recipe (see tip)
- 6 slices OSCAR MAYER Bacon, cut into 1/2-inch pieces
- 1/2 lb. sliced fresh mushrooms
- 1 baking potato (5 oz.), peeled, cut into 1/2-inch pieces
- 1 onion, chopped
- 1 carrot, chopped
- 2 cloves garlic, minced
- 2 Tbsp. flour
- 2-1/4 cups fat-free reduced-sodium chicken broth
- 4 oz. (1/2 of 8-oz. pkg.) PHILADELPHIA Cream Cheese, cubed
- 3 cups shredded cooked chicken

Direction

- Prepare dough for Foolproof PHILLY Pie Crust Recipe and refrigerate as directed.
- Cook and stir bacon in Dutch oven or large deep skillet on medium heat until crisp. Remove bacon from pan with slotted spoon; drain on paper towels. Discard all but 2 tsp. drippings from pan.
- Add vegetables and garlic to reserved drippings in pan; cook 5 min., stirring occasionally. Add flour; cook and stir 1 min. Gradually stir in broth. Bring to boil. Add cream cheese; cook and stir 1 min. or until

cream cheese is completely melted and mixture is well blended. Remove from heat; stir in chicken. Spoon into 9-inch deep-dish pie plate sprayed with cooking spray; top with bacon.
- Heat oven to 400°F. Roll out pie crust dough into 10-inch round between 2 sheets of waxed paper; place over chicken mixture. Flute edge, sealing crust to edge of pie plate. Cut several slits in crust to allow steam to escape. Place on baking sheet.
- Bake 40 min. or until golden brown, covering edge of crust with foil for the last 10 min. if necessary to prevent overbrowning.

Nutrition Information

- Calories: 460
- Total Carbohydrate: 0 g
- Saturated Fat: 16 g
- Cholesterol: 120 mg
- Protein: 24 g
- Total Fat: 29 g
- Fiber: 2 g
- Sodium: 510 mg
- Sugar: 0 g

73. Chicken & Pepper Pasta Bake

Serving: 0 | Prep: 25mins | Cook: 20mins | Ready in: 45mins

Ingredients

- 3 cups rigatoni pasta, uncooked
- 1 lb. boneless skinless chicken breasts, cut into bite-size pieces
- 1 each large green and red pepper, coarsely chopped
- 1 jar (24 oz.) CLASSICO Tomato and Basil Pasta Sauce
- 2 oz. (1/4 of 8-oz. pkg.) PHILADELPHIA Cream Cheese, cubed
- 1 cup KRAFT Shredded Mozzarella Cheese
- 1/4 cup KRAFT Grated Parmesan Cheese

Direction

- Heat oven to 375°F.
- Cook pasta as directed on package, omitting salt. Meanwhile, cook and stir chicken in large nonstick skillet on medium-high heat 2 min. Add peppers; cook and stir 3 min. Stir in pasta sauce; simmer 6 to 8 min. or until chicken is done and peppers are crisp-tender, stirring occasionally. Add cream cheese; cook and stir 1 to 2 min. or until melted.
- Drain pasta. Add to chicken mixture; toss to coat. Spoon half into 8- or 9-inch square baking dish; top with 1/2 cup mozzarella and 2 Tbsp. Parmesan. Repeat layers.
- Bake 20 min. or until heated through.

Nutrition Information

- Calories: 620
- Fiber: 7 g
- Cholesterol: 110 mg
- Total Carbohydrate: 0 g
- Sodium: 1160 mg
- Protein: 46 g
- Total Fat: 19 g
- Sugar: 0 g
- Saturated Fat: 9 g

74. Chicken & Rice Casserole

Serving: 4 | Prep: 25mins | Cook: 30mins | Ready in: 55mins

Ingredients

- 1 cup KRAFT Shredded Cheddar Cheese, divided
- 1/2 lb. boneless skinless chicken breasts, cooked, shredded
- 2 cups cooked instant white rice

- 1 jar (12 oz.) HEINZ HomeStyle Classic Chicken Gravy
- 1 pkg. (10 oz.) frozen chopped broccoli, thawed, drained
- 1/4 tsp. garlic powder

Direction

- Heat oven to 350°F.
- Reserve 1/2 cup cheese for later use. Combine remaining cheese with all remaining ingredients.
- Spoon into 8-inch-square baking dish sprayed with cooking spray; top with reserved cheese.
- Bake 25 to 30 min. until heated through.

Nutrition Information

- Calories: 330
- Cholesterol: 65 mg
- Sodium: 590 mg
- Sugar: 0 g
- Total Fat: 14 g
- Total Carbohydrate: 0 g
- Fiber: 3 g
- Protein: 22 g
- Saturated Fat: 7 g

75. Chicken & Rice With Asparagus

Serving: 0 | Prep: 10mins | Cook: 35mins | Ready in: 45mins

Ingredients

- 4 slices OSCAR MAYER Bacon
- 4 skinless bone-in chicken breast halves (2 lb.)
- 1 Tbsp. ground chipotle chile pepper
- 1/2 cup KRAFT Zesty Italian Dressing, divided
- 2 red peppers, stemmed, seeded
- 1 bunch green onions, sliced, divided
- 1 jalapeño pepper, stemmed
- 1 lb. fresh asparagus, cut into 2-inch pieces
- 3/4 cup quartered Spanish olives, divided
- 4 cups hot cooked brown rice

Direction

- Cook bacon in large skillet on medium heat 8 to 10 min. or to desired crispness, turning frequently. Remove bacon from skillet; place on paper towels to drain. Drain grease from skillet.
- Cut each chicken breast crosswise in half; sprinkle evenly with chipotle pepper. Heat 1/4 cup of the dressing in same skillet on medium-high heat. Add chicken; cook 3 min. on each side or until browned on both sides. Meanwhile, place remaining 1/4 cup dressing, red peppers, 1/2 cup of the onions and jalapeno pepper in blender; cover. Blend until smooth.
- Move chicken pieces to outside edge of skillet. Add red pepper mixture; bring to boil. Coarsely crumble bacon over ingredients in skillet. Add 1/2 cup of the olives and 1/4 cup of the onions; mix well. Cover. Reduce heat to medium-low; simmer 15 min. or until chicken is cooked through (165°F). Add asparagus; cover. Cook 5 min. or until asparagus is tender. Serve over rice. Top with remaining 1/4 cup olives and onions.

Nutrition Information

- Calories: 280
- Protein: 19 g
- Fiber: 4 g
- Sugar: 0 g
- Total Fat: 10 g
- Sodium: 620 mg
- Saturated Fat: 1.5 g
- Cholesterol: 40 mg
- Total Carbohydrate: 0 g

76. Chicken & Summer Squash Skillet

Serving: 6 | Prep: 40mins | Cook: | Ready in: 40mins

Ingredients

- 1 Tbsp. butter
- 6 small boneless skinless chicken breasts (1-1/2 lb.)
- 1 tub (8 oz.) PHILADELPHIA Cream Cheese Spread
- 3 Tbsp. milk, divided
- 1 tsp. dried Italian seasoning
- 1/2 tsp. garlic powder
- 2 small each yellow squash and zucchini, cut lengthwise in half, then sliced crosswise
- 3 cups cooked orzo pasta
- 2 Tbsp. thinly sliced fresh basil

Direction

- Melt butter in large skillet on medium heat. Add chicken; cook 6 to 7 min. on each side or until done (165ºF). Transfer to plate; cover to keep warm.
- Mix cream cheese spread, 2 Tbsp. milk and dry seasonings until blended. Mix 1/4 cup with remaining milk in small microwaveable bowl; set aside. Add vegetables to same skillet; cook 5 min. or until crisp-tender, stirring frequently. Stir in remaining cream cheese mixture; cook and stir 2 min. Add orzo; cook and stir 2 min. or until heated through.
- Spoon orzo mixture onto 4 plates; top with chicken. Microwave reserved cream cheese mixture on HIGH 15 to 20 sec. or until heated through; stir. Spoon over chicken; top with basil.

Nutrition Information

- Calories: 440
- Cholesterol: 95 mg
- Total Carbohydrate: 42 g
- Protein: 34 g
- Saturated Fat: 8 g
- Sodium: 240 mg
- Fiber: 3 g
- Sugar: 4 g
- Total Fat: 15 g

77. Chicken Bacon Ranch Pita Pizzas

Serving: 0 | Prep: 10mins | Cook: 10mins | Ready in: 20mins

Ingredients

- 2 pita breads
- 2 tablespoons KRAFT Buttermilk Ranch Dressing
- 2 oz. OSCAR MAYER CARVING BOARD Rotisserie Seasoned Chicken Breast, diced
- 2 pieces OSCAR MAYER Fully Cooked Bacon, chopped
- 1/2 cup KRAFT Shredded Mozzarella Cheese

Direction

- Using the stove: Preheat the broiler. Heat a heavy skillet over medium high heat. Place one pita in the pan. After the underside has browned in spots (about 3-4 minutes), remove to a baking sheet placing the browned side down and repeat with second pita. Top each pita with 1 Tablespoon of dressing and layer on chicken, bacon and ¼ cup of mozzarella cheese. Place under broiler until cheese is golden. Serve immediately.
- Using the grill: Preheat the grill using medium heat. Place the pitas on the grill and watch them closely until they are slightly charred on the underside. Flip over and quickly spread 1 Tablespoon of dressing on each pita. Layer on chicken, bacon and ¼ cup of mozzarella cheese onto each pita. Lower the heat to low and close the grill until the cheese is melted. Serve immediately.

Nutrition Information

- Calories: 0 g
- Saturated Fat: 0 g
- Total Fat: 0 g
- Sodium: 0 g
- Cholesterol: 0 g
- Fiber: 0 g
- Total Carbohydrate: 0 g
- Sugar: 0 g
- Protein: 0 g

78. Chicken Breasts In Sour Cream Sauce

Serving: 4 | Prep: 20mins | Cook: 30mins | Ready in: 50mins

Ingredients

- 1/4 cup flour
- 1/4 tsp. pepper
- 4 small bone-in chicken breasts (1-1/2 lb.)
- 2 Tbsp. butter or margarine
- 1 tomato, seeded, chopped
- 2 Tbsp. tomato sauce
- 2 cloves garlic, minced
- 1/2 cup fat-free reduced-sodium chicken broth
- 1/2 cup BREAKSTONE'S or KNUDSEN Sour Cream

Direction

- Mix flour and pepper in shallow dish. Add chicken; turn to evenly coat both sides of each breast. Gently shake off excess flour mixture.
- Melt butter in large skillet on medium-high heat. Add chicken; cook 10 to 12 min. on each side or until done (165°F). Transfer chicken to platter; cover to keep warm.
- Add tomatoes, tomato sauce and garlic to skillet; cook 3 min. or until heated through, stirring frequently. Stir in broth; bring to boil. Simmer on medium-low heat 3 min., stirring frequently. Whisk in sour cream; cook and stir 2 min. or until heated through. (Do not let sauce come to boil.) Spoon over chicken.

Nutrition Information

- Calories: 380
- Saturated Fat: 10 g
- Cholesterol: 145 mg
- Total Carbohydrate: 0 g
- Sodium: 250 mg
- Fiber: 1 g
- Protein: 40 g
- Sugar: 0 g
- Total Fat: 21 g

79. Chicken Burritos El Grande

Serving: 6 | Prep: 30mins | Cook: | Ready in: 30mins

Ingredients

- 2 tsp. olive oil
- 1 small onion, chopped
- 1 small green pepper, chopped
- 1 lb. ground chicken
- 1 pkg. (1 oz.) TACO BELL® Taco Seasoning Mix
- 1-1/2 cups water
- 1 cup instant brown rice, uncooked
- 1 cup TACO BELL® Refried Beans
- 6 flour tortillas (10 inch), warmed
- 1 cup KRAFT Mexican Style Finely Shredded Cheddar Pepper Jack Cheese
- 6 Tbsp. BREAKSTONE'S or KNUDSEN Sour Cream
- 1 cup shredded lettuce
- 1 tomato, chopped

Direction

- Heat oil in large skillet on medium heat. Add onions and peppers; cook 5 min. or until crisp-tender. Add chicken; cook 5 min. or until done, stirring frequently. Add seasoning mix

and water; bring to boil. Stir in rice; cover. Cook on medium-low heat 5 min. Let stand 5 min.
- Spoon beans down centers of tortillas; top with chicken mixture and cheese. Fold in opposite sides of each tortilla, then roll up burrito-style.
- Serve topped with sour cream, lettuce and tomatoes.

Nutrition Information

- Calories: 560
- Protein: 28 g
- Saturated Fat: 9 g
- Sodium: 1170 mg
- Total Fat: 22 g
- Total Carbohydrate: 62 g
- Fiber: 5 g
- Cholesterol: 95 mg
- Sugar: 4 g

80. Chicken Cacciatore Pronto

Serving: 4 | Prep: 45mins | Cook: | Ready in: 45mins

Ingredients

- 1 Tbsp. KRAFT Lite Zesty Italian Dressing
- 4 bone-in chicken thighs (1-1/2 lb.), skin removed
- 2 small red peppers, chopped
- 1 can (14-1/2 oz.) Italian-style diced tomatoes, undrained
- 1/3 cup tomato paste
- 3 cloves garlic, minced
- 1/2 lb. whole wheat spaghetti, uncooked
- 1/4 cup KRAFT Grated Parmesan Cheese
- 1/2 cup KRAFT 2% Milk Shredded Mozzarella Cheese

Direction

- Heat dressing in large nonstick skillet on medium-high heat. Add chicken; cook 10 min. or until evenly browned, turning occasionally.
- Stir in next 4 ingredients; cover. Simmer on medium-low heat 20 min. or until chicken is done (165°F), stirring occasionally. Meanwhile, cook spaghetti as directed on package, omitting salt.
- Remove skillet from heat. Add Parmesan to chicken mixture; stir. Sprinkle with mozzarella; let stand 5 min. or until melted.
- Drain spaghetti; place on platter. Top with chicken mixture.

Nutrition Information

- Calories: 460
- Sodium: 1060 mg
- Total Carbohydrate: 0 g
- Saturated Fat: 4 g
- Protein: 39 g
- Fiber: 9 g
- Total Fat: 10 g
- Sugar: 0 g
- Cholesterol: 120 mg

81. Chicken Caesar Salad Pizza

Serving: 6 | Prep: 10mins | Cook: 8mins | Ready in: 18mins

Ingredients

- 1 ready-to-use baked pizza crust (12 inch)
- 1-1/2 cups KRAFT Shredded Mozzarella Cheese
- 1 pkg. (10 oz.) torn salad greens
- 1 pkg. (6 oz.) OSCAR MAYER CARVING BOARD Flame Grilled Chicken Breast Strips
- 1 cup seasoned croutons
- 1/3 cup KRAFT Grated Parmesan Cheese
- 1/2 cup KRAFT Classic Caesar Dressing, divided

Direction

- Heat oven to 425°F.
- Place pizza crust on baking sheet; top with mozzarella.
- Bake 7 to 8 min. or until cheese is melted. Meanwhile, toss greens with remaining ingredients.
- Top pizza with salad just before serving.

Nutrition Information

- Calories: 400
- Protein: 22 g
- Total Carbohydrate: 32 g
- Sodium: 1160 mg
- Saturated Fat: 7 g
- Cholesterol: 50 mg
- Sugar: 1 g
- Fiber: 2 g
- Total Fat: 20 g

82. Chicken Fettuccine Primavera

Serving: 0 | Prep: 35mins | Cook: | Ready in: 35mins

Ingredients

- 1 tub (8 oz.) PHILADELPHIA Cream Cheese Spread
- 1/4 cup milk
- 1 tsp. garlic powder
- 1 tsp. dried Italian seasoning
- 1-1/2 lb. boneless skinless chicken breasts, cut into bite-size pieces
- 1/2 cup each chopped broccoli, carrots and yellow peppers
- 2 Tbsp. water
- 1/2 cup halved grape tomatoes
- 3 cups hot cooked fettuccine
- 1/4 cup KRAFT Shredded Parmesan Cheese

Direction

- Mix cream cheese spread, milk and seasonings until blended.
- Cook and stir chicken in large nonstick skillet on medium heat 8 to 10 min. or until done. Remove from skillet; cover to keep warm. Add broccoli, carrots, peppers and water to skillet; mix well. Cover; cook 6 min. or until vegetables are crisp-tender, stirring occasionally.
- Return chicken to skillet. Add cream cheese mixture and tomatoes; cook and stir 3 min. or until heated through. Add pasta; toss to evenly coat. Sprinkle with Parmesan.

Nutrition Information

- Calories: 380
- Total Carbohydrate: 28 g
- Cholesterol: 95 mg
- Sugar: 3 g
- Fiber: 2 g
- Saturated Fat: 7 g
- Total Fat: 14 g
- Sodium: 300 mg
- Protein: 33 g

83. Chicken Fiesta Chili Dip

Serving: 0 | Prep: 15mins | Cook: | Ready in: 15mins

Ingredients

- 1 lb. (16 oz.) VELVEETA, cut into 1/2-inch cubes
- 1 pkg. (6 oz.) OSCAR MAYER CARVING BOARD Flame Grilled Chicken Breast Strips, chopped
- 1 can (15 oz.) chili with beans
- 1/2 cup chopped green peppers
- 2 cloves garlic, minced
- 1 tsp. hot pepper sauce

Direction

- Mix ingredients in 2-qt. microwaveable bowl.
- Microwave on HIGH 6 to 8 min. or until VELVEETA is completely melted and mixture is blended, stirring every 3 min.
- Serve hot with tortilla chips, crackers or assorted cut-up fresh vegetables.

Nutrition Information

- Calories: 60
- Saturated Fat: 2 g
- Sodium: 290 mg
- Fiber: 1 g
- Total Fat: 3 g
- Total Carbohydrate: 3 g
- Sugar: 2 g
- Protein: 5 g
- Cholesterol: 15 mg

84. Chicken Harvest Salad

Serving: 0 | Prep: 15mins | Cook: | Ready in: 15mins

Ingredients

- 1 pkg. (10 oz.) torn salad greens
- 1 cup dried apple slices
- 1 pkg. (6 oz.) OSCAR MAYER CARVING BOARD Flame Grilled Chicken Breast Strips
- 4 oz. KRAFT Monterey Jack Cheese, cubed
- 1/4 cup OSCAR MAYER Real Bacon Recipe Pieces
- 1/3 cup KRAFT Creamy Poppyseed Dressing

Direction

- Place greens in large bowl.
- Top with all remaining ingredients except dressing.
- Add dressing just before serving; mix lightly.

Nutrition Information

- Calories: 350
- Fiber: 5 g
- Sugar: 20 g
- Protein: 21 g
- Cholesterol: 70 mg
- Saturated Fat: 7 g
- Total Fat: 18 g
- Total Carbohydrate: 26 g
- Sodium: 1020 mg

85. Chicken Harvest Stir Fry

Serving: 3 | Prep: 10mins | Cook: 7mins | Ready in: 17mins

Ingredients

- 1 Tbsp. olive oil
- 1 medium red pepper, coarsely chopped
- 1 cup baby carrots, cut in half lengthwise
- 1 pkg. (6 oz.) OSCAR MAYER CARVING BOARD Flame Grilled Chicken Breast Strips
- 1/4 cup lemon-herb stir-fry sauce
- 3 cups hot cooked rice pilaf

Direction

- Heat oil in medium skillet on medium-high heat. Add peppers and carrots; cook and stir 5 min. or until crisp-tender.
- Add chicken breast strips and stir-fry sauce; mix well. Cover; simmer 2 min. or until heated through.
- Serve spooned over the rice pilaf.

Nutrition Information

- Calories: 400
- Total Fat: 11 g
- Sodium: 1800 mg
- Protein: 19 g
- Saturated Fat: 3.5 g
- Total Carbohydrate: 60 g
- Fiber: 3 g
- Cholesterol: 50 mg

- Sugar: 7 g

86. Chicken Herb Quiche Squares

Serving: 0 | Prep: 15mins | Cook: 30mins | Ready in: 45mins

Ingredients

- 1 can (10 oz.) refrigerated pizza crust
- 1 pkg. (6 oz.) OSCAR MAYER CARVING BOARD Flame Grilled Chicken Breast Strips
- 1 medium tomato, chopped
- 1/2 of a medium green pepper, chopped
- 1/2 of a medium onion, chopped
- 1/4 cup KRAFT Grated Parmesan Cheese
- 4 eggs
- 3 Tbsp. water
- 1/2 tsp. dried Italian seasoning

Direction

- Preheat oven to 375°F. Press dough evenly onto bottom and halfway up sides of greased 13x9-inch baking dish. Top with chicken, tomato, green pepper and onion. Sprinkle with Parmesan cheese.
- Beat eggs, water and seasoning in small bowl with wire whisk until well blended; pour over ingredients in baking dish.
- Bake 30 min. or until center is puffed and edges are set. Let stand 5 min. Cut into 6 squares to serve.

Nutrition Information

- Calories: 230
- Saturated Fat: 2.5 g
- Cholesterol: 165 mg
- Sodium: 860 mg
- Protein: 17 g
- Sugar: 4 g
- Total Fat: 7 g
- Total Carbohydrate: 24 g

- Fiber: 1 g

87. Chicken Italiano Skillet

Serving: 0 | Prep: 35mins | Cook: | Ready in: 35mins

Ingredients

- 1 lb. boneless skinless chicken breasts, cut into bite-size pieces
- 1 green pepper, chopped
- 1 small onion, cut into thin wedges
- 1 can (14-1/2 oz.) diced tomatoes, undrained
- 1 cup water
- 1 pkg. (14 oz.) KRAFT Deluxe Macaroni & Cheese Dinner

Direction

- Cook and stir chicken in large skillet sprayed with cooking spray on medium-high heat 5 min. or until chicken is no longer pink. Add peppers and onions; cook and stir 5 min. or until chicken is done.
- Stir in tomatoes, water and Macaroni. Bring to boil; cover. Simmer on low heat 10 min. or until macaroni is tender, stirring occasionally.
- Add Cheese Sauce; stir until blended.

Nutrition Information

- Calories: 310
- Fiber: 2 g
- Sodium: 740 mg
- Cholesterol: 50 mg
- Saturated Fat: 2 g
- Total Carbohydrate: 0 g
- Protein: 24 g
- Sugar: 0 g
- Total Fat: 9 g

88. Chicken Kiev

Serving: 6 | Prep: 30mins | Cook: 3hours50mins | Ready in: 4hours20mins

Ingredients

- 6 Tbsp. unsalted butter, softened
- 1 Tbsp. chopped fresh chives
- 3 Tbsp. chopped fresh parsley, divided
- 1/2 tsp. ground black pepper, divided
- 6 small boneless skinless chicken breasts (1-1/2 lb.)
- 1 pkt. SHAKE 'N BAKE Seasoned Panko Seasoned Coating Mix
- 1/4 cup milk
- 2 Tbsp. water
- 1 Tbsp. GREY POUPON Dijon Mustard

Direction

- Mix butter, chives, 1 Tbsp. parsley and 1/4 tsp. pepper until blended. Place on sheet of plastic wrap or waxed paper; roll into 3x2-inch log. Wrap in plastic wrap. Freeze 3 hours or until firm.
- Pound chicken to 1/4-inch thickness; place, top sides down on cutting board. Cut frozen butter mixture into 6 pieces; place 1 piece in center of each breast. Roll chicken breasts up, starting at one short end of each. Secure with wooden toothpicks. Refrigerate 10 min.
- Heat oven to 425°F. Spray rimmed baking sheet with cooking spray. Combine coating mix, remaining parsley and remaining pepper in shallow dish. Mix milk, water and mustard in separate shallow dish until blended. Dip chicken roll-ups, 1 at a time, in milk mixture, then in coating mix, turning to evenly coat each roll-up with each ingredient; place on prepared baking sheet.
- Bake 35 to 40 min. or until chicken is done.

Nutrition Information

- Calories: 270
- Fiber: 0 g
- Sugar: 1 g
- Protein: 26 g
- Cholesterol: 100 mg
- Total Fat: 15 g
- Saturated Fat: 8 g
- Sodium: 340 mg
- Total Carbohydrate: 7 g

89. Chicken Lo Mein

Serving: 0 | Prep: 25mins | Cook: | Ready in: 25mins

Ingredients

- 1/2 lb. spaghetti, uncooked
- 1/4 cup KRAFT Asian Toasted Sesame Dressing
- 1 lb. boneless skinless chicken breasts, cut into thin strips
- 2 cloves garlic, minced
- 1 pkg. (16 oz.) frozen bell pepper and onion strips, thawed, drained
- 1/2 cup fat-free reduced-sodium chicken broth
- 1 Tbsp. creamy peanut butter
- 1/4 cup lite soy sauce
- 2 Tbsp. chopped fresh cilantro
- 2 Tbsp. chopped PLANTERS COCKTAIL Peanuts

Direction

- Cook spaghetti in large saucepan as directed on package, omitting salt.
- Meanwhile, heat dressing in large nonstick skillet on medium-high heat. Add chicken and garlic; stir-fry 5 min. or until chicken is no longer pink. Add vegetables, broth and peanut butter; stir-fry 3 to 4 min. or until chicken is done.
- Drain spaghetti; return to pan. Add chicken mixture and soy sauce; mix lightly.
- Spoon onto platter; top with cilantro and nuts.

Nutrition Information

- Calories: 310
- Sugar: 0 g
- Saturated Fat: 1.5 g
- Fiber: 3 g
- Cholesterol: 40 mg
- Total Carbohydrate: 0 g
- Sodium: 420 mg
- Total Fat: 7 g
- Protein: 19 g

90. Chicken Marsala Sandwiches

Serving: 4 | Prep: 20mins | Cook: | Ready in: 20mins

Ingredients

- 1 Tbsp. oil
- 1 pkg. (8 oz.) sliced fresh mushrooms
- 1 large onion, thinly sliced
- 2 cloves garlic, minced
- 1 pkg. (7.5 oz.) OSCAR MAYER CARVING BOARD Rotisserie Seasoned Chicken Breast
- 3/4 cup Marsala wine
- 1/4 cup fat-free reduced-sodium chicken broth
- 1/2 tsp. dried Italian seasoning
- 4 small ciabatta sandwich rolls, cut in half horizontally, toasted
- 2 KRAFT Slim Cut Mozzarella Cheese Slices, cut in half, divided

Direction

- Heat oil in large skillet on medium-high heat. Add mushrooms, onions and garlic; cook and stir 10 min. or until onions are tender.
- Stir in chicken, wine, broth and seasoning; cook 2 min. or until wine is cooked off, stirring occasionally.
- Fill rolls with cheese and chicken mixture.

Nutrition Information

- Calories: 430
- Sodium: 960 mg
- Total Carbohydrate: 0 g
- Protein: 24 g
- Saturated Fat: 2.5 g
- Total Fat: 12 g
- Fiber: 3 g
- Sugar: 0 g
- Cholesterol: 35 mg

91. Chicken Milanese With Apple Salad

Serving: 4 | Prep: 30mins | Cook: | Ready in: 30mins

Ingredients

- 2 Granny Smith apples, cut into matchlike sticks
- 1/2 cup chopped fresh parsley
- 3 green onions, sliced
- 1/2 cup KRAFT Honey Mustard Dressing
- 4 small boneless skinless chicken breasts (1 lb.), pounded to 1/4-inch thickness
- 1 pkt. SHAKE 'N BAKE Parmesan Crusted Seasoned Coating Mix
- 2 Tbsp. oil

Direction

- Combine first 4 ingredients.
- Coat chicken with coating mix as directed on package.
- Heat oil in large nonstick skillet on medium heat. Add chicken; cook 4 to 6 min. or until done, turning after 3 min.
- Serve chicken with apple salad.

Nutrition Information

- Calories: 0
- Fiber: 0 g
- Total Fat: 0 g
- Cholesterol: 0 mg
- Saturated Fat: 0 g
- Protein: 0 g

- Total Carbohydrate: 0 g
- Sugar: 0 g
- Sodium: 0 mg

92. Chicken Nicoise Salad Recipe

Serving: 0 | Prep: 10mins | Cook: | Ready in: 10mins

Ingredients

- 2 heads Boston lettuce, separated into leaves
- 2 pkg. (6 oz. each) OSCAR MAYER CARVING BOARD Flame Grilled Chicken Breast Strips
- 2 hard-cooked eggs, cut into wedges
- 2 cups steamed green beans
- 2 cups cubed cooked new potatoes
- 3 tomatoes (3/4 lb.), cut into wedges
- 1/2 cup KRAFT Lite House Italian Dressing

Direction

- Place lettuce in large serving bowl; top decoratively with chicken, eggs, beans, potatoes and tomatoes.
- Refrigerate until ready to serve.
- Add dressing; toss to coat.

Nutrition Information

- Calories: 290
- Total Fat: 8 g
- Cholesterol: 165 mg
- Protein: 31 g
- Saturated Fat: 2.5 g
- Sugar: 0 g
- Sodium: 1010 mg
- Total Carbohydrate: 0 g
- Fiber: 6 g

93. Chicken Parm Snackers

Serving: 0 | Prep: 20mins | Cook: | Ready in: 20mins

Ingredients

- 2 oz. (1/4 of 8-oz. pkg.) KRAFT Low-Moisture Part-Skim Mozzarella Cheese
- 1 cooked small boneless skinless chicken breast half (4 oz.), cut into 16 thin slices
- 1/4 cup CLASSICO Tomato and Basil Pasta Sauce
- 16 cracked pepper and olive oil woven wheat crackers
- 1/2 tsp. dried oregano leaves

Direction

- Heat oven to 350ºF.
- Cut cheese into 8 slices, then cut each slice in half. Toss chicken with pasta sauce.
- Place crackers in single layer on baking sheet; top with chicken mixture, cheese and oregano.
- Bake 5 to 6 min. or until cheese is melted.

Nutrition Information

- Calories: 90
- Fiber: 1 g
- Protein: 7 g
- Saturated Fat: 1 g
- Total Carbohydrate: 0 g
- Total Fat: 3.5 g
- Sugar: 0 g
- Sodium: 135 mg
- Cholesterol: 15 mg

94. Chicken Parmesan Spaghetti

Serving: 4 | Prep: 15mins | Cook: 20mins | Ready in: 35mins

Ingredients

- 4 small boneless skinless chicken breasts (1 lb.)
- 1/4 cup KRAFT Real Mayo Mayonnaise
- 1/2 cup dry Italian-style bread crumbs
- 1 pt. grape tomato

- 1-1/2 cups CLASSICO Tomato and Basil Pasta Sauce
- 8 oz. spaghetti, cooked, drained
- 2 Tbsp. KRAFT Grated Parmesan Cheese

Direction

- Heat oven to 425° F.
- Brush chicken with mayo, then coat with bread crumbs, turning to evenly coat both sides of each breast. Place on foil-covered baking sheet.
- Bake 20 min. or until chicken is done (165°F). Meanwhile, heat large heavy skillet on high heat. Add tomatoes; cook 7 min. or until charred on all sides, stirring constantly. Add pasta sauce, cook 3 to 4 min. on medium heat or until heated through, crushing tomatoes with the back of a spoon.
- Toss spaghetti with sauce; top with chicken and cheese.

Nutrition Information

- Calories: 570
- Sugar: 0 g
- Total Carbohydrate: 0 g
- Saturated Fat: 3.5 g
- Protein: 37 g
- Total Fat: 18 g
- Fiber: 5 g
- Sodium: 960 mg
- Cholesterol: 75 mg

95. Chicken Pasta Bowl

Serving: 6 | Prep: 20mins | Cook: | Ready in: 20mins

Ingredients

- 12 oz. linguine, uncooked
- 1 Tbsp. oil
- 1 lb. boneless skinless chicken breasts, cut into bite-size pieces
- 1 can (10-3/4 oz.) condensed cream of chicken soup
- 1/2 cup milk
- 1/4 cup KRAFT Classic Ranch Dressing
- 2 cups cherry tomatoes, halved
- 1/2 cup KRAFT Shredded Cheddar Cheese

Direction

- Cook pasta as directed on package, omitting salt.
- Meanwhile, heat oil in large skillet on medium heat. Add chicken; cook 5 min. or until lightly browned, stirring occasionally. Add soup, milk and dressing; stir. Bring to boil; cover. Simmer on low heat 5 min. or until chicken is done. Stir in tomatoes; cook 1 min.
- Drain pasta. Add to sauce in skillet; mix lightly. Top with cheese.

Nutrition Information

- Calories: 430
- Protein: 27 g
- Total Fat: 13 g
- Sodium: 310 mg
- Total Carbohydrate: 49 g
- Cholesterol: 55 mg
- Saturated Fat: 3.5 g
- Fiber: 3 g
- Sugar: 4 g

96. Chicken Pesto Cavatappi

Serving: 6 | Prep: 20mins | Cook: | Ready in: 20mins

Ingredients

- 1-1/2 cups cavatappi, uncooked
- 1 lb. boneless skinless chicken breasts, cut into bite-size pieces
- 1/2 lb. asparagus, cut into 1-inch lengths
- 1/2 cup chopped tomatoes

- 1 tub (8 oz.) PHILADELPHIA Cream Cheese Spread
- 2 Tbsp. CLASSICO Traditional Basil Pesto Sauce and Spread
- 2 Tbsp. milk
- 1/2 cup KRAFT Shredded Mozzarella Cheese

Direction

- Cook pasta as directed on package; omitting salt. Meanwhile, cook and stir chicken in large nonstick skillet on medium heat 5 to 7 min. or until done. Add asparagus and tomatoes; cook 2 to 3 min. or until heated through, stirring occasionally.
- Mix cream cheese spread, pesto sauce and milk until blended; add to skillet. Cook and stir 2 to 3 min. or until heated through.
- Drain pasta; add to chicken mixture. Top with mozzarella.

Nutrition Information

- Calories: 320
- Total Carbohydrate: 0 g
- Total Fat: 15 g
- Fiber: 2 g
- Protein: 24 g
- Cholesterol: 75 mg
- Saturated Fat: 8 g
- Sodium: 320 mg
- Sugar: 0 g

97. Chicken Pho Recipe

Serving: 6 | Prep: 40mins | Cook: | Ready in: 40mins

Ingredients

- 6 oz. rice stick noodles, uncooked
- 1 qt. (4 cups) fat-free reduced-sodium chicken broth
- 1 piece fresh ginger (1 inch), cut into thin slices
- 1 Tbsp. MR. YOSHIDA'S Cracked Pepper & Garlic Sauce
- 1 Tbsp. Sriracha sauce (hot chili sauce)
- 2 Tbsp. KRAFT Asian Toasted Sesame Dressing
- 1 lb. boneless skinless chicken breasts and thighs, cut into bite-size pieces
- 1 small onion, cut into thin slices
- 1/4 cup finely chopped fresh cilantro
- 1/4 cup fresh mint
- 1 fresh jalapeño pepper, cut into thin slices
- 4 fresh Thai basil sprigs
- 1 lime, cut into 4 wedges

Direction

- Cook noodles as directed on package, omitting salt; drain. Place in 4 bowls; cover to keep warm.
- Bring broth, ginger, Cracked Pepper & Garlic Sauce and Sriracha sauce to boil in large saucepan, stirring frequently. Simmer on medium-low heat 5 min.
- Heat dressing in medium skillet on medium heat. Add chicken; cook and stir 8 to 10 min. or until done. Stir into broth mixture. Ladle over noodles.
- Top with all remaining ingredients except lime wedges.
- Squeeze lime wedges over each serving before serving.

Nutrition Information

- Calories: 220
- Fiber: 2 g
- Saturated Fat: 1 g
- Total Carbohydrate: 0 g
- Protein: 17 g
- Cholesterol: 55 mg
- Total Fat: 4 g
- Sodium: 510 mg
- Sugar: 0 g

98. Chicken Pie

Serving: 8 | Prep: 10mins | Cook: 25mins | Ready in: 35mins

Ingredients

- 3 cups chopped cooked chicken
- 1 pkg. (16 oz.) frozen mixed vegetables (carrots, corn, green beans, peas), thawed, drained
- 1/2 lb. (8 oz.) 2% Milk VELVEETA, cut into 1/2-inch cubes
- 1 can (10-3/4 oz.) 98%-fat-free condensed cream of chicken soup
- 1 can (8 oz.) refrigerated reduced-fat crescent dinner rolls

Direction

- Heat oven to 375°F.
- Combine first 4 ingredients in 13x9-inch baking dish.
- Unroll dough; place over chicken mixture.
- Bake 20 to 25 min. or until crust is golden brown.

Nutrition Information

- Calories: 480
- Total Carbohydrate: 0 g
- Sugar: 0 g
- Saturated Fat: 8 g
- Total Fat: 25 g
- Cholesterol: 110 mg
- Sodium: 1460 mg
- Fiber: 2 g
- Protein: 40 g

99. Chicken Pot Pie Bubble Bread Bake

Serving: 8 | Prep: 10mins | Cook: 35mins | Ready in: 45mins

Ingredients

- 1 can (16.3 oz.) refrigerated big buttermilk biscuits (8 biscuits)
- 2 cups chopped cooked chicken
- 1-1/2 cups frozen mixed vegetables (carrots, corn, green beans, peas)
- 3/4 cup HEINZ HomeStyle Classic Chicken Gravy
- 1-1/2 cups KRAFT Shredded Mild Cheddar Cheese

Direction

- Heat oven to 350°F.
- Cut biscuits into quarters; place in even layer in 13x9-inch baking dish sprayed with cooking spray. Top with chicken.
- Combine vegetables and gravy; spoon over chicken.
- Bake 20 min. Top with cheese; bake 15 min. or until biscuits are golden brown and cheese is melted.

Nutrition Information

- Calories: 350
- Total Fat: 16 g
- Sodium: 740 mg
- Total Carbohydrate: 31 g
- Fiber: 2 g
- Saturated Fat: 8 g
- Cholesterol: 50 mg
- Protein: 18 g
- Sugar: 5 g

100. Chicken Ranch BLT

Serving: 2 | Prep: 10mins | Cook: | Ready in: 10mins

Ingredients

- 1 cup OSCAR MAYER CARVING BOARD Flame Grilled Chicken Breast Strips

- 1 Tbsp. OSCAR MAYER Real Bacon Recipe Pieces
- 1 Tbsp. KRAFT Classic Ranch Dressing
- 2 98% fat-free hot dog buns
- 2 KRAFT Slim Cut Sharp Cheddar Cheese Slices
- 1/2 cup shredded lettuce
- 1 tomato, cut into 4 slices, then cut crosswise in half

Direction

- Heat broiler.
- Combine chicken, bacon and dressing.
- Open buns; place, cut-sides up, on foil-covered baking sheet. Top with cheese and chicken mixture.
- Broil 3 to 4 min. or until cheese is melted and sandwiches are heated through.
- Top with lettuce and tomatoes. Fold buns in half.

Nutrition Information

- Calories: 370
- Cholesterol: 80 mg
- Protein: 32 g
- Saturated Fat: 6 g
- Total Fat: 15 g
- Total Carbohydrate: 26 g
- Fiber: 3 g
- Sugar: 5 g
- Sodium: 1030 mg

101. Chicken Rollatini

Serving: 6 | Prep: 15mins | Cook: 40mins | Ready in: 55mins

Ingredients

- 3 large boneless skinless chicken breasts (1-1/2 lb.)
- 1/2 tsp. ground black pepper
- 12 slices OSCAR MAYER Hard Salami
- 6 KRAFT Provolone Cheese Slices
- 18 fresh asparagus spears
- 1-1/2 cups CLASSICO Marinara with Plum Tomatoes & Olive Oil Pasta Sauce
- 1/4 cup KRAFT Shredded Parmesan Cheese

Direction

- Heat oven to 350°F.
- Cut each chicken breast horizontally in half to make 2 cutlets; place between 2 sheets of plastic wrap. Pound to 1/4-inch thickness; sprinkle with pepper. Top with salami, provolone and asparagus; roll up tightly, starting at one short end of each cutlet. Secure with wooden toothpicks.
- Spread 1/2 cup pasta sauce onto bottom of 11x7-inch baking dish sprayed with cooking spray. Top with chicken; cover with remaining pasta sauce. Sprinkle with Parmesan.
- Bake 30 to 40 min. or until chicken is done. Remove and discard toothpicks before serving.

Nutrition Information

- Calories: 310
- Sodium: 740 mg
- Saturated Fat: 6 g
- Total Carbohydrate: 0 g
- Total Fat: 15 g
- Cholesterol: 100 mg
- Sugar: 0 g
- Fiber: 2 g
- Protein: 35 g

102. Chicken Salad Cuban Sandwich

Serving: 10 | Prep: 10mins | Cook: | Ready in: 10mins

Ingredients

- 3/4 cup KRAFT Mayo Homestyle Real Mayonnaise
- 2 Tbsp. chopped fresh cilantro
- 2 Tbsp. fresh lemon juice
- 1 tsp. black pepper
- 3/4 tsp. garlic powder
- 4 cups chopped cooked chicken
- 2 avocados, chopped
- 10 Cuban rolls, split
- 20 slices OSCAR MAYER Natural Applewood Smoked Ham
- 10 KRAFT Big Slice Aged Swiss Cheese Slices
- 10 CLAUSSEN Bread 'N Butter Pickle Sandwich Slices

Direction

- Heat panini grill.
- Mix first 5 ingredients in large bowl until blended. Add chicken; mix lightly. Stir in avocados.
- Fill rolls with chicken mixture, ham, cheese, and pickles.
- Grill 2 to 3 min. or until cheese is melted and sandwiches are golden brown.

Nutrition Information

- Calories: 580
- Cholesterol: 85 mg
- Fiber: 4 g
- Protein: 35 g
- Sugar: 0 g
- Sodium: 610 mg
- Saturated Fat: 8 g
- Total Carbohydrate: 0 g
- Total Fat: 30 g

103. Chicken Salad Sandwich Recipe

Serving: 4 | Prep: 10mins | Cook: | Ready in: 10mins

Ingredients

- 4 oz. (1/2 of 8-oz. pkg.) PHILADELPHIA Neufchatel Cheese, softened
- 1/4 cup MIRACLE WHIP Light Dressing
- 2 cups chopped cooked chicken breast
- 2 stalks celery, finely chopped
- 1/4 cup finely chopped onions
- 2 Tbsp. chopped fresh tarragon
- 8 slices whole wheat bread, toasted
- 8 lettuce leaves
- 1 tomato, cut into 8 thin slices

Direction

- Mix cream cheese and dressing in medium bowl until blended. Stir in chicken, celery, onions and tarragon.
- Fill toast slices with lettuce, tomatoes and chicken salad to make 4 sandwiches.

Nutrition Information

- Calories: 360
- Total Carbohydrate: 30 g
- Cholesterol: 80 mg
- Fiber: 4 g
- Saturated Fat: 5 g
- Sugar: 6 g
- Protein: 31 g
- Sodium: 580 mg
- Total Fat: 12 g

104. Chicken Salad Stuffed Zucchini

Serving: 2 | Prep: 10mins | Cook: | Ready in: 10mins

Ingredients

- 1 small zucchini
- 3 oz. OSCAR MAYER CARVING BOARD Flame Grilled Chicken Breast Strips, finely chopped
- 1 Tbsp. chopped tomatoes
- 1 tsp. green onion slices

- 1 KRAFT Slim Cut Sharp Cheddar Cheese Slice, halved

Direction

- Cut zucchini lengthwise in half; scoop out centers with spoon, leaving 1/4-inch-thick shells. Chop removed zucchini; place in small bowl. Add chicken, tomatoes and onions; mix lightly.
- Spoon into zucchini shells; place on microwaveable plate. Microwave on HIGH 1 min.
- Top with cheese. Microwave 30 sec. or until cheese is melted.

Nutrition Information

- Calories: 80
- Cholesterol: 35 mg
- Total Carbohydrate: 0 g
- Protein: 13 g
- Total Fat: 2.5 g
- Fiber: 1 g
- Saturated Fat: 1 g
- Sodium: 320 mg
- Sugar: 0 g

105. Chicken Stir Fry With Jicama, Tomatillos And Red Peppers

Serving: 0 | Prep: 15mins | Cook: 45mins | Ready in: 1hours

Ingredients

- 1 lb. boneless skinless chicken breasts, cut into strips
- 1/4 cup KRAFT Zesty Italian Dressing
- 4 slices OSCAR MAYER Bacon, chopped
- 1 cup sliced jicama (about 1 medium)
- 1 cup quartered tomatillos
- 1 cup sliced red bell peppers (about 1 medium)
- 1/2 tsp. crushed red pepper
- 2 cups hot cooked rice

Direction

- Place chicken in resealable plastic bag. Add dressing; seal bag. Turn bag over several times to evenly coat chicken with dressing. Refrigerate at least 30 min. or up to 1 hour to marinate.
- Cook bacon in large skillet on medium heat until crisp. Drain fat from skillet; set bacon aside. Remove chicken from marinade; discard marinade. Add chicken to same skillet; cook 4 min. or until evenly browned, stirring frequently. Add jicama, tomatillos, red bell peppers and crushed red pepper; mix well. Cook 3 min. or until chicken is cooked through, stirring occasionally.
- Serve over the rice.

Nutrition Information

- Calories: 320
- Cholesterol: 75 mg
- Protein: 29 g
- Fiber: 3 g
- Total Carbohydrate: 0 g
- Sugar: 0 g
- Saturated Fat: 2.5 g
- Sodium: 410 mg
- Total Fat: 9 g

106. Chicken TV Dinner Roll Up

Serving: 9 | Prep: 15mins | Cook: 25mins | Ready in: 40mins

Ingredients

- 1 can (13.8 oz.) refrigerated pizza crust

- 1 cup KRAFT Shredded Cheddar Cheese
- 2 cups chopped leftover cooked chicken
- 1 cup leftover cooked mixed vegetables (carrots, green beans, peas)
- 1 cup leftover mashed ORE-IDA STEAM N' MASH Cut Russet Potatoes
- 1 jar (12 oz.) HEINZ HomeStyle Classic Chicken Gravy, divided

Direction

- Heat oven to 400°F.
- Unroll pizza dough onto baking sheet sprayed with cooking spray; press into 15x8-inch rectangle. Top with cheese, chicken, mixed vegetables and mashed potatoes, leaving a 1/2-inch-wide border around all sides of dough. Drizzle with 1/2 cup gravy.
- Roll up, starting at one long side. Rearrange if necessary so roll is seam side down on baking sheet.
- Bake 20 to 25 min. or until golden brown.
- Warm remaining gravy. Cut roll-up into 9 slices. Serve topped with gravy.

Nutrition Information

- Calories: 260
- Sodium: 650 mg
- Sugar: 3 g
- Total Fat: 9 g
- Cholesterol: 40 mg
- Saturated Fat: 4 g
- Total Carbohydrate: 29 g
- Fiber: 1 g
- Protein: 16 g

107. Chicken Taco Casserole

Serving: 6 | Prep: 35mins | Cook: 15mins | Ready in: 50mins

Ingredients

- 1 Tbsp. oil
- 1-1/2 lb. boneless skinless chicken thighs, cut into bite-size pieces
- 2 green onions, chopped
- 1 pkg. (14.6 oz.) TACO BELL® Soft Tortilla Taco Dinner Kit
- 3/4 cup water
- 1/2 cup frozen corn
- 1/2 cup BREAKSTONE'S or KNUDSEN Sour Cream
- 1 pkg. (8 oz.) KRAFT Shredded Cheddar Cheese, divided

Direction

- Heat oven to 350°F.
- Heat oil in large skillet on medium heat. Add chicken and onions; cook and stir 8 to 10 min. or until chicken is done. Add Seasoning Mix and water; stir. Bring to boil; simmer on medium-low heat 10 min., stirring occasionally. Remove from heat; stir in corn and sour cream.
- Cover bottom of 13x9-inch baking dish sprayed with cooking spray with 5 Tortillas; top with 1 cup cheese, chicken mixture and remaining tortillas. Drizzle with Taco Sauce.
- Bake 15 min. or until heated through. Sprinkle with remaining cheese; bake 5 min. or until melted.

Nutrition Information

- Calories: 530
- Cholesterol: 150 mg
- Sugar: 3 g
- Total Fat: 29 g
- Sodium: 1080 mg
- Total Carbohydrate: 35 g
- Fiber: 2 g
- Protein: 32 g
- Saturated Fat: 13 g

108. Chicken Thighs With Fennel And Dried Apricots

Serving: 6 | Prep: 10mins | Cook: 7hours | Ready in: 7hours10mins

Ingredients

- 1 fennel bulb, trimmed, cut into 1/2-inch-thick wedges
- 2 jars (6 oz. each) sliced mushrooms, drained
- 1/2 cup chopped dried apricots
- 2 Tbsp. MINUTE Tapioca
- 1-1/2 lb. boneless skinless chicken thighs
- 3/4 tsp. dried sage leaves, crushed
- 1/2 tsp. dried thyme leaves, crushed
- 1/4 tsp. crushed red pepper
- 1 cup apricot nectar

Direction

- Place first 4 ingredients in slow cooker sprayed with cooking spray. Add chicken; sprinkle with seasonings.
- Pour nectar over ingredients in slow cooker; cover with lid.
- Cook on LOW 7 to 8 hours (or on HIGH 3-1/2 to 4 hours).

Nutrition Information

- Calories: 220
- Fiber: 3 g
- Protein: 21 g
- Sodium: 270 mg
- Sugar: 14 g
- Total Carbohydrate: 23 g
- Total Fat: 6 g
- Saturated Fat: 2 g
- Cholesterol: 100 mg

109. Chicken Tinga Recipe

Serving: 0 | Prep: 20mins | Cook: 10mins | Ready in: 30mins

Ingredients

- 1/2 cup water
- 2 tomatoes
- 2 canned chipotle peppers in adobo sauce
- 1/4 cup KRAFT Zesty Italian Dressing
- 1 large onion, sliced
- 2 cups shredded cooked chicken
- 1/2 cup BREAKSTONE'S or KNUDSEN Sour Cream
- 2 pkg. (12 oz. each) tortilla chips

Direction

- Blend water, tomatoes and peppers in blender until smooth.
- Heat dressing in large saucepan on medium-high heat. Add onions; cook 5 min. or until crisp-tender, stirring frequently. Stir in tomato mixture; bring to boil, stirring occasionally.
- Add chicken; stir. Cover; simmer on low heat 10 min. or until heated through, stirring occasionally.
- Spoon dip into serving dish; top with sour cream. Serve with chips.

Nutrition Information

- Calories: 180
- Total Carbohydrate: 21 g
- Sodium: 140 mg
- Cholesterol: 15 mg
- Protein: 6 g
- Total Fat: 8 g
- Sugar: 1 g
- Saturated Fat: 1.5 g
- Fiber: 2 g

110. Chicken Tortellini Soup

Serving: 0 | Prep: 30mins | Cook: | Ready in: 30mins

Ingredients

- 1/4 cup KRAFT Sun Dried Tomato Vinaigrette Dressing made with Extra Virgin Olive Oil
- 3/4 lb. boneless skinless chicken breasts, cut into bite-size pieces
- 2 stalks celery, thinly sliced
- 3/4 cup chopped onions
- 2 cloves garlic, minced
- 1 carton (32 oz.) fat-free reduced-sodium chicken broth
- 2 cups water
- 1-1/2 cups frozen mixed vegetables (carrots, corn, green beans, peas)
- 1/4 cup CLASSICO Sun-Dried Tomato Pesto Sauce and Spread
- 1 pkg. (9 oz.) refrigerated cheese tortellini
- 1/4 cup KRAFT Grated Parmesan Cheese

Direction

- Heat dressing in large saucepan on medium-high heat. Add chicken, celery and onions; cook and stir 5 min. or until onions are tender and chicken is no longer pink. Add garlic; cook and stir 1 min.
- Add broth, water, vegetables and pesto sauce; bring to boil. Simmer on medium-low heat 5 min. Stir in pasta; return to boil. Cook on medium heat 3 min. Remove from heat. Let stand 2 min.
- Serve topped with Parmesan.

Nutrition Information

- Calories: 170
- Total Carbohydrate: 17 g
- Fiber: 2 g
- Cholesterol: 30 mg
- Saturated Fat: 1.5 g
- Sodium: 500 mg
- Sugar: 4 g
- Protein: 14 g
- Total Fat: 5 g

111. Chicken Waldorf Salad

Serving: 0 | Prep: 15mins | Cook: | Ready in: 15mins

Ingredients

- 3 cups chopped cooked chicken
- 1 cup grapes, halved
- 2 stalks celery, finely chopped
- 1 apple, chopped
- 1/2 cup chopped PLANTERS Walnuts, toasted
- 1/2 cup KRAFT Real Mayo Mayonnaise
- 1/4 cup BREAKSTONE'S or KNUDSEN Sour Cream
- 1/4 cup GREY POUPON Savory Honey Mustard

Direction

- Combine first 5 ingredients in large bowl.
- Mix remaining ingredients until blended. Add to chicken mixture; mix lightly.

Nutrition Information

- Calories: 170
- Sodium: 75 mg
- Saturated Fat: 2 g
- Total Carbohydrate: 5 g
- Sugar: 4 g
- Fiber: 1 g
- Protein: 10 g
- Total Fat: 12 g
- Cholesterol: 30 mg

112. Chicken And Dumplings In Green Salsa

Serving: 6 | Prep: 1hours | Cook: | Ready in: 1hours

Ingredients

- 6 slices OSCAR MAYER Bacon, chopped
- 1 whole chicken (3 lb.), cut up
- 1 jar (16 oz.) green salsa
- 1 can (10.5 oz.) chicken broth
- 1/2 lb. prepared corn masa dough
- 1/2 cup KRAFT Shredded Cheddar Cheese
- 1/4 cup chopped fresh cilantro

Direction

- Cook and stir bacon in Dutch oven or large deep skillet on medium heat until crisp. Remove bacon from pan with slotted spoon; drain on paper towels. Remove drippings from pan; reserve 1 Tbsp. drippings for later use.
- Add chicken, in batches, to pan; cook 3 min. on each side or until browned on both sides. Return all chicken to pan. Stir in salsa and broth. Bring to boil; cover. Simmer on medium-low heat 15 min. Meanwhile, mix masa dough, cheese and reserved bacon drippings; shape into 18 balls, using about 1 Tbsp. dough for each.
- Add dough balls to chicken mixture; cook 5 to 8 min. or until dumplings and chicken are done (165°F). Remove from heat. Stir in bacon and cilantro.

Nutrition Information

- Calories: 400
- Total Fat: 21 g
- Fiber: 1 g
- Cholesterol: 95 mg
- Sodium: 1140 mg
- Saturated Fat: 7 g
- Sugar: 0 g
- Total Carbohydrate: 17 g
- Protein: 31 g

113. Chicken And Ham Lemon Soup

Serving: 0 | Prep: 15mins | Cook: 15mins | Ready in: 30mins

Ingredients

- 1 lb. boneless skinless chicken breasts
- 2 cups water
- 1 bay leaf
- 1 clove garlic, chopped
- 3 cups chicken broth
- 1/2 cup wild rice
- zest and juice of 1 lemon
- 1 cup chopped OSCAR MAYER Deli Fresh Smoked Ham
- 20 dino kale leaves, rinsed, ribs removed and torn
- 1 lemon thinly sliced in rounds

Direction

- In a large pot, combine water and chicken over medium heat. Cook for 15 minutes or until chicken is tender. Remove from heat. Remove chicken from broth and let cool. Reserve broth.
- Strain chicken broth into a 5-quart stock pot. Heat over medium heat. Add bay leaf, salt, garlic, 3 cups chicken broth, rice, lemon zest and lemon juice. Cook for 10 minutes.
- Shred chicken breast and add to soup. Add ham. Cook for 5 minutes more. Remove soup from heat, stir in kale, lemon slices and serve.

Nutrition Information

- Calories: 0 g
- Protein: 0 g
- Fiber: 0 g
- Sodium: 0 g
- Sugar: 0 g
- Total Fat: 0 g
- Saturated Fat: 0 g
- Total Carbohydrate: 0 g
- Cholesterol: 0 g

114. Chicken And Peanut Stew

Serving: 12 | Prep: 30mins | Cook: 1hours30mins | Ready in: 2hours

Ingredients

- 1 Tbsp. PLANTERS Peanut Oil
- 4 lb. mixed bone-in chicken breasts, legs and thighs
- 1/2 cup creamy peanut butter
- 2 Tbsp. tomato paste
- 1 can (14.5 oz.) diced tomatoes, drained
- 2 cans (14-1/2 oz. each) fat-free reduced-sodium chicken broth
- 2 onions, chopped
- 4 carrots, chopped
- 3 cloves garlic, minced
- 2 cups long-grain white rice, uncooked
- 1/2 cup PLANTERS COCKTAIL Peanuts, chopped

Direction

- Heat oil in large skillet on medium heat. Add chicken; cook 8 to 10 min. or until all pieces are evenly browned on both sides, turning occasionally. Remove chicken from skillet, reserving drippings in skillet; cover chicken to keep warm.
- Mix peanut butter and tomato paste in medium bowl until blended. Add tomatoes and chicken broth; mix well.
- Add onions, carrots and garlic to reserved chicken drippings in skillet; cook 5 min. or until crisp-tender, stirring frequently. Add peanut butter mixture; mix well.
- Return chicken to skillet; stir until evenly coated with sauce. Bring to boil; partially cover skillet with lid. Simmer on medium-low heat 1-1/2 hours or until chicken is done (165°F). About 20 min. before stew is done, cook rice as directed on package, omitting salt.
- Serve stew over rice; sprinkle with nuts.

Nutrition Information

- Calories: 390
- Fiber: 3 g
- Protein: 24 g
- Cholesterol: 50 mg
- Sodium: 300 mg
- Sugar: 0 g
- Saturated Fat: 4 g
- Total Fat: 18 g
- Total Carbohydrate: 0 g

115. Chicken With Apple Walnut Stuffing

Serving: 6 | Prep: 15mins | Cook: 40mins | Ready in: 55mins

Ingredients

- 1 pkg. (6 oz.) STOVE TOP Stuffing Mix for Chicken
- 1 small Granny Smith apple, chopped
- 3/4 cup chopped PLANTERS Walnuts
- 1/2 cup raisins
- 6 small boneless skinless chicken breasts (1-1/2 lb.)
- 3/4 cup fat-free reduced-sodium chicken broth
- 4 oz. (1/2 of 8-oz. pkg.) PHILADELPHIA Cream Cheese, cubed
- 1 tsp. GREY POUPON Dijon Mustard
- 2 Tbsp. chopped fresh parsley

Direction

- Heat oven to 375°F.
- Prepare stuffing in large saucepan as directed on package. Add apples, nuts and raisins; mix lightly. Spoon into 13x9-inch baking dish; top with chicken.
- Bake 35 to 40 min. or until chicken is done (165°F). Meanwhile, bring broth to boil in medium saucepan on medium-high heat. Add cream cheese and mustard; cook on medium-low heat 4 to 5 min. or until cream cheese is

melted and sauce begins to thicken, stirring constantly with whisk.
- Pour sauce over chicken just before serving; sprinkle with parsley.

Nutrition Information

- Calories: 510
- Fiber: 3 g
- Sodium: 730 mg
- Total Fat: 26 g
- Sugar: 13 g
- Saturated Fat: 7 g
- Cholesterol: 90 mg
- Total Carbohydrate: 36 g
- Protein: 32 g

116. Chicken, Apple & Spinach Salad

Serving: 0 | Prep: 5mins | Cook: | Ready in: 5mins

Ingredients

- 1 cup tightly packed fresh spinach
- 1/2 cup apple slices
- 1/2 cup chopped cooked chicken breast
- 1/4 cup slivered red onions
- 2 Tbsp. golden raisins
- 2 Tbsp. KRAFT Chunky Blue Cheese Dressing

Direction

- Combine all ingredients except dressing in medium bowl.
- Add dressing; toss to coat.

Nutrition Information

- Calories: 350
- Fiber: 4 g
- Cholesterol: 60 mg
- Saturated Fat: 3 g
- Total Carbohydrate: 0 g

- Sugar: 0 g
- Sodium: 410 mg
- Total Fat: 15 g
- Protein: 25 g

117. Chicken, Broccoli & Pinto Beans Recipe

Serving: 6 | Prep: 10mins | Cook: 10mins | Ready in: 20mins

Ingredients

- 4 slices OSCAR MAYER Bacon, chopped
- 1 lb. boneless skinless chicken breasts, cut into thin strips
- 1 onion, sliced and slices cut in half
- 1 lb. broccoli, broken into small florets and stems sliced
- 1 red bell pepper, cut into thin strips
- 1 can (15 oz.) pinto beans, drained
- 1 tsp. crushed red pepper
- 1/4 cup lite soy sauce
- 1 Tbsp. cornstarch
- 1/4 cup PLANTERS Dry Roasted Peanuts
- 3 cups hot cooked brown rice

Direction

- Cook bacon in large nonstick skillet on medium-high heat until completely browned. Remove from skillet; set aside. Add chicken to skillet; cook 2 to 3 min. or until cooked through, stirring constantly. Remove from skillet; set aside.
- Add onions to skillet; cook 3 to 4 min. until crisp-tender. Add broccoli, bell peppers, beans and crushed red pepper; cover. Cook 5 min. until vegetables are tender.
- Combine soy sauce and cornstarch in small bowl; add to skillet with chicken. Bring to boil; cook 1 min., stirring constantly. Stir in cooked bacon and peanuts.

Nutrition Information

- Calories: 370
- Protein: 28 g
- Saturated Fat: 2 g
- Sugar: 0 g
- Total Fat: 9 g
- Cholesterol: 50 mg
- Sodium: 580 mg
- Total Carbohydrate: 0 g
- Fiber: 7 g

118. Chicken, Broccoli And Rice Casserole

Serving: 6 | Prep: 15mins | Cook: 35mins | Ready in: 50mins

Ingredients

- 2 cups cooked long-grain white rice
- 2 Tbsp. butter
- 2 Tbsp. flour
- 1 cup milk
- 3 cups chopped cooked chicken
- 1 container (8 oz.) BREAKSTONE'S or KNUDSEN Sour Cream
- 2 cups small broccoli florets
- 2 green onions, sliced
- 6 oz. VELVEETA, cut into 1/2-inch cubes
- 1 cup french-fried onions

Direction

- Heat oven to 375°F.
- Spread rice onto bottom of 2-qt. casserole sprayed with cooking spray.
- Melt butter in large skillet on medium heat. Add flour; cook and stir 1 min. or until hot and bubbly. Gradually whisk in milk. Bring to boil, stirring constantly. Simmer on medium-low heat 2 min., stirring constantly. Add all remaining ingredients except french fried onions; mix well. Spoon over rice; sprinkle with onions.
- Bake 30 to 35 min. or until heated through.

Nutrition Information

- Calories: 480
- Cholesterol: 120 mg
- Total Carbohydrate: 28 g
- Fiber: 1 g
- Protein: 30 g
- Total Fat: 27 g
- Sodium: 590 mg
- Saturated Fat: 14 g
- Sugar: 7 g

119. Chicken Parmesan Bake

Serving: 0 | Prep: 10mins | Cook: 35mins | Ready in: 45mins

Ingredients

- 1 jar (24 oz.) CLASSICO Tomato and Basil Pasta Sauce
- 1/3 cup KRAFT Grated Parmesan Cheese, divided
- 8 small boneless skinless chicken breasts (2 lb.)
- 1 pkg. (11.25 oz.) frozen garlic Texas toast
- 1 cup KRAFT Shredded Mozzarella Cheese

Direction

- Heat oven to 375°F.
- Pour sauce into 13x9-inch baking dish; stir in half the Parmesan. Add chicken; turn to evenly coat both sides of each breast.
- Bake 30 min. or until chicken is done (165°F). Meanwhile prepare garlic toast as directed on package.
- Top chicken with mozzarella and remaining Parmesan; bake 5 min. or until mozzarella is melted. Serve with garlic toast.

Nutrition Information

- Calories: 410
- Cholesterol: 80 mg
- Total Carbohydrate: 0 g
- Sodium: 870 mg
- Protein: 33 g
- Fiber: 3 g
- Saturated Fat: 6 g
- Sugar: 0 g
- Total Fat: 16 g

120. Chicken Parmesan Bundles

Serving: 6 | Prep: 30mins | Cook: 25mins | Ready in: 55mins

Ingredients

- 6 small boneless skinless chicken breasts (1-1/2 lb.)
- 4 oz. (1/2 of 8-oz. pkg.) PHILADELPHIA Cream Cheese, softened
- 1 pkg. (10 oz.) frozen chopped spinach, thawed, well drained
- 1-1/4 cups KRAFT Shredded Low-Moisture Part-Skim Mozzarella Cheese, divided
- 6 Tbsp. KRAFT Grated Parmesan Cheese, divided
- 1 egg
- 10 RITZ Crackers, crushed
- 1-1/2 cups CLASSICO Tomato and Basil Pasta Sauce

Direction

- Heat oven to 375°F.
- Pound chicken to 1/4-inch-thickness on work surface; turn smooth sides down. Mix cream cheese, spinach, 1 cup mozzarella and 3 Tbsp. Parmesan until blended; spread onto chicken. Starting at one short end of each breast, roll up chicken tightly. Secure with wooden toothpicks, if desired.
- Whisk egg in shallow dish until blended. Combine cracker crumbs and remaining Parmesan in separate shallow dish. Spray 13x9-inch baking dish with cooking spray. Dip chicken, 1 bundle at a time, into egg, then into crumb mixture, turning to evenly coat all sides with crumb mixture. Place, seam sides down, in prepared baking dish.
- Bake 30 min. or until chicken is done (165°F). About 5 min. before chicken is done, cook pasta sauce on medium-low heat until heated through, stirring occasionally.
- Remove and discard toothpicks from chicken. Spoon pasta sauce over chicken; top with remaining mozzarella.

Nutrition Information

- Calories: 330
- Cholesterol: 130 mg
- Fiber: 2 g
- Total Fat: 19 g
- Protein: 31 g
- Saturated Fat: 9 g
- Sodium: 540 mg
- Sugar: 0 g
- Total Carbohydrate: 0 g

121. Chicken Parmesan Pasta

Serving: 0 | Prep: 10mins | Cook: 30mins | Ready in: 40mins

Ingredients

- 6 small boneless skinless chicken breasts (1-1/2 lb.)
- 2 egg whites, lightly beaten
- 1 cup dry Italian-style bread crumbs
- 3 cups CLASSICO Tomato and Basil Pasta Sauce, divided
- 1-1/2 cups KRAFT 2% Milk Shredded Mozzarella Cheese
- 1/4 cup KRAFT Grated Parmesan Cheese
- 1 tsp. dried oregano leaves
- 6 oz. spaghetti, cooked, drained

Direction

- Heat oven to 400°F.
- Dip chicken in egg whites, then in bread crumbs, turning to evenly coat both sides of each breast. Place in 13x9-inch pan sprayed with cooking spray.
- Bake 20 to 25 min. or until chicken is done (165°F). Top with 2 cups sauce, cheeses and oregano. Bake 5 min. or until mozzarella is melted. Meanwhile, heat remaining sauce.
- Toss spaghetti with sauce; place on plate. Top with chicken.

Nutrition Information

- Calories: 470
- Fiber: 4 g
- Sodium: 1350 mg
- Cholesterol: 85 mg
- Total Fat: 12 g
- Saturated Fat: 4.5 g
- Protein: 43 g
- Total Carbohydrate: 0 g
- Sugar: 0 g

122. Chicken Penne Florentine Bake

Serving: 0 | Prep: 25mins | Cook: 18mins | Ready in: 43mins

Ingredients

- 2 cups multi-grain penne pasta, uncooked
- 1 lb. boneless skinless chicken breasts, cut into bite-size pieces
- 2 Tbsp. flour
- 2 Tbsp. KRAFT Sun Dried Tomato Vinaigrette Dressing
- 1 cup fat-free reduced-sodium chicken broth
- 2 oz. (1/4 of 8-oz. pkg.) PHILADELPHIA Neufchatel Cheese, cubed
- 1 pkg. (10 oz.) frozen chopped spinach, thawed, well drained
- 1 cup KRAFT Shredded Mozzarella Cheese
- 2 Tbsp. KRAFT Grated Parmesan Cheese

Direction

- Heat oven to 375°F.
- Cook pasta as directed on package, omitting salt.
- Meanwhile, toss chicken with flour. Heat dressing in large skillet on medium heat. Add chicken; cook and stir 3 min. or until evenly browned. Add broth and Neufchatel; cook 3 min. or until Neufchatel is melted, stirring frequently. Stir in spinach.
- Drain pasta. Add to chicken mixture; mix lightly. Spoon half into 2-qt. casserole sprayed with cooking spray; top with half the mozzarella. Repeat layers. Sprinkle with Parmesan.
- Bake 16 to 18 min. or until mozzarella is melted and casserole is heated through.

Nutrition Information

- Calories: 350
- Cholesterol: 60 mg
- Total Carbohydrate: 0 g
- Sugar: 0 g
- Sodium: 430 mg
- Saturated Fat: 5 g
- Total Fat: 11 g
- Protein: 29 g
- Fiber: 5 g

123. Chinese Sweet And Sour Chicken Recipe

Serving: 6 | Prep: 30mins | Cook: | Ready in: 30mins

Ingredients

- 1-1/2 cups long-grain white rice, uncooked

- 1 can (8 oz.) pineapple chunks in juice, undrained
- 1/4 cup KRAFT Lite Asian Toasted Sesame Dressing
- 1-1/2 lb. boneless skinless chicken breasts, cut into bite-size pieces
- 1 red pepper, coarsely chopped
- 1 small red onion, coarsely chopped
- 3/4 cup KRAFT Sweet'N Sour Sauce

Direction

- Cook rice as directed on package, omitting salt.
- Drain pineapple, reserving juice. Mix dressing with reserved juice; pour half into large skillet. Add chicken; stir-fry 8 to 10 min. or until done. Add vegetables and remaining dressing mixture; stir-fry 2 to 4 min. or until vegetables are crisp-tender. Stir in sweet-and-sour sauce and pineapple; stir-fry 1 to 2 min. or until heated through.
- Serve chicken mixture over rice.

Nutrition Information

- Calories: 370
- Cholesterol: 55 mg
- Sugar: 0 g
- Saturated Fat: 0.5 g
- Fiber: 2 g
- Total Carbohydrate: 0 g
- Sodium: 260 mg
- Protein: 21 g
- Total Fat: 3 g

124. Chipotle Chicken & Vegetable Skillet

Serving: 8 | Prep: 25mins | Cook: 25mins | Ready in: 50mins

Ingredients

- 1/2 cup KRAFT Zesty Italian Dressing, divided
- 8 small boneless skinless chicken breasts (2 lb.)
- 1 large onion, sliced
- 2 cans (14.5 oz. each) diced tomatoes, undrained
- 1 lb. new potatoes, quartered
- 2 carrots, chopped
- 3 canned chipotle peppers in adobo sauce, chopped
- 1/2 cup BREAKSTONE'S or KNUDSEN Sour Cream

Direction

- Heat 1/4 cup dressing in large skillet on medium heat. Add chicken breasts; cook 5 min. or until evenly browned on both sides, turning after 3 min. Remove from skillet; cover to keep warm.
- Add onions and remaining dressing to skillet; cook and stir 3 min. or until onions are crisp-tender. Return chicken to skillet. Add tomatoes, potatoes, carrots and peppers. Bring to boil; cover. Simmer on low heat 25 min. or until chicken is done (165°F) and potatoes are tender, uncovering after 10 min.
- Serve topped with sour cream.

Nutrition Information

- Calories: 230
- Cholesterol: 70 mg
- Saturated Fat: 2.5 g
- Fiber: 3 g
- Total Carbohydrate: 0 g
- Sodium: 350 mg
- Total Fat: 7 g
- Protein: 20 g
- Sugar: 0 g

125. Chopped Greek Chicken Salad

Serving: 0 | Prep: 10mins | Cook: | Ready in: 10mins

Ingredients

- 2 cups chopped iceberg lettuce
- 1 pkg. (6 oz.) OSCAR MAYER CARVING BOARD Lemon Pepper Chicken Breast Strips
- 1/2 cup halved grape tomatoes
- 1/2 cup chopped cucumbers
- 1/2 cup chopped radishes
- 1/2 cup chopped green bell peppers
- 1/4 cup chopped red onions
- 1/4 cup chopped Kalamata olives
- 1/4 cup ATHENOS Traditional Crumbled Feta Cheese
- 1/4 cup KRAFT Greek Vinaigrette Dressing

Direction

- Combine ingredients.

Nutrition Information

- Calories: 370
- Cholesterol: 85 mg
- Saturated Fat: 5 g
- Fiber: 4 g
- Sodium: 1290 mg
- Protein: 29 g
- Total Carbohydrate: 0 g
- Sugar: 0 g
- Total Fat: 21 g

126. Cider Glazed Stuffed Chicken

Serving: 6 | Prep: 20mins | Cook: 40mins | Ready in: 1hours

Ingredients

- 1 pkg. (6 oz.) STOVE TOP Stuffing Mix for Chicken
- 2 cups apple cider, divided
- 1/4 cup butter, divided
- 1 stalk celery, minced
- 2 apples, peeled, chopped and divided
- 6 small boneless skinless chicken breasts (1-1/2 lb.), pounded to 1/4-inch thickness
- 1/4 tsp. paprika
- 3 Tbsp. brown sugar

Direction

- Heat oven to 350°F.
- Combine stuffing mix, 1-1/2 cups cider and 1 Tbsp. butter in microwaveable bowl; cover with waxed paper. Microwave on HIGH 5 to 6 min. or until heated through. Fluff with fork. Add celery and half the apples; mix lightly.
- Place chicken, top-sides down, on cutting board; spread with stuffing. Roll up, starting at one short end of each breast. Place, seam-sides down, in 13x9-inch baking dish sprayed with cooking spray. Melt 1 Tbsp. of the remaining butter; mix with paprika. Brush onto chicken.
- Bake 40 min. or until chicken is done (165°F). Transfer chicken to platter; cover to keep warm.
- Melt 1 Tbsp. of the remaining butter in medium skillet on medium-high heat. Add sugar, remaining cider and apples; cook 5 to 6 min. or until thickened, stirring frequently. Remove from heat; stir in remaining butter until melted. Pour over chicken.

Nutrition Information

- Calories: 380
- Protein: 28 g
- Fiber: 2 g
- Cholesterol: 85 mg
- Sodium: 530 mg
- Total Carbohydrate: 0 g
- Sugar: 0 g
- Total Fat: 12 g

- Saturated Fat: 6 g

127. Classic Balsamic Marinade For Chicken

Serving: 6 | Prep: 20mins | Cook: 30mins | Ready in: 50mins

Ingredients

- 6 Tbsp. LEA & PERRINS Worcestershire Sauce
- 3 Tbsp. olive oil
- 3 Tbsp. HEINZ Balsamic Vinegar
- 6 small boneless skinless chicken breasts (1-1/2 lb.)

Direction

- Whisk Worcestershire sauce, oil and vinegar until blended. Reserve 1/4 cup Worcestershire sauce mixture for later use.
- Pour remaining Worcestershire sauce mixture over chicken in shallow dish; turn to evenly coat both sides of chicken breasts.
- Refrigerate 30 min. to marinate.
- Heat grill to medium heat. Remove chicken from marinade; discard marinade.
- Grill chicken 6 to 8 min. on each side or until done (165°F), turning and brushing with reserved Worcestershire sauce mixture for the last 5 min.

Nutrition Information

- Calories: 170
- Saturated Fat: 1.5 g
- Total Carbohydrate: 0 g
- Protein: 24 g
- Cholesterol: 65 mg
- Sugar: 0 g
- Fiber: 0 g
- Sodium: 170 mg
- Total Fat: 7 g

128. Cobb Salad

Serving: 0 | Prep: 20mins | Cook: | Ready in: 20mins

Ingredients

- 6 slices OSCAR MAYER Fully Cooked Bacon
- 6 cups torn mixed salad greens
- 1 pkg. (6 oz.) OSCAR MAYER CARVING BOARD Flame Grilled Chicken Breast Strips
- 2 tomatoes, seeded, chopped
- 2 hard-cooked eggs, chopped
- 1 avocado, peeled, chopped
- 3/4 cup KRAFT Shredded Cheddar Cheese
- 1/2 cup KRAFT Classic Ranch Dressing
- 1/4 cup ATHENOS Crumbled Blue Cheese

Direction

- Heat bacon as directed on package. Cut into bite-size pieces.
- Place greens on large serving platter; top with rows of chicken, tomatoes, eggs and avocado. Sprinkle with bacon and cheddar cheese.
- Drizzle with dressing. Sprinkle with blue cheese.

Nutrition Information

- Calories: 490
- Sugar: 4 g
- Cholesterol: 185 mg
- Total Carbohydrate: 12 g
- Saturated Fat: 12 g
- Total Fat: 38 g
- Sodium: 1110 mg
- Protein: 23 g
- Fiber: 5 g

129. Coconut Chicken Dippers

Serving: 8 | Prep: 15mins | Cook: 14mins | Ready in: 29mins

Ingredients

- 1 pkt. SHAKE 'N BAKE Extra Crispy Seasoned Coating Mix
- 1 cup BAKER'S ANGEL FLAKE Coconut, toasted
- 1/4 tsp. each curry powder and ground red pepper (cayenne)
- 1 egg
- 1 lb. boneless skinless chicken breasts, cut into 1-inch-wide strips
- 1/2 cup MIRACLE WHIP Dressing
- 2 Tbsp. mango chutney

Direction

- Heat oven to 400°F.
- Combine coating mix, coconut and dry seasonings in pie plate. Beat egg in second pie plate until blended.
- Dip chicken in egg, then coating mixture, turning to evenly coat both sides of each strip with each ingredient; place in 15x10x1-inch pan sprayed with cooking spray. Discard any remaining coating mix.
- Bake 12 to 14 min. or until chicken is done. Meanwhile, mix MIRACLE WHIP and chutney until blended.
- Serve chicken with MIRACLE WHIP mixture.

Nutrition Information

- Calories: 200
- Protein: 14 g
- Sodium: 420 mg
- Saturated Fat: 6 g
- Sugar: 0 g
- Fiber: 1 g
- Total Carbohydrate: 0 g
- Cholesterol: 60 mg
- Total Fat: 9 g

130. Cool Fruited Chicken Salad

Serving: 4 | Prep: 20mins | Cook: 1hours | Ready in: 1hours20mins

Ingredients

- 1/2 cup KRAFT Lite Raspberry Vinaigrette Dressing, divided
- 1 lb. boneless skinless chicken breasts, cooked, cut into bite-size pieces
- 1/4 cup thin red onion slices, separated into rings
- 1 pkg. (10 oz.) torn salad greens
- 1 cup cantaloupe chunks (1 inch)
- 2 kiwis, sliced
- 1 cup raspberries
- 24 woven wheat crackers

Direction

- Pour 1/4 cup dressing over chicken and onions in medium bowl; toss to coat. Refrigerate 1 hour.
- Drain chicken mixture; discard dressing. Place greens on 4 serving plates; top with chicken mixture and fruit.
- Drizzle with remaining dressing. Serve with crackers.

Nutrition Information

- Calories: 360
- Sodium: 460 mg
- Fiber: 9 g
- Total Carbohydrate: 0 g
- Cholesterol: 65 mg
- Sugar: 0 g
- Protein: 29 g
- Saturated Fat: 1 g
- Total Fat: 10 g

131. Cordon Bleu Chicken Casserole

Serving: 6 | Prep: 15mins | Cook: 25mins | Ready in: 40mins

Ingredients

- 6 small boneless skinless chicken breasts (1-1/2 lb.)
- 6 slices OSCAR MAYER Deli Fresh Smoked Ham
- 6 KRAFT Extra Thin Swiss Cheese Slices
- 2 cups tightly packed baby spinach leaves
- 1 red pepper, cut into strips
- 1 can (10-3/4 oz.) reduced-fat reduced-sodium condensed cream of chicken soup
- 1/2 cup BREAKSTONE'S Reduced Fat or KNUDSEN Light Sour Cream
- 1 Tbsp. GREY POUPON Dijon Mustard
- 1 cup croutons, coarsely crushed

Direction

- Heat oven to 400°F.
- Place chicken in 13x9-inch baking dish sprayed with cooking spray; top with ham, cheese, spinach and peppers.
- Mix soup, sour cream and mustard until blended. Spoon over ingredients in baking dish; spread to evenly cover all ingredients. Top with crushed croutons.
- Bake 25 min. or until chicken is done (165°F) and remaining ingredients are heated through.

Nutrition Information

- Calories: 300
- Total Fat: 12 g
- Fiber: 1 g
- Saturated Fat: 6 g
- Total Carbohydrate: 0 g
- Sugar: 0 g
- Cholesterol: 100 mg
- Sodium: 500 mg
- Protein: 34 g

132. Cornbread Topped Creamy Chicken Bake

Serving: 0 | Prep: 15mins | Cook: 25mins | Ready in: 40mins

Ingredients

- 1 can (10-3/4 oz.) reduced-fat reduced-sodium condensed cream of chicken soup
- 1/2 cup milk
- 1/4 tsp. pepper
- 2 cups chopped cooked chicken
- 1 cup frozen corn
- 1-1/2 cups KRAFT Shredded Triple Cheddar Cheese with a TOUCH OF PHILADELPHIA, divided
- 1 pkg. (8.5 oz.) corn muffin mix
- 1 green onion, sliced

Direction

- Heat oven to 425°F.
- Whisk first 3 ingredients in large bowl until blended. Stir in chicken, corn and 1 cup cheese; spoon into 2-qt. casserole sprayed with cooking spray.
- Prepare cornbread batter as directed on package; stir in onions and remaining cheese. Drop large spoonfuls of batter over chicken mixture.
- Bake 20 to 25 min. or until chicken mixture is hot and bubbly, and cornbread topping is golden brown.

Nutrition Information

- Calories: 450
- Protein: 26 g
- Saturated Fat: 10 g
- Sugar: 12 g
- Fiber: 2 g
- Cholesterol: 105 mg
- Sodium: 770 mg
- Total Fat: 20 g

- Total Carbohydrate: 43 g

133. Cranberry Glazed Chicken Dinner

Serving: 4 | Prep: 25mins | Cook: | Ready in: 25mins

Ingredients

- 1 can (14-1/2 oz.) fat-free reduced-sodium vegetable broth
- 1-1/2 cups each small broccoli and cauliflower florets
- 2 cups whole wheat couscous, uncooked
- 4 boneless skinless chicken thighs (1 lb.)
- 1/4 cup KRAFT Sweet & Spicy Barbecue Sauce
- 1/4 cup low-calorie cranberry juice cocktail
- 3 Tbsp. maple-flavored or pancake syrup
- 2 Tbsp. PLANTERS Dry Roasted Sunflower Kernels

Direction

- Bring broth and vegetables to boil in large saucepan on medium heat. Stir in couscous; cover. Remove from heat. Let stand 5 min. or until broth is completely absorbed.
- Meanwhile, cook chicken in large skillet sprayed with cooking spray on medium heat 5 to 6 min. on each side or until done (165°F). Remove from skillet; cover to keep warm.
- Add barbecue sauce, cranberry juice cocktail and syrup to skillet; stir. Bring to boil on medium-high heat; simmer on medium-low heat 3 min. or until thickened, stirring constantly.
- Serve chicken and couscous mixture topped with barbecue sauce mixture; sprinkle with sunflower kernels.

Nutrition Information

- Calories: 550
- Protein: 33 g
- Cholesterol: 100 mg
- Fiber: 7 g
- Total Fat: 12 g
- Sodium: 510 mg
- Saturated Fat: 2 g
- Total Carbohydrate: 0 g
- Sugar: 0 g

134. Cranberry Pecan Glazed Chicken Dinner

Serving: 4 | Prep: 25mins | Cook: | Ready in: 25mins

Ingredients

- 1 can (14-1/2 oz.) fat-free reduced-sodium chicken broth
- 2 cups instant brown rice, uncooked
- 2-1/2 cups small broccoli florets
- 1/4 cup dried cranberries
- 4 boneless skinless chicken thighs (1 lb.), 1/2 inch thick
- 1/4 cup KRAFT Thick & Spicy Barbecue Sauce
- 1/4 cup cranberry juice
- 3 Tbsp. maple-flavored or pancake syrup
- 2 Tbsp. chopped PLANTERS Pecans, toasted

Direction

- Bring broth to boil in medium saucepan on medium-high heat; stir in rice. Cover; simmer on medium-low heat 3 min. Add broccoli and cranberries; stir. Simmer, covered, 2 min. Remove from heat; let stand 5 min. or until broth is completely absorbed.
- Meanwhile, heat large nonstick skillet sprayed with cooking spray on medium heat. Add chicken thighs; cook 8 to 10 min. on each side or until done (170°F). Remove from skillet; cover to keep warm.
- Add barbecue sauce, juice and syrup to same skillet; stir. Bring to boil; cook on medium-high heat 3 min. or until thickened, stirring occasionally. Fluff rice with fork. Serve chicken and rice topped with sauce and nuts.

Nutrition Information

- Calories: 420
- Total Fat: 11 g
- Cholesterol: 50 mg
- Total Carbohydrate: 0 g
- Protein: 26 g
- Fiber: 4 g
- Sodium: 450 mg
- Sugar: 0 g
- Saturated Fat: 2.5 g

135. Creamed Chicken On Toast

Serving: 4 | Prep: 5mins | Cook: 5mins | Ready in: 10mins

Ingredients

- 1 pkg. (6 oz.) OSCAR MAYER CARVING BOARD Flame Grilled Chicken Breast Strips
- 1 can (10-3/4 oz.) low sodium condensed cream of mushroom soup
- 1-1/2 cups broccoli florets, cooked, drained
- 1/2 cup milk
- 1/2 cup KRAFT Shredded Swiss Cheese
- 1 tsp. LEA & PERRINS Worcestershire Sauce
- 8 slices bread, toasted, cut diagonally in half

Direction

- Combine chicken breast strips, soup, broccoli, milk, cheese and Worcestershire sauce in saucepan; cook on medium heat 5 min. or until mixture is heated through and cheese is melted, stirring occasionally.
- Serve spooned toast slices.

Nutrition Information

- Calories: 310
- Sodium: 1000 mg
- Saturated Fat: 4 g
- Sugar: 4 g
- Fiber: 2 g
- Cholesterol: 50 mg
- Total Carbohydrate: 35 g
- Total Fat: 9 g
- Protein: 21 g

136. Creamy Broccoli Stuffed Chicken Breasts

Serving: 0 | Prep: 15mins | Cook: 30mins | Ready in: 45mins

Ingredients

- 1 pkg. (6 oz.) STOVE TOP Stuffing Mix for Chicken
- 1 cup water
- 6 small boneless skinless chicken breasts (1-1/2 lb.)
- 1 pkg. (10 oz.) frozen chopped broccoli, thawed, drained
- 1 can (10-3/4 oz.) 98% fat-free condensed cream of chicken soup
- 1/2 cup fat-free milk
- 1 tsp. paprika
- 2 Tbsp. KRAFT Grated Parmesan Cheese

Direction

- Heat oven to 400°F.
- Combine stuffing mix and water in large bowl. Let stand 5 min. Meanwhile, pound chicken to 1/4-inch thickness. Add broccoli to stuffing; mix lightly. Spread onto chicken to within 1/2 inch of edges; roll up starting at one short end of each.
- Place, seam-sides down, in 13x9-inch baking dish. Mix soup and milk; pour over chicken. Top with paprika and cheese.
- Bake 30 min. or until chicken is done (165°F).

Nutrition Information

- Calories: 300
- Saturated Fat: 2 g
- Sodium: 740 mg
- Protein: 31 g
- Sugar: 0 g
- Cholesterol: 75 mg
- Fiber: 2 g
- Total Carbohydrate: 0 g
- Total Fat: 6 g

137. Creamy Chicken & Cheddar Rice Bake

Serving: 6 | Prep: 10mins | Cook: 40mins | Ready in: 50mins

Ingredients

- 1 can (10-3/4 oz.) condensed cream of mushroom soup
- 1 soup can milk
- 1 tsp. garlic powder
- 2 cups instant white rice, uncooked
- 1 lb. boneless skinless chicken breasts, cut into bite-size pieces
- 1 pkg. (10 oz.) frozen chopped broccoli, thawed, drained
- 1-1/2 cups KRAFT Shredded Triple Cheddar Cheese with a TOUCH OF PHILADELPHIA, divided

Direction

- Heat oven to 375°F.
- Mix soup, milk and garlic powder in 13x9-inch baking dish with whisk until blended.
- Add rice, chicken, broccoli and 1 cup cheese; mix well. Cover.
- Bake 30 min.; stir. Top with remaining cheese; bake, uncovered, 5 to 10 min. or until cheese is melted and chicken is done. Let stand 5 min. or until liquid is absorbed.

Nutrition Information

- Calories: 390
- Saturated Fat: 8 g
- Fiber: 2 g
- Protein: 29 g
- Total Fat: 16 g
- Total Carbohydrate: 0 g
- Sugar: 0 g
- Cholesterol: 75 mg
- Sodium: 620 mg

138. Creamy Chicken & Corn Soup

Serving: 0 | Prep: 25mins | Cook: | Ready in: 25mins

Ingredients

- 1/4 cup KRAFT Zesty Italian Dressing
- 1 cup chopped onion s
- 1 jalapeño pepper, finely chopped
- 4 oz. (1/2 of 8-oz. pkg.) PHILADELPHIA Cream Cheese, cubed
- 1 can (14-1/2 oz.) fat-free reduced-sodium chicken broth
- 1 pkt. sazon adobo seasoning with saffron
- 1 can (14.7 oz.) cream-style corn
- 1 cup shredded cooked chicken
- 1 Tbsp. chopped fresh parsley
- RITZ Crackers

Direction

- Heat dressing in medium saucepan on medium-high heat. Add onions and peppers; cook 5 min. or until crisp-tender, stirring frequently. Add cream cheese; cook 5 min. or until cream cheese is completely melted and mixture is well blended, stirring constantly.
- Add broth and adobo seasoning; stir until blended. Stir in corn and chicken; simmer on medium-low heat 10 min. or until heated through, stirring occasionally.
- Sprinkle with parsley. Serve with crackers.

Nutrition Information

- Calories: 370
- Total Carbohydrate: 35 g
- Protein: 16 g
- Total Fat: 20 g
- Saturated Fat: 8 g
- Fiber: 3 g
- Cholesterol: 70 mg
- Sugar: 15 g
- Sodium: 1030 mg

139. Creamy Chicken Broccoli Stuffed Potato

Serving: 0 | Prep: 10mins | Cook: 15mins | Ready in: 25mins

Ingredients

- 1/3 cup MIRACLE WHIP Dressing
- 1 lb. boneless skinless chicken breasts, cut into bite-sized pieces
- 1 pkg. (10 oz.) frozen chopped broccoli, thawed, drained
- 1/2 lb. (8 oz.) VELVEETA, cut up
- 6 large baking potatoes, baked, split

Direction

- Heat dressing in large skillet on medium-high heat. Add chicken; cook 8 minutes or until chicken is cooked through, stirring occasionally.
- Add broccoli; cook and stir until tender.
- Stir in VELVEETA. Reduce heat to low; cook until VELVEETA is completely melted, stirring frequently. Spoon over hot potatoes.

Nutrition Information

- Calories: 430
- Protein: 29 g
- Cholesterol: 75 mg
- Sodium: 770 mg
- Sugar: 8 g
- Total Fat: 13 g
- Saturated Fat: 6 g
- Fiber: 6 g
- Total Carbohydrate: 51 g

140. Creamy Chicken Casserole

Serving: 0 | Prep: 25mins | Cook: 40mins | Ready in: 1hours5mins

Ingredients

- 2 cups chopped cooked chicken
- 2 cups cooked long-grain white rice
- 1 can (10-3/4 oz.) condensed cream of mushroom soup
- 1/3 cup KRAFT Real Mayo Mayonnaise
- 3 hard-cooked eggs, chopped
- 2 green onions, sliced
- 1 cup corn flakes
- 1 Tbsp. butter or margarine, melted

Direction

- Heat oven to 350°F.
- Combine all ingredients except corn flakes and butter.
- Spoon into 1-1/2-qt. casserole sprayed with cooking spray; top with combined remaining ingredients.
- Bake 35 to 40 min. or until heated through.

Nutrition Information

- Calories: 350
- Fiber: 1 g
- Cholesterol: 145 mg
- Sodium: 530 mg
- Saturated Fat: 5 g
- Sugar: 0 g
- Total Fat: 20 g

- Protein: 19 g
- Total Carbohydrate: 0 g

141. Creamy Chicken Mac & Cheese With Sour Cream

Serving: 4 | Prep: 20mins | Cook: |Ready in: 20mins

Ingredients

- 1 pkg. (14 oz.) KRAFT Deluxe Macaroni & Cheese Dinner
- 1-1/2 cups frozen mixed vegetables (carrots, corn, green beans, peas)
- 1 cup chopped cooked chicken
- 1/4 cup BREAKSTONE'S or KNUDSEN Sour Cream
- 1/2 tsp. garlic powder
- 1/4 tsp. pepper

Direction

- Prepare Dinner in large saucepan as directed on package, adding vegetables to the boiling water for the last 5 min. of the Macaroni cooking time.
- Stir in remaining ingredients; cook and stir 5 min. or until heated through.

Nutrition Information

- Calories: 450
- Total Fat: 15 g
- Cholesterol: 60 mg
- Total Carbohydrate: 53 g
- Fiber: 3 g
- Sodium: 960 mg
- Sugar: 6 g
- Protein: 24 g
- Saturated Fat: 5 g

142. Creamy Chicken Pomodoro

Serving: 6 | Prep: 30mins | Cook: |Ready in: 30mins

Ingredients

- 2 Tbsp. olive oil, divided
- 6 small boneless skinless chicken breasts (1-1/2 lb.)
- 4 cloves garlic, minced
- 1/4 tsp. crushed red pepper
- 1 can (14-1/2 oz.) diced tomatoes, undrained
- 4 oz. (1/2 of 8-oz. pkg.) PHILADELPHIA Cream Cheese, cubed
- 2 cups penne pasta, uncooked
- 1 cup KRAFT Shredded Mozzarella Cheese with a TOUCH OF PHILADELPHIA
- 2 Tbsp. KRAFT Grated Parmesan Cheese
- 2 Tbsp. chopped fresh basil

Direction

- Heat 1 Tbsp. oil in large nonstick skillet on medium heat. Add chicken; cook 3 min. on each side or until golden brown on both sides. Transfer to plate.
- Add remaining oil to skillet. Stir in garlic and red pepper; cook and stir 30 sec. Add tomatoes and cream cheese; cook and stir 2 to 3 min. or until cream cheese is melted and sauce is well blended. Return chicken to skillet along with any meat juices; cover. Simmer 8 to 10 min. or until chicken is done (165°F). Meanwhile, cook pasta as directed on package, omitting salt.
- Sprinkle chicken with cheeses and basil. Remove from heat. Let stand, covered, 2 to 3 min. or until mozzarella is melted. Serve over drained pasta.

Nutrition Information

- Calories: 440
- Sodium: 380 mg
- Total Carbohydrate: 30 g
- Sugar: 4 g
- Total Fat: 19 g

- Fiber: 3 g
- Saturated Fat: 8 g
- Cholesterol: 105 mg
- Protein: 36 g

143. Creamy Chicken Salad Pizza

Serving: 6 | Prep: 10mins | Cook: 12mins | Ready in: 22mins

Ingredients

- 1 ready-to-use baked pizza crust (12 inch)
- 3/4 cup KRAFT Three Cheese Ranch Dressing, divided
- 1-1/2 cups KRAFT Shredded Mozzarella Cheese
- 1 pkg. (10 oz.) mixed salad greens
- 1 cup chopped cooked chicken
- 3/4 cup sliced cucumbers

Direction

- Heat oven to 400°F.
- Spread pizza crust with 1/4 cup dressing; top with cheese. Bake 12 min. or until cheese is melted.
- Toss salad greens with chicken, cucumbers and remaining dressing.
- Serve pizza wedges topped with salad.

Nutrition Information

- Calories: 390
- Fiber: 1 g
- Total Carbohydrate: 0 g
- Cholesterol: 40 mg
- Sugar: 0 g
- Total Fat: 22 g
- Protein: 19 g
- Saturated Fat: 7 g
- Sodium: 800 mg

144. Creamy Chicken Sausage And Pasta Skillet

Serving: 0 | Prep: 30mins | Cook: | Ready in: 30mins

Ingredients

- 3 cups penne pasta, uncooked
- 1 each green and red pepper, cut into thin strips
- 1 jar (24 oz.) CLASSICO Tomato and Basil Pasta Sauce
- 1 tsp. fennel seed
- dash crushed red pepper
- 4 oz. (1/2 of 8-oz. pkg.) PHILADELPHIA Cream Cheese, cubed
- 1/4 cup KRAFT Shredded Parmesan Cheese

Direction

- Cook pasta as directed on package, omitting salt.
- Meanwhile, crumble sausage into large skillet; cook and stir on medium heat 8 min. or until done. Drain. Add peppers; cook and stir 5 min. or until crisp-tender. Stir in next 3 ingredients; cook 5 min. or until heated through. Add cream cheese; cook 2 min. or until melted, stirring frequently.
- Drain pasta. Add to sausage mixture; mix lightly. Top with Parmesan.

Nutrition Information

- Calories: 620
- Sugar: 0 g
- Saturated Fat: 9 g
- Cholesterol: 110 mg
- Protein: 33 g
- Total Carbohydrate: 0 g
- Fiber: 7 g
- Total Fat: 21 g
- Sodium: 1490 mg

145. Creamy Chicken Soup With Matzo

Serving: 0 | Prep: | Cook: | Ready in:

Ingredients

- 3 eggs
- 3/4 cup matzo meal
- 3 Tbsp. oil
- 3 Tbsp. water
- 2 Tbsp. KRAFT Zesty Italian Dressing, divided
- 1 small onion, finely chopped
- 3 cans (14.5 oz. each) fat-free reduced-sodium chicken broth
- 2 cups chopped cooked chicken breasts
- 3 carrots, peeled, finely chopped
- 1 large stalk celery, finely chopped
- 1 tsp. peppercorns
- 3 whole cloves
- 1 bay leaf
- 1/4 tsp. ground black pepper
- 4 oz. (1/2 of 8-oz. pkg.) PHILADELPHIA Cream Cheese, softened
- 1 Tbsp. flour
- 2 Tbsp. chopped fresh parsley

Direction

- Mix first 4 ingredients until blended. Refrigerate 15 min.
- Meanwhile, heat dressing in medium saucepan on medium-high heat. Add onions; cook and stir 6 to 8 min. or until tender. Stir in broth, chicken, carrots, celery, peppercorns, cloves, bay leaf and pepper.
- Wet hands and shape matzo dough into 16 (1-inch) balls. Bring soup to boil. Add matzo balls; cover. Simmer 20 min. or until vegetables are tender and matzo balls are cooked through.
- Meanwhile, whisk cream cheese and flour with 1/4 cup hot broth in medium bowl until smooth. Gradually stir cream cheese mixture into soup until blended; cover and simmer 5 min.
- Ladle soup into bowls, placing 2 matzo balls in each. Sprinkle with parsley.

Nutrition Information

- Calories: 0 g
- Cholesterol: 0 g
- Sugar: 0 g
- Sodium: 0 g
- Total Fat: 0 g
- Saturated Fat: 0 g
- Total Carbohydrate: 0 g
- Fiber: 0 g
- Protein: 0 g

146. Creamy Chicken Cauliflower Pasta

Serving: 0 | Prep: 10mins | Cook: 20mins | Ready in: 30mins

Ingredients

- 2-1/2 cups penne pasta, uncooked
- 1 Tbsp. oil
- 2-1/2 cups small cauliflower florets (about 1/2 small head), finely chopped
- 1-1/2 lb. boneless skinless chicken breasts, cut into bite-size pieces
- 6 KRAFT Singles, cut up
- 1/2 cup KRAFT Shredded Low-Moisture Part-Skim Mozzarella Cheese
- 1/4 cup chopped fresh parsley
- 2 Tbsp. KRAFT Grated Parmesan Cheese

Direction

- Cook pasta as directed on package.
- Meanwhile, heat oil in large nonstick skillet on medium-high heat. Add cauliflower; cook and stir 5 min. Remove from skillet; cover to keep warm. Add chicken, in batches, to skillet; cook

3 min. or until evenly browned, stirring frequently. Return all chicken and cauliflower to skillet; cover. Cook on medium-low heat 2 min. or until heated through, stirring occasionally.
- Drain pasta, reserving 1-1/2 cups cooking water. Return pasta to pan; stir in reserved water and Singles. Cook on medium heat 2 min. or until Singles are completely melted and sauce is well blended. Add to chicken mixture in skillet with mozzarella; cook 2 min. or until mozzarella is melted, stirring frequently. Sprinkle with parsley and Parmesan.

Nutrition Information

- Calories: 380
- Cholesterol: 95 mg
- Fiber: 2 g
- Sodium: 460 mg
- Total Fat: 13 g
- Saturated Fat: 6 g
- Total Carbohydrate: 0 g
- Protein: 37 g
- Sugar: 0 g

147. Creamy Curried Chicken Salad

Serving: 0 | Prep: 15mins | Cook: 2hours | Ready in: 2hours15mins

Ingredients

- 2 pkg. (6 oz. each) OSCAR MAYER CARVING BOARD Flame Grilled Chicken Breast Strips
- 1/4 cup KRAFT Real Mayo Mayonnaise
- 1/4 cup green onion slices
- 2 Tbsp. raisins
- 2 Tbsp. PLANTERS Slivered Almonds, toasted
- 1 tsp. curry powder

Direction

- Mix all ingredients until well blended; cover.
- Refrigerate several hours or overnight.
- Serve with assorted crackers and mini pita halves. Or, serve in Boston or Red Leaf lettuce cups.

Nutrition Information

- Calories: 250
- Total Carbohydrate: 6 g
- Cholesterol: 65 mg
- Total Fat: 17 g
- Saturated Fat: 3 g
- Fiber: 1 g
- Sugar: 4 g
- Sodium: 850 mg
- Protein: 20 g

148. Creamy Garlic Chicken & Broccoli Mac & Cheese

Serving: 4 | Prep: 30mins | Cook: | Ready in: 30mins

Ingredients

- 4 small boneless skinless chicken breasts (1 lb.)
- 4 Tbsp. butter or margarine, divided
- 1 pkg. (7-1/4 oz.) KRAFT Macaroni & Cheese Dinner
- 1-1/2 cups water
- 2 cups broccoli florets
- 1 tsp. garlic powder
- 1/4 cup milk
- 2 Tbsp. KRAFT Grated Parmesan Cheese

Direction

- Cook chicken in 1 Tbsp. butter in skillet on medium heat 6 to 7 min. on each side or until done (165ºF). Remove chicken from skillet; cover to keep warm.
- Stir in Macaroni, water, broccoli and garlic powder. Cover; cook on medium heat 7 min. or until macaroni is tender.

- Stir in milk, remaining butter and Cheese Sauce Mix. Return chicken to skillet; cover. Cook 2 to 3 min. or until heated through. Top with Parmesan.

Nutrition Information

- Calories: 460
- Total Carbohydrate: 38 g
- Protein: 34 g
- Sugar: 1 g
- Saturated Fat: 9 g
- Sodium: 670 mg
- Fiber: 2 g
- Total Fat: 16 g
- Cholesterol: 110 mg

149. Creamy Guajillo Chicken Pasta

Serving: 0 | Prep: 10mins | Cook: 27mins | Ready in: 37mins

Ingredients

- 1-1/2 cups guajillo salsa
- 4 oz. (1/2 of 8-oz. pkg.) PHILADELPHIA Cream Cheese, cubed, softened
- 6 small boneless skinless chicken breasts (1-1/2 lb.)
- 2 red peppers, cut into strips
- 1 cup frozen corn
- 3/4 lb. spaghetti, uncooked
- 1/2 cup KRAFT Shredded Low-Moisture Part-Skim Mozzarella Cheese
- 2 Tbsp. KRAFT Grated Parmesan Cheese
- 3 green onions, chopped

Direction

- Blend salsa and cream cheese in blender until smooth.
- Cook chicken in large nonstick skillet sprayed with cooking spray on medium heat 2 min. on each side or until browned on both sides. Remove from skillet; cover to keep warm. Add peppers and corn to skillet; cook and stir 3 min. Stir in cream cheese mixture; top with chicken. Cover; cook on medium-low heat 20 min. or until chicken is done (165°F). Meanwhile, cook spaghetti as directed on package.
- Drain spaghetti; place on large platter. Top with mozzarella, chicken and cream cheese sauce. Sprinkle with Parmesan and onions.

Nutrition Information

- Calories: 560
- Sodium: 660 mg
- Total Fat: 17 g
- Saturated Fat: 7 g
- Total Carbohydrate: 0 g
- Sugar: 0 g
- Protein: 39 g
- Fiber: 4 g
- Cholesterol: 100 mg

150. Creamy Mexican Chicken Casserole

Serving: 4 | Prep: 20mins | Cook: 25mins | Ready in: 45mins

Ingredients

- 3/4 lb. boneless skinless chicken breasts, cut into bite-size pieces
- 1 green pepper, chopped
- 1-1/2 cups TACO BELL® Thick & Chunky Salsa
- 1 tsp. ground cumin
- 1/4 tsp. ground black pepper
- 2 oz. (1/4 of 8-oz. pkg.) PHILADELPHIA Neufchatel Cheese, cubed
- 1 can (15 oz.) no-salt-added black beans, rinsed
- 1 tomato, chopped
- 2 whole wheat tortillas (6 inch)

- 1/2 cup KRAFT Mexican Style 2% Milk Finely Shredded Four Cheese, divided
- 2 Tbsp. chopped fresh cilantro

Direction

- Heat oven to 375°F.
- Cook and stir chicken in large nonstick skillet on medium heat 2 min. Add green peppers; cook 2 min., stirring occasionally. Add salsa, cumin and black pepper; stir. Cook 2 min., stirring frequently. Add Neufchatel; cook and stir 2 min. or until melted. Stir in beans and tomatoes.
- Spread 1/3 of chicken mixture onto bottom of 8-inch square baking dish sprayed with cooking spray; cover with 1 tortilla and half each of the remaining chicken mixture and shredded cheese. Top with remaining tortilla and chicken mixture; cover.
- Bake 20 min. or until heated through. Sprinkle with remaining shredded cheese, then cilantro; bake, uncovered, 5 min. or until cheese is melted.

Nutrition Information

- Calories: 140
- Sodium: 100 mg
- Total Carbohydrate: 0 g
- Fiber: 0 g
- Cholesterol: 70 mg
- Saturated Fat: 2.5 g
- Sugar: 0 g
- Protein: 20 g
- Total Fat: 5 g

151. Creamy Mexican Chicken Pasta

Serving: 0 | Prep: 10mins | Cook: 15mins | Ready in: 25mins

Ingredients

- 3 cups farfalle (bow-tie pasta), uncooked
- 1-1/4 lb. boneless skinless chicken breasts, cut into strips
- 1/2 lb. (8 oz.) VELVEETA, cut into 1/2-inch cubes
- 1 can (10-3/4 oz.) condensed cream of mushroom soup
- 1 cup TACO BELL® Thick & Chunky Salsa
- 1/4 cup milk

Direction

- Cook pasta in large saucepan as directed on package. Meanwhile, cook chicken in skillet sprayed with cooking spray on medium heat 4 to 5 min. or until done, stirring occasionally.
- Drain pasta; return to saucepan. Stir in chicken and all remaining ingredients. Cook on low heat until VELVEETA is completely melted and mixture is well blended, stirring occasionally.

Nutrition Information

- Calories: 360
- Sodium: 1030 mg
- Saturated Fat: 4.5 g
- Cholesterol: 70 mg
- Sugar: 6 g
- Total Carbohydrate: 36 g
- Total Fat: 11 g
- Protein: 26 g
- Fiber: 3 g

152. Creamy Parmesan Chicken Salad

Serving: 4 | Prep: 30mins | Cook: 2hours | Ready in: 2hours30mins

Ingredients

- 1/4 cup KRAFT Grated Parmesan Cheese
- 1/4 cup KRAFT Real Mayo Mayonnaise

- 1 Tbsp. chopped fresh cilantro
- 1 Tbsp. fresh lime juice
- 1 clove garlic, minced
- 3/4 tsp. minced jalapeño peppers
- 1/2 lb. boneless skinless chicken breasts, cooked, shredded
- 1 small tomato, chopped
- 2 avocados

Direction

- Mix first 6 ingredients in small bowl until blended.
- Combine chicken and tomatoes in medium bowl Add cheese mixture; mix lightly.
- Refrigerate 1 hour. Serve spooned over sliced avocados.

Nutrition Information

- Calories: 360
- Cholesterol: 45 mg
- Sugar: 0 g
- Saturated Fat: 5 g
- Fiber: 7 g
- Protein: 17 g
- Total Fat: 29 g
- Total Carbohydrate: 0 g
- Sodium: 230 mg

153. Creamy Salsa Verde Chicken

Serving: 6 | Prep: 20mins | Cook: | Ready in: 20mins

Ingredients

- 1 cup green salsa
- 2 oz. PHILADELPHIA Cream Cheese
- 6 boneless skinless chicken breasts (1-1/2 lb.)
- 1 Tbsp. chopped fresh cilantro

Direction

- Blend salsa and cream cheese in blender until smooth.
- Cook chicken in skillet on medium-high heat 2 min. on each side or until browned on both sides. Top with salsa mixture; cover. Cook on medium-low heat 8 min. Uncover; cook 5 min. or until chicken is done (165°F).
- Top with cilantro just before serving.

Nutrition Information

- Calories: 170
- Sodium: 470 mg
- Total Fat: 6 g
- Cholesterol: 80 mg
- Total Carbohydrate: 3 g
- Saturated Fat: 2.5 g
- Protein: 25 g
- Sugar: 0 g
- Fiber: 0 g

154. Creole Chicken Salad Sandwich

Serving: 0 | Prep: 10mins | Cook: | Ready in: 10mins

Ingredients

- 1/3 cup MIRACLE WHIP Light Dressing
- 1/2 tsp. hot pepper sauce
- 1/2 tsp. dried thyme leaves
- 1/4 tsp. black pepper
- 1 pkg. (9 oz.) OSCAR MAYER Deli Fresh Rotisserie Seasoned Chicken Breast, finely chopped
- 1/2 cup finely chopped celery
- 1/2 cup finely chopped green peppers
- 1/2 cup finely chopped tomatoes
- 4 kaiser rolls, partially split
- 4 lettuce leaves

Direction

- Mix dressing, hot sauce and seasonings in large bowl.
- Add chicken, celery, green peppers and tomatoes; mix lightly.
- Fill rolls with lettuce and chicken salad.

Nutrition Information

- Calories: 270
- Sodium: 1160 mg
- Total Fat: 6 g
- Cholesterol: 35 mg
- Sugar: 0 g
- Saturated Fat: 1.5 g
- Fiber: 2 g
- Total Carbohydrate: 0 g
- Protein: 18 g

155. Crispy Baked Pesto Chicken

Serving: 4 | Prep: 15mins | Cook: 20mins | Ready in: 35mins

Ingredients

- 4 small boneless skinless chicken breasts (1 lb.)
- 1 pkt. SHAKE 'N BAKE Chicken Coating Mix
- 2 Tbsp. CLASSICO Traditional Basil Pesto Sauce and Spread
- 1/4 cup KRAFT Shredded Mozzarella Cheese

Direction

- Heat oven to 400°F.
- Coat chicken with coating mix; place in 8-inch square baking dish sprayed with cooking spray.
- Bake 20 min. or until done (165°F).
- Top with pesto and cheese; bake 5 min. or until cheese is melted.

Nutrition Information

- Calories: 260
- Sugar: 0 g
- Protein: 28 g
- Total Fat: 9 g
- Cholesterol: 70 mg
- Sodium: 630 mg
- Fiber: 1 g
- Saturated Fat: 2.5 g
- Total Carbohydrate: 0 g

156. Crispy Cheddar Chicken Nuggets Recipe

Serving: 6 | Prep: 10mins | Cook: 18mins | Ready in: 28mins

Ingredients

- 1-1/2 lb. boneless skinless chicken breasts, cut into 1-1/2- to 2-inch pieces
- 1 Tbsp. GREY POUPON Dijon Mustard
- 1 pkt. SHAKE 'N BAKE Crispy Cheddar Seasoned Coating Mix
- 1/3 cup KRAFT Original Barbecue Sauce
- 2 Tbsp. KRAFT Real Mayo Mayonnaise

Direction

- Heat oven to 400°F.
- Toss chicken with mustard.
- Coat chicken, in batches, with coating mix, then bake as directed on package.
- Mix barbecue sauce and mayo until blended. Serve with chicken.

Nutrition Information

- Calories: 240
- Fiber: 0 g
- Sugar: 0 g
- Total Fat: 8 g
- Total Carbohydrate: 0 g
- Saturated Fat: 1.5 g
- Sodium: 580 mg

- Protein: 26 g
- Cholesterol: 70 mg

- Sodium: 450 mg
- Fiber: 1 g
- Total Fat: 16 g
- Saturated Fat: 3.5 g

157. Crispy Chicken Parmesan With Avocado Salsa

Serving: 6 | Prep: 25mins | Cook: | Ready in: 25mins

Ingredients

- 1/3 cup dry bread crumbs
- 1/3 cup KRAFT Grated Parmesan Cheese, divided
- 1/4 cup KRAFT Real Mayo Mayonnaise
- 1/2 tsp. chili powder
- 6 small boneless skinless chicken breasts (1-1/2 lb.), pounded to 1/4-inch thickness
- 1 Tbsp. olive oil
- 1/2 cup chopped avocados
- 1/2 cup tomatillo salsa
- 1/2 cup chopped tomatoes

Direction

- Combine bread crumbs and 1/4 cup cheese in shallow dish; set aside. Mix mayo and chili powder; spread onto both sides of chicken breasts. Coat evenly with bread crumb mixture.
- Heat oil in large skillet on medium heat. Add chicken; cook 4 to 5 min. on each side or until done (165°F). Meanwhile, mash avocados with salsa.
- Place chicken on serving plate; top with avocado mixture, tomatoes and remaining cheese.

Nutrition Information

- Calories: 290
- Cholesterol: 75 mg
- Protein: 28 g
- Sugar: 0 g
- Total Carbohydrate: 0 g

158. Crispy Chicken With Honey Dipping Sauce

Serving: 0 | Prep: 15mins | Cook: 14mins | Ready in: 29mins

Ingredients

- 1 cup MIRACLE WHIP Dressing
- 1/4 cup honey
- 2 Tbsp. GREY POUPON Dijon Mustard
- 2 Tbsp. creamy peanut butter
- 4 boneless skinless chicken breasts (1-1/4 lb.), each cut into 4 lengthwise strips
- 1-1/2 cups finely crushed potato chips

Direction

- Preheat oven to 425°F. Mix dressing, honey, mustard and peanut butter until well blended. Remove 1 cup of the dressing mixture; set aside for later use.
- Brush chicken with remaining dressing mixture; coat with crushed chips. Place on greased baking sheet.
- Bake 8 min. Turn chicken over; bake an additional 5 to 6 min. or until lightly browned. Serve with the reserved 1 cup dressing mixture as a dipping sauce.

Nutrition Information

- Calories: 140
- Cholesterol: 25 mg
- Fiber: 0 g
- Protein: 9 g
- Saturated Fat: 1.5 g
- Sugar: 6 g
- Total Fat: 8 g

- Sodium: 220 mg
- Total Carbohydrate: 10 g

159. Crispy Oven Baked Chicken Parmesan

Serving: 6 | Prep: 10mins | Cook: 20mins | Ready in: 30mins

Ingredients

- 6 small boneless skinless chicken breasts (1-1/2 lb.)
- 1 pkt. SHAKE 'N BAKE Chicken Coating Mix
- 2 cups CLASSICO Tomato and Basil Pasta Sauce
- 1-1/2 cups KRAFT Finely Shredded Italian* Five Cheese Blend
- 1/4 cup KRAFT Grated Parmesan Cheese
- 1/2 tsp. dried Italian seasoning

Direction

- Heat oven to 400°F.
- Coat chicken with coating mix as directed on package; place in 13x9-inch pan.
- Bake 20 min. or until done (165°F).
- Top with remaining ingredients; bake 5 min. or until shredded cheese is melted.

Nutrition Information

- Calories: 330
- Sugar: 0 g
- Fiber: 2 g
- Total Carbohydrate: 0 g
- Protein: 35 g
- Cholesterol: 90 mg
- Sodium: 1020 mg
- Total Fat: 13 g
- Saturated Fat: 6 g

160. Crispy Santa Fe Chicken

Serving: 4 | Prep: 15mins | Cook: 20mins | Ready in: 35mins

Ingredients

- 4 small boneless skinless chicken breasts (1 lb.)
- 1 egg, beaten
- 12 saltine crackers, finely crushed (about 1/2 cup)
- 2 Tbsp. butter, melted
- 1 cup TACO BELL® Thick & Chunky Salsa
- 1 cup KRAFT Mexican Style Finely Shredded Four Cheese

Direction

- Heat oven to 425°F.
- Dip chicken in egg then in cracker crumbs, turning to evenly coat both sides of each breast with each ingredient.
- Place in 13x9-inch baking dish sprayed with cooking spray; drizzle with butter.
- Bake 20 min. or until chicken is done (165°F). Top with salsa and cheese; bake 5 min. or until cheese is melted.

Nutrition Information

- Calories: 370
- Sodium: 810 mg
- Total Carbohydrate: 14 g
- Saturated Fat: 10 g
- Protein: 34 g
- Total Fat: 19 g
- Fiber: 1 g
- Cholesterol: 150 mg
- Sugar: 2 g

161. Crunchy Topped Chicken & Rice Casserole

Serving: 0 | Prep: 25mins | Cook: 40mins | Ready in: 1hours5mins

Ingredients

- 2 cups cooked long grain & wild rice
- 2 cups chopped cooked chicken
- 1 can (10-3/4 oz.) condensed cheddar cheese soup
- 1/3 cup KRAFT Light Mayo Reduced Fat Mayonnaise
- 1/4 cup finely chopped onions
- 1/4 cup chopped green peppers
- 1 cup corn flakes
- 1 Tbsp. butter or margarine, melted

Direction

- Heat oven to 350°F.
- Combine all ingredients except corn flakes and butter; spoon into 1-1/2-qt. casserole sprayed with cooking spray.
- Top with combined remaining ingredients.
- Bake 35 to 40 min. or until heated through.

Nutrition Information

- Calories: 270
- Sodium: 580 mg
- Total Fat: 11 g
- Protein: 17 g
- Total Carbohydrate: 0 g
- Fiber: 1 g
- Sugar: 0 g
- Cholesterol: 55 mg
- Saturated Fat: 4 g

162. Curried BBQ Chicken Thighs

Serving: 8 | Prep: 15mins | Cook: 30mins | Ready in: 45mins

Ingredients

- 3 Tbsp. brown sugar
- 2 Tbsp. HEINZ Ketchup Blended with Sriracha Flavors
- 2 Tbsp. HEINZ Apple Cider Vinegar
- 2 cloves garlic, minced
- 1 Tbsp. yellow curry paste
- 1/4 tsp. coriander seed
- 1/2 tsp. curry powder
- 1/2 tsp. ground allspice
- 1/4 tsp. ground red pepper (cayenne)
- 8 bone-in skinless chicken thighs (3 lb.)

Direction

- Heat grill to medium heat.
- Bring first 6 ingredients to boil in small saucepan on medium heat, stirring frequently. Stir until sugar is dissolved. Remove from heat; set aside.
- Combine curry powder, allspice and pepper; rub onto chicken.
- Grill chicken 15 min. on each side. Brush with sauce mixture; grill 3 to 5 min. or until done (165°F).

Nutrition Information

- Calories: 180
- Fiber: 0 g
- Saturated Fat: 2 g
- Protein: 22 g
- Total Fat: 7 g
- Sodium: 210 mg
- Total Carbohydrate: 0 g
- Cholesterol: 115 mg
- Sugar: 0 g

163. Curried Chicken Bites

Serving: 12 | Prep: 30mins | Cook: 15mins | Ready in: 45mins

Ingredients

- 6 slices white bread, crusts removed
- 2 Tbsp. butter, melted
- 2 cups chopped cooked chicken
- 2 Tbsp. BAKER'S ANGEL FLAKE Coconut, toasted
- 2 Tbsp. PLANTERS Slivered Almonds, toasted
- 3 Tbsp. KRAFT Real Mayo Mayonnaise
- 1 tsp. GREY POUPON Savory Honey Mustard
- 1 Tbsp. curry powder
- 1 Tbsp. apricot jam

Direction

- Heat oven to 375°F.
- Use rolling pin to flatten bread to 1/8-inch thickness; brush with butter. Brush 24 mini muffin pan cups with any remaining butter. Cut each bread slice into 4 squares; press 1 square, buttered side up, onto bottom and up side of each muffin cup.
- Bake 7 to 8 min. or until golden brown; cool completely.
- Combine chicken, coconut and nuts in large bowl. Mix remaining ingredients until blended. Add to chicken mixture; mix lightly. Spoon into toast cups just before serving.

Nutrition Information

- Calories: 130
- Cholesterol: 25 mg
- Fiber: 1 g
- Sugar: 2 g
- Saturated Fat: 2.5 g
- Protein: 8 g
- Sodium: 115 mg
- Total Carbohydrate: 8 g
- Total Fat: 8 g

164. Curried Chicken Spread

Serving: 0 | Prep: 15mins | Cook: 1hours | Ready in: 1hours15mins

Ingredients

- 1 pkg. (8 oz.) PHILADELPHIA Cream Cheese, softened
- 3 Tbsp. orange juice
- 1 Tbsp. KRAFT Real Mayo Mayonnaise
- 1/2 tsp. curry powder
- 1 cup finely chopped cooked chicken
- 2 Tbsp. finely chopped celery
- 28 stoned wheat crackers

Direction

- Beat cream cheese, orange juice, mayo and curry powder in small bowl with electric mixer on medium speed until well blended. Stir in chicken and celery; cover.
- Refrigerate at least 1 hour before serving.
- Garnish as desired. Serve as a spread with the crackers.

Nutrition Information

- Calories: 140
- Total Carbohydrate: 11 g
- Sugar: 1 g
- Sodium: 220 mg
- Total Fat: 9 g
- Saturated Fat: 4 g
- Protein: 6 g
- Cholesterol: 25 mg
- Fiber: 0 g

165. Deep Dish Chicken Pot Pie Recipe

Serving: 6 | Prep: 25mins | Cook: 30mins | Ready in: 55mins

Ingredients

- 1 lb. boneless skinless chicken breasts, cut into bite-size pieces
- 1/4 cup KRAFT Lite Zesty Italian Dressing
- 4 oz. (1/2 of 8-oz. pkg.) PHILADELPHIA Neufchatel Cheese, cubed
- 2 Tbsp. flour
- 1/2 cup fat-free reduced-sodium chicken broth
- 3 cups frozen mixed vegetables (peas, carrots, corn, green beans), thawed, drained
- 1 ready-to-use refrigerated pie crust (1/2 of 14.1-oz. pkg.)

Direction

- Heat oven to 375°F.
- Cook chicken in hot dressing in large skillet on medium heat 2 min., stirring frequently. Add Neufchatel; cook and stir 2 to 3 min. or until melted. Add flour; mix well. Stir in broth; cook and stir 2 to 3 min. or until thickened. Add vegetables; stir. Simmer 5 min. or until heated through, stirring frequently.
- Spoon into 10-inch deep-dish pie plate sprayed with cooking spray; cover with pie crust. Use tines of fork to seal edge of crust to rim of pie plate. Cut slits in crust to permit steam to escape.
- Bake 30 min. or until golden brown.

Nutrition Information

- Calories: 360
- Sugar: 0 g
- Sodium: 490 mg
- Protein: 22 g
- Fiber: 2 g
- Total Fat: 18 g
- Saturated Fat: 6 g
- Total Carbohydrate: 0 g
- Cholesterol: 55 mg

166. Dijon Balsamic Herb Chicken

Serving: 0 | Prep: 20mins | Cook: 20mins | Ready in: 40mins

Ingredients

- 2 tsp. dried tarragon leaves
- 1 tsp. dried rosemary leaves
- 1/2 tsp. ground black pepper
- 2 Tbsp. margarine or butter, divided
- 6 small boneless skinless chicken breasts (1-1/2 lb.)
- 2 Tbsp. minced shallots
- 2 Tbsp. HEINZ Balsamic Vinegar
- 1 can (14-1/2 oz.) chicken broth
- 1 tsp. sugar
- 1 Tbsp. GREY POUPON Dijon Mustard
- 2 tsp. cornstarch
- 2 tsp. water

Direction

- Combine tarragon, rosemary and pepper; spread evenly onto chicken. Melt 1 Tbsp. of the margarine in large skillet on medium heat. Add chicken; cook 6 to 7 min. on each side or until cooked through (170°F). Remove from skillet; cover to keep warm.
- Melt remaining 1 Tbsp. margarine in same skillet. Add shallots; cook 1 to 2 min. or until tender, stirring occasionally. Add vinegar; cook 1 min. Stir in broth and sugar; bring to boil. Cook until sauce is reduced by one third, stirring occasionally. Stir in mustard.
- Mix cornstarch and water until well blended. Add to ingredients in skillet; mix well. Bring to boil; cook until thickened, stirring occasionally. Serve spooned over the chicken.

Nutrition Information

- Calories: 190
- Total Carbohydrate: 4 g
- Total Fat: 7 g
- Cholesterol: 65 mg
- Sugar: 2 g
- Sodium: 390 mg
- Protein: 26 g
- Saturated Fat: 1.5 g
- Fiber: 0 g

167. Dijon Chicken Elegant

Serving: 0 | Prep: 30mins | Cook: 30mins | Ready in: 1hours

Ingredients

- 1/4 cup GREY POUPON Dijon Mustard
- 1 tsp. dill weed
- 8 small boneless skinless chicken breasts (2 lb.), pounded to 1/2-inch thickness
- 4 KRAFT Big Slice Swiss Cheese Slices, cut in half
- 1 pkg. (17.3 oz.) frozen puff pastry sheets (2 sheets), thawed
- 1 egg white
- 1 Tbsp. cold water

Direction

- Heat oven to 375°F
- Mix mustard and dill; spread onto chicken. Top with cheese; roll up, starting at one short end of each.
- Roll each pastry sheet on lightly floured surface to 12-inch square; cut into 4 (6-inch) squares. Whisk egg white and water until blended; brush onto edges of squares. Top with chicken. Bring corners of each pastry square together over chicken; press together to seal. Place, seam-sides down, on baking sheet sprayed with cooking spray. Brush with remaining egg.
- Bake 30 min. or until pastry is lightly browned and chicken is done (165°F).

Nutrition Information

- Calories: 530
- Cholesterol: 75 mg
- Saturated Fat: 9 g
- Total Carbohydrate: 29 g
- Fiber: 1 g
- Sodium: 420 mg
- Sugar: 2 g
- Protein: 33 g
- Total Fat: 30 g

168. Dijon Chicken Salad Sandwich

Serving: 0 | Prep: 15mins | Cook: | Ready in: 15mins

Ingredients

- 4 cups chopped cooked chicken
- 1-1/2 cups chopped celery
- 1/2 cup KRAFT Real Mayo Mayonnaise
- 1/4 cup GREY POUPON Dijon Mustard
- 2 Tbsp. lemon juice
- 1/8 tsp. ground black pepper
- 16 slices rye bread
- 8 lettuce leaves

Direction

- Combine chicken, celery, mayonnaise, mustard, lemon juice and pepper.
- Top 8 bread slices with lettuce, chicken salad and remaining bread slices.

Nutrition Information

- Calories: 410
- Cholesterol: 65 mg
- Protein: 27 g
- Sodium: 760 mg
- Saturated Fat: 3.5 g

- Total Fat: 19 g
- Sugar: 1 g
- Total Carbohydrate: 33 g
- Fiber: 4 g

169. Dijon Marinade

Serving: 16 | Prep: 10mins | Cook: 1hours30mins | Ready in: 1hours40mins

Ingredients

- 1 cup LEA & PERRINS Worcestershire Sauce
- 1/4 cup GREY POUPON Dijon Mustard
- 1/4 cup olive oil
- 8 chicken leg quarters (5-1/2 lb.)

Direction

- Whisk all ingredients except chicken until blended; pour over chicken in shallow dish. Turn to evenly coat both sides of chicken pieces.
- Refrigerate 1 hour to marinate, turning after 30 min.
- Heat grill to medium heat. Remove chicken from marinade; discard marinade.
- Grill chicken 25 to 30 min. or until done (165°F), turning after 15 min. Cut in half before serving.

Nutrition Information

- Calories: 190
- Total Carbohydrate: 0 g
- Protein: 23 g
- Cholesterol: 125 mg
- Sodium: 190 mg
- Sugar: 0 g
- Fiber: 0 g
- Total Fat: 10 g
- Saturated Fat: 2.5 g

170. Doner Kebab (Turkish Style Kebab) Wrap

Serving: 12 | Prep: 40mins | Cook: 3hours35mins | Ready in: 4hours15mins

Ingredients

- 3 Tbsp. tomato paste
- 1-1/2 cups BREAKSTONE'S or KNUDSEN Sour Cream, divided
- 1/2 cup KRAFT Greek Vinaigrette Dressing, divided
- 2 tsp. each garlic powder, ground coriander and ground cumin, divided
- 2 lb. boneless skinless chicken thighs
- 12 pita breads
- 1 pkg. (7 oz.) ATHENOS Original Hummus
- 3 cups loosely packed shredded romaine lettuce
- 1 large tomato, cut into 12 slices
- 1 pkg. (4 oz.) ATHENOS Traditional Crumbled Feta Cheese

Direction

- Mix tomato paste with 1 cup sour cream; 1/4 cup dressing; and 1-1/2 tsp. each garlic powder, coriander and cumin until blended. Pour over chicken in shallow dish; turn to evenly coat both sides of each thigh with sour cream mixture. Refrigerate 3 hours to marinate.
- Heat oven to 400°F. Cover rimmed baking sheet with foil; spray with cooking spray. Place 2 large skewers, parallel to each other and 1-1/2 inches apart, on prepared baking sheet. Repeat with 2 additional skewers.
- Remove chicken from marinade; discard marinade. Fold chicken thighs in half, then thread evenly onto skewers, tightly threading half the thighs onto each set of parallel skewers.
- Drizzle with 2 Tbsp. of the remaining dressing.

- Bake 30 to 35 min. or until chicken is done (165°F). Remove chicken from oven. Heat broiler.
- Broil chicken, 4 inches from heat, 5 min. on each side or until golden brown on both sides. Meanwhile, mix remaining sour cream, dressing and seasonings until blended. Reserve for later use.
- Stand 1 kebab on work surface, then use sharp knife to cut chicken vertically, from top to bottom, into thin strips.
- Stack pita breads on microwaveable plate; cover with damp paper towel. Microwave on HIGH 30 sec.
- Spread pita breads with hummus; top with lettuce, tomatoes, cheese and chicken. Drizzle with reserved sour cream mixture; roll up.

Nutrition Information

- Calories: 350
- Fiber: 3 g
- Sodium: 710 mg
- Saturated Fat: 5 g
- Sugar: 0 g
- Protein: 17 g
- Total Carbohydrate: 0 g
- Total Fat: 13 g
- Cholesterol: 60 mg

171. Double Chipotle BBQ Chicken Rolls

Serving: 16 | Prep: 15mins | Cook: | Ready in: 15mins

Ingredients

- 1 flour tortilla (13 inch)
- 1/2 cup PHILADELPHIA Chipotle Cream Cheese Spread
- 8 slices OSCAR MAYER Deli Fresh Bold Chipotle Seasoned Chicken Breast
- 4 KRAFT Singles
- 3 Tbsp. finely chopped red peppers
- 2 Tbsp. chopped red onions
- 1/3 cup KRAFT Original Barbecue Sauce
- 2 Tbsp. chopped fresh cilantro

Direction

- Spread tortilla with cream cheese spread. Top with chicken, Singles, peppers and onions, leaving 3/4-inch border around edge.
- Cut tortilla in half. Working with 1 half at a time, roll up tightly, beginning at cut edge of tortilla. Cut roll evenly into 10 pieces; discard 2 end pieces. Repeat with second tortilla half.
- Serve slices, cut-side up, topped with a drizzle of barbecue sauce and a sprinkle of cilantro.

Nutrition Information

- Calories: 60
- Sodium: 260 mg
- Protein: 3 g
- Total Carbohydrate: 0 g
- Total Fat: 2.5 g
- Fiber: 0 g
- Saturated Fat: 1.5 g
- Cholesterol: 10 mg
- Sugar: 0 g

172. Easy 30 Minute Skillet Chicken Mac & Cheese

Serving: 0 | Prep: 10mins | Cook: 15mins | Ready in: 25mins

Ingredients

- 1 Tbsp. oil
- 4 boneless skinless chicken thighs (1 lb.)
- 1 pkg. (7-1/4 oz.) KRAFT Macaroni & Cheese Dinner
- 1 can (14-1/2 oz.) diced tomatoes, undrained
- 2 green onions, sliced
- 1/2 cup chopped fresh parsley

Direction

- Heat oil in medium skillet on medium-high heat. Add chicken; cook 7 min. on each side or until cooked through (170°F).
- Meanwhile, prepare Dinner as directed on package, substituting large skillet for the saucepan.
- Add tomatoes, onions and parsley to prepared Dinner; mix lightly. Top with the chicken.

Nutrition Information

- Calories: 490
- Sodium: 770 mg
- Sugar: 0 g
- Total Carbohydrate: 0 g
- Cholesterol: 115 mg
- Fiber: 3 g
- Saturated Fat: 4.5 g
- Total Fat: 21 g
- Protein: 27 g

173. Easy BBQ Glazed Chicken

Serving: 4 | Prep: 30mins | Cook: 10mins | Ready in: 40mins

Ingredients

- 1/2 cup KRAFT Zesty Italian Dressing, divided
- 4 small boneless skinless chicken breasts (1 lb.)
- 1/4 cup KRAFT Original Barbecue Sauce
- 2 Tbsp. orange marmalade

Direction

- Heat grill to medium heat.
- Pour 1/4 cup dressing over chicken in shallow dish; turn to evenly coat both sides of each breast. Refrigerate 10 min.
- Meanwhile, mix barbecue sauce, marmalade and remaining dressing.
- Remove chicken from dressing; discard dressing. Grill chicken 5 to 7 min. on each side or until done (165°F), brushing occasionally with barbecue sauce mixture for the last few minutes.

Nutrition Information

- Calories: 250
- Sugar: 0 g
- Cholesterol: 65 mg
- Total Carbohydrate: 0 g
- Protein: 25 g
- Saturated Fat: 1.5 g
- Fiber: 0 g
- Total Fat: 8 g
- Sodium: 530 mg

174. Easy Cheesy Chicken Bake

Serving: 0 | Prep: 20mins | Cook: 10mins | Ready in: 30mins

Ingredients

- 1 pkg. (12 oz.) VELVEETA Shells & Cheese Dinner Made With 2% Milk Cheese
- 1 can (12.5 oz.) chicken, drained
- 1 green pepper, chopped
- 1 cup frozen corn, thawed
- 1/3 cup KRAFT Original Barbecue Sauce
- 1/4 cup BREAKSTONE'S Reduced Fat or KNUDSEN Light Sour Cream
- 1/2 cup KRAFT 2% Milk Shredded Mild Cheddar Cheese

Direction

- Heat oven to 400°F.
- Prepare Dinner in large saucepan as directed on package. Stir in all remaining ingredients except shredded cheese.

- Spoon into 8-inch square baking dish sprayed with cooking spray; top with shredded cheese.
- Bake 10 min. or until heated through.

Nutrition Information

- Calories: 270
- Total Carbohydrate: 0 g
- Sodium: 720 mg
- Sugar: 0 g
- Total Fat: 10 g
- Cholesterol: 35 mg
- Fiber: 1 g
- Protein: 16 g
- Saturated Fat: 3.5 g

175. Easy Chicken & Pasta Skillet With Parmesan

Serving: 0 | Prep: 30mins | Cook: | Ready in: 30mins

Ingredients

- 1-1/2 lb. boneless skinless chicken breasts, cut into thin strips
- 1 Tbsp. oil
- 4 cups rotini pasta, uncooked
- 3 cups water
- 2 cups fat-free reduced-sodium chicken broth
- 1 Tbsp. lemon zest
- 1 red pepper, cut into strips
- 1 cup halved grape tomatoes
- 3 Tbsp. KRAFT Grated Parmesan Cheese

Direction

- Cook and stir chicken in hot oil in large skillet on medium heat 4 min. or until done.
- Add pasta, water, broth and zest; stir. Bring to boil; simmer on medium-low heat 15 min. Add peppers and tomatoes; cook 5 min. or until peppers are crisp-tender, stirring frequently.
- Sprinkle with cheese.

Nutrition Information

- Calories: 380
- Saturated Fat: 2 g
- Total Fat: 7 g
- Total Carbohydrate: 0 g
- Cholesterol: 70 mg
- Fiber: 3 g
- Sugar: 0 g
- Sodium: 280 mg
- Protein: 34 g

176. Easy Chicken Cacciatore Recipe

Serving: 0 | Prep: 10mins | Cook: 40mins | Ready in: 50mins

Ingredients

- 2 tsp. oil
- 1 broiler-fryer chicken (3-1/2 lb.), cut up
- 1 env. GOOD SEASONS Italian Dressing Mix
- 1 jar (24 oz.) CLASSICO Tomato and Basil Pasta Sauce
- 1 small green pepper, sliced
- 6 cups hot cooked ziti pasta

Direction

- Heat oil in large skillet on medium heat. Add chicken; cook until browned on all sides, turning occasionally.
- Sprinkle dressing mix over chicken. Add pasta sauce and green pepper. Bring to boil. Reduce heat to low; cover.
- Simmer 25 to 30 min. or until chicken is cooked through, stirring occasionally. Serve over pasta.

Nutrition Information

- Calories: 1180

- Fiber: 9 g
- Sugar: 0 g
- Saturated Fat: 6 g
- Total Carbohydrate: 0 g
- Sodium: 1060 mg
- Cholesterol: 235 mg
- Total Fat: 27 g
- Protein: 100 g

177. Easy Chicken Parmesan

Serving: 6 | Prep: 15mins | Cook: 30mins | Ready in: 45mins

Ingredients

- 1 jar (24 oz.) CLASSICO Tomato and Basil Pasta Sauce
- 6 Tbsp. KRAFT Grated Parmesan Cheese, divided
- 6 small boneless skinless chicken breasts (1-1/2 lb.)
- 3/4 lb. spaghetti, uncooked
- 1-1/2 cups KRAFT Shredded Mozzarella Cheese

Direction

- Heat oven to 375°F.
- Pour sauce into 13x9-inch baking dish sprayed with cooking spray. Stir in 1/4 cup (4 Tbsp.) Parmesan. Add chicken; turn to evenly coat both sides of each breast with pasta sauce mixture. Cover.
- Bake 30 min. or until chicken is done (165°F). Meanwhile, cook spaghetti as directed on package, omitting salt.
- Top chicken with remaining cheeses; bake, uncovered, 5 min. or until mozzarella is melted.
- Drain spaghetti. Serve topped with chicken and pasta sauce mixture.

Nutrition Information

- Calories: 550
- Sugar: 0 g
- Total Carbohydrate: 0 g
- Fiber: 6 g
- Cholesterol: 80 mg
- Saturated Fat: 6 g
- Protein: 41 g
- Total Fat: 14 g
- Sodium: 860 mg

178. Easy Chicken Quesadillas

Serving: 6 | Prep: 20mins | Cook: 10mins | Ready in: 30mins

Ingredients

- 1 lb. lean ground chicken
- 1 pkg. (1 oz.) TACO BELL® Reduced Sodium Taco Seasoning Mix
- 6 flour tortillas (8 inch), warmed
- 1 cup KRAFT Mexican Style 2% Milk Finely Shredded Four Cheese
- 3/4 cup TACO BELL® Thick & Chunky Salsa

Direction

- Heat oven to 425°F.
- Cook chicken with seasoning mix as directed on package.
- Spoon onto tortillas; top with cheese.
- Fold tortillas in half; place on baking sheet sprayed with cooking spray.
- Bake 8 to 10 min. or until heated through. Cut into wedges. Serve with salsa.

Nutrition Information

- Calories: 310
- Sodium: 980 mg
- Fiber: 2 g
- Sugar: 2 g
- Cholesterol: 55 mg
- Protein: 27 g

- Saturated Fat: 3.5 g
- Total Carbohydrate: 31 g
- Total Fat: 9 g

179. Easy Chicken Rigatoni

Serving: 6 | Prep: 35mins | Cook: | Ready in: 35mins

Ingredients

- 2 Tbsp. butter
- 1-1/2 lb. boneless skinless chicken breasts, cut into bite-size pieces
- 1 onion, chopped
- 2 cloves garlic, minced
- 1 red pepper, chopped
- 1/4 lb. portobello mushrooms, chopped
- 1 jar (15 oz.) CLASSICO Spicy Tomato & Parmesan Cream Pasta Sauce
- 1/4 tsp. ground black pepper
- 3-1/2 cups rigatoni pasta, uncooked
- 4 oz. (1/2 of 8-oz. pkg.) PHILADELPHIA Cream Cheese, cubed
- 1/2 cup chopped fresh basil
- 1 can (2.22 oz.) sliced black olives, drained

Direction

- Melt butter in large skillet on medium heat. Add chicken; cook and stir 5 to 6 min. or until no longer pink. Add onions and garlic; cook and stir 1 min. Add red peppers and mushrooms; cook 5 min., stirring frequently. Stir in pasta sauce and black pepper; simmer on medium-low heat 10 min., stirring occasionally.
- Meanwhile, cook pasta as directed on package, omitting salt.
- Add cream cheese, basil and olives to chicken mixture; cook and stir 1 to 2 min. or until cream cheese is completely melted and sauce is well blended. Drain pasta. Add to pasta sauce mixture; stir until evenly coated.

Nutrition Information

- Calories: 520
- Saturated Fat: 8 g
- Total Fat: 17 g
- Cholesterol: 110 mg
- Sodium: 440 mg
- Protein: 35 g
- Sugar: 0 g
- Total Carbohydrate: 0 g
- Fiber: 4 g

180. Easy Chicken Stir Fry Skillet

Serving: 0 | Prep: 10mins | Cook: 10mins | Ready in: 20mins

Ingredients

- 2 tsp. oil
- 1 lb. boneless skinless chicken breasts, cut into strips
- 3 cups frozen stir-fry vegetables (broccoli, carrots, red peppers, snow peas), thawed
- 1/4 cup KRAFT Asian Toasted Sesame Dressing
- 2 Tbsp. soy sauce
- 1 Tbsp. honey
- 1/4 cup chopped PLANTERS COCKTAIL Peanuts
- 4 cups hot cooked instant white rice

Direction

- Heat oil in large skillet on medium-high heat. Add chicken; cook and stir 7 min. or until no longer pink.
- Add vegetables, dressing, soy sauce and honey; mix well. Cook an additional 2 min. or until heated through. Sprinkle with peanuts.
- Serve over the rice.

Nutrition Information

- Calories: 480
- Total Fat: 13 g
- Cholesterol: 65 mg
- Sodium: 710 mg
- Saturated Fat: 2 g
- Protein: 30 g
- Fiber: 3 g
- Total Carbohydrate: 0 g
- Sugar: 0 g

181. Easy Chicken À La King

Serving: 4 | Prep: 15mins | Cook: 15mins | Ready in: 30mins

Ingredients

- 1/3 cup MIRACLE WHIP Light Dressing
- 2 Tbsp. flour
- 1 cup fat-free milk
- 2 pkg. (6 oz. each) OSCAR MAYER CARVING BOARD Flame Grilled Chicken Breast Strips, chopped
- 1 cup each frozen peas and sliced fresh mushrooms
- 1/2 cup chopped red pepper
- dash black pepper
- 2 cups hot cooked long-grain white rice

Direction

- Mix dressing, flour and milk in medium microwaveable bowl. Microwave on HIGH 3 to 4 min. or until thickened, stirring after 2 min.
- Stir in all remaining ingredients except rice. Microwave on MEDIUM (50%) 10 min. or until heated through, stirring every 4 min.
- Serve over rice.

Nutrition Information

- Calories: 310
- Fiber: 3 g

- Protein: 29 g
- Total Carbohydrate: 0 g
- Sodium: 760 mg
- Total Fat: 4.5 g
- Sugar: 0 g
- Saturated Fat: 1 g
- Cholesterol: 70 mg

182. Easy Chile Stuffed Chicken Breasts

Serving: 4 | Prep: 20mins | Cook: 20mins | Ready in: 40mins

Ingredients

- 4 small boneless skinless chicken breasts (1 lb.)
- 1/4 cup KRAFT Mexican Style Shredded Queso Quesadilla Cheese
- 2 Tbsp. canned chopped green chiles, drained
- 2 Tbsp. chopped roasted poblano chiles
- 1 egg
- 1/4 cup chopped fresh cilantro
- 2 Tbsp. KRAFT Grated Parmesan Cheese

Direction

- Heat oven to 350°F.
- Make 2-inch-long cut in one long side of each chicken breast to form pocket; fill with shredded cheese and chiles. Press cut edges of pockets together to seal.
- Whisk egg in pie plate. Combine cilantro and Parmesan in separate pie plate. Dip chicken, 1 breast at a time, in egg, then in parsley mixture, turning to evenly coat both sides of each breast. Place in 8-inch square baking dish sprayed with cooking spray.
- Bake 18 to 20 min. or until chicken is done (165°F).

Nutrition Information

- Calories: 190

- Total Fat: 7 g
- Cholesterol: 120 mg
- Protein: 29 g
- Saturated Fat: 3 g
- Sugar: 0 g
- Sodium: 210 mg
- Total Carbohydrate: 0 g
- Fiber: 0 g

183. Easy Enchilada Recipe

Serving: 6 | Prep: 30mins | Cook: | Ready in: 30mins

Ingredients

- 1 lb. lean ground chicken
- 1/2 tsp. onion powder
- 1/4 tsp. garlic powder
- 1/4 tsp. ground red pepper (cayenne)
- 1 pkg. (8 oz.) KRAFT Mexican Style Shredded Four Cheese with a TOUCH OF PHILADELPHIA, divided
- 1 jar (16 oz.) TACO BELL® Thick & Chunky Salsa, divided
- 12 flour tortillas (6 inch)

Direction

- Cook chicken in large nonstick skillet sprayed with cooking spray until done, stirring occasionally. Remove from heat. Add dry seasonings, 1 cup cheese and 1/2 cup salsa; mix well.
- Spread 1/2 cup of the remaining salsa onto each of 2 microwaveable plates. Spoon 1/4 cup chicken mixture down center of each tortilla; roll up. Place 6 roll-ups, seam sides down, in single layer on each prepared plate. Top with remaining salsa and cheese. Cover loosely with waxed paper.
- Microwave enchiladas, 1 plate at a time, on HIGH 2 to 3 min. or until cheese is melted and enchiladas are heated through.

Nutrition Information

- Calories: 400
- Total Carbohydrate: 37 g
- Protein: 27 g
- Total Fat: 17 g
- Saturated Fat: 8 g
- Fiber: 3 g
- Sugar: 3 g
- Cholesterol: 70 mg
- Sodium: 1180 mg

184. Easy Feta Chicken Bake

Serving: 0 | Prep: 10mins | Cook: 40mins | Ready in: 50mins

Ingredients

- 6 boneless skinless chicken breasts (1-1/2 lb.)
- 2 Tbsp. lemon juice, divided
- 1/4 tsp. black pepper
- 1 pkg. (4 oz.) ATHENOS Crumbled Feta Cheese with Basil & Tomato
- 1/4 cup finely chopped red peppers
- 1/4 cup finely chopped fresh parsley

Direction

- Heat oven to 350°F.
- Place chicken in 13x9-inch baking dish sprayed with cooking spray.
- Drizzle with 1 Tbsp. lemon juice. Season with black pepper. Top with cheese; drizzle with remaining lemon juice.
- Bake 35 to 40 min. or until chicken is done (165°F). Top with red peppers and parsley.

Nutrition Information

- Calories: 190
- Saturated Fat: 3 g
- Cholesterol: 80 mg
- Protein: 28 g
- Sodium: 270 mg

- Fiber: 1 g
- Total Carbohydrate: 0 g
- Total Fat: 7 g
- Sugar: 0 g

185. Easy Glazed Chicken Dinner

Serving: 4 | Prep: 35mins | Cook: 15mins | Ready in: 50mins

Ingredients

- 1 can (14 oz.) fat-free reduced-sodium chicken broth
- 2 cups quinoa, rinsed
- 3 cups small broccoli florets
- 4 small boneless skinless chicken breasts (1 lb.)
- 1/4 cup KRAFT Zesty CATALINA Dressing
- 1/4 cup orange juice
- 3 Tbsp. maple-flavored or pancake syrup
- 2 Tbsp. PLANTERS Sliced Almonds, toasted

Direction

- Bring broth to boil in medium saucepan. Stir in quinoa; cover. Simmer on medium-low heat 15 min. Add broccoli; stir. Simmer, covered, 3 min. Remove from heat; let stand 5 min. or until broth is completely absorbed.
- Meanwhile, cook chicken in large nonstick skillet sprayed with cooking spray on medium heat 6 to 7 min. on each side or until done (165°F). Remove from skillet; cover to keep warm.
- Add dressing, juice and syrup to skillet; stir. Bring to boil; simmer on medium heat 3 min. or until thickened, stirring occasionally.
- Place chicken and quinoa on platter. Drizzle dressing mixture over chicken. Sprinkle with nuts.

Nutrition Information

- Calories: 590
- Fiber: 8 g
- Total Fat: 16 g
- Sodium: 450 mg
- Total Carbohydrate: 0 g
- Saturated Fat: 2.5 g
- Protein: 39 g
- Sugar: 0 g
- Cholesterol: 65 mg

186. Easy Greek Grilled Chicken Salads With Feta

Serving: 4 | Prep: 30mins | Cook: 20mins | Ready in: 50mins

Ingredients

- 2/3 cup KRAFT Greek Vinaigrette Dressing, divided
- 4 small boneless skinless chicken breasts (1 lb.)
- 1 pkg. (10 oz.) torn mixed salad greens
- 1 small red onion, chopped
- 1 tomato, chopped
- 1/2 cup cucumber slices
- 1/2 cup pitted black olives
- 1 pkg. (4 oz.) ATHENOS Traditional Crumbled Feta Cheese

Direction

- Heat grill to medium-high heat.
- Pour 1/3 cup dressing over chicken in shallow dish; turn to evenly coat both sides of each breast. Refrigerate 20 min. to marinate. Remove chicken from marinade; discard marinade.
- Grill chicken 6 to 8 min. on each side or until done (165°F). Meanwhile, combine salad greens, onions, tomatoes, cucumbers, olives and cheese in large bowl. Add remaining dressing; toss to coat.
- Place salad on 4 plates. Top each with 1 sliced chicken breast.

Nutrition Information

- Calories: 360
- Fiber: 4 g
- Sugar: 0 g
- Cholesterol: 85 mg
- Saturated Fat: 6 g
- Sodium: 820 mg
- Total Carbohydrate: 0 g
- Protein: 32 g
- Total Fat: 21 g

187. Easy Grilled BBQ Chicken

Serving: 8 | Prep: 20mins | Cook: 1hours | Ready in: 1hours20mins

Ingredients

- 1/2 cup KRAFT Original Barbecue Sauce, divided
- 8 small boneless skinless chicken breasts (2 lb.)

Direction

- Pour 1/4 cup barbecue sauce over chicken in shallow dish; turn to evenly coat both sides of each breast. Refrigerate 1 hour to marinate.
- Heat grill to medium heat. Remove chicken from marinade; discard marinade.
- Grill chicken 5 to 7 min. on each side or until done (165ºF), brushing occasionally with remaining barbecue sauce for the last few minutes.

Nutrition Information

- Calories: 150
- Sodium: 200 mg
- Total Carbohydrate: 6 g
- Sugar: 5 g
- Total Fat: 3 g
- Fiber: 0 g
- Cholesterol: 65 mg
- Protein: 24 g
- Saturated Fat: 1 g

188. Easy Grilled Chicken Parmesan Dinner

Serving: 6 | Prep: 25mins | Cook: | Ready in: 25mins

Ingredients

- 1/2 cup KRAFT Shredded Low-Moisture Part-Skim Mozzarella Cheese
- 1/3 cup KRAFT Grated Parmesan Cheese, divided
- 6 KRAFT Singles, divided
- 4 cups gemelli pasta, uncooked
- 6 small boneless skinless chicken breasts (1-1/2 lb.), pounded to 1/2-inch thickness
- 1 jar (24 oz.) CLASSICO Tomato and Basil Pasta Sauce, divided
- 2 Tbsp. chopped fresh basil

Direction

- Heat grill to medium heat.
- Combine mozzarella and 1/4 cup Parmesan. Cut 3 Singles in half. Cook pasta in large saucepan as directed on package, omitting salt.
- Meanwhile, grill chicken 6 to 8 min. on each side or until done. Top each breast with 1 Tbsp. pasta sauce, about 1-1/2 Tbsp. of the mozzarella mixture and 1 Singles piece. Grill 1 min. or until cheeses are melted. Remove from grill; cover to keep warm.
- Drain pasta; return to pan. Stir in remaining sauce and Singles; cook and stir 3 min. or until sauce is heated through and Singles are melted.
- Spoon pasta onto platter; top with chicken, remaining Parmesan and basil.

Nutrition Information

- Calories: 600
- Cholesterol: 90 mg
- Protein: 44 g
- Total Carbohydrate: 0 g
- Fiber: 5 g
- Saturated Fat: 6 g
- Sodium: 820 mg
- Total Fat: 15 g
- Sugar: 0 g

189. Easy Skillet Fried Chicken

Serving: 4 | Prep: 50mins | Cook: 2hours | Ready in: 2hours50mins

Ingredients

- 2-1/2 lb. chicken pieces
- 1 env. (0.7 oz.) GOOD SEASONS Garlic & Herb Dressing Mix, divided
- 2 tsp. chili powder, divided
- 1 cup panko bread crumbs
- 2 Tbsp. finely chopped fresh parsley
- 1-1/2 cups oil

Direction

- Sprinkle chicken with 1 Tbsp. dressing mix and 1 tsp. chili powder in shallow glass dish; turn to coat. Refrigerate 1 to 2 hours to marinate.
- Mix bread crumbs, parsley, remaining dressing mix and chili powder in resealable plastic bag. Add chicken, 1 piece at a time; shake to coat.
- Heat oil in large skillet on medium-high heat. Add chicken; cook 10 min. or until browned on all sides, turning frequently. Cover. Cook on medium heat 30 min. or until chicken is done (165°F), turning occasionally. Drain on paper towels.

Nutrition Information

- Calories: 240
- Sodium: 530 mg
- Protein: 21 g
- Total Fat: 15 g
- Total Carbohydrate: 0 g
- Saturated Fat: 3.5 g
- Fiber: 1 g
- Cholesterol: 65 mg
- Sugar: 0 g

190. Easy Weeknight Pasta Toss

Serving: 4 | Prep: 25mins | Cook: | Ready in: 25mins

Ingredients

- 3 cups rotini pasta, uncooked
- 1 lb. boneless skinless chicken breasts, thinly sliced
- 1 Tbsp. oil
- 1/4 cup KRAFT Sun Dried Tomato Vinaigrette Dressing
- 1 large carrot, thinly sliced
- 1 red pepper, chopped
- 1/2 cup KRAFT Shredded Colby & Monterey Jack Cheeses

Direction

- Cook pasta as directed on package, omitting salt.
- Meanwhile, cook and stir chicken in hot oil in large skillet on medium heat 5 min. or until chicken is done. Remove from skillet; cover to keep warm. Add dressing and vegetables to skillet; cook 4 to 5 min. or until vegetables are crisp-tender, stirring occasionally.
- Drain pasta, reserving 1/4 cup of the cooking water. Place pasta in large bowl. Add chicken and vegetable mixture; mix lightly. Gradually stir in reserved pasta water, if needed, until pasta mixture is of desired consistency. Top with cheese.

Nutrition Information

- Calories: 500
- Sugar: 0 g
- Saturated Fat: 4.5 g
- Sodium: 350 mg
- Protein: 36 g
- Fiber: 4 g
- Total Fat: 14 g
- Total Carbohydrate: 0 g
- Cholesterol: 80 mg

191. Fiesta Chicken Enchiladas

Serving: 4 | Prep: 25mins | Cook: 20mins | Ready in: 45mins

Ingredients

- 1 small onion, chopped
- 1 clove garlic, minced
- 1 lb. cooked boneless skinless chicken breasts, shredded
- 1 cup TACO BELL® Thick & Chunky Salsa, divided
- 4 oz. (1/2 of 8-oz. pkg.) PHILADELPHIA Cream Cheese, cubed
- 1 Tbsp. chopped fresh cilantro
- 1 tsp. ground cumin
- 1 cup KRAFT Shredded Cheddar & Monterey Jack Cheeses, divided
- 8 flour tortillas (6 inch)

Direction

- Heat oven to 350°F.
- Cook and stir onions and garlic in large skillet spayed with cooking spray on medium heat 2 min. Add chicken, 1/4 cup salsa, cream cheese, cilantro and cumin; mix well. Cook 5 min. or until heated through, stirring occasionally. Add 1/2 cup shredded cheese; mix well.
- Spoon about 1/3 cup chicken mixture down center of each tortilla; roll up. Place, seam-sides down, in 13x9-inch baking dish sprayed with cooking spray; top with remaining salsa and shredded cheese.
- Bake 15 to 20 min. or until heated through.

Nutrition Information

- Calories: 560
- Saturated Fat: 13 g
- Sodium: 1150 mg
- Total Carbohydrate: 0 g
- Fiber: 3 g
- Sugar: 0 g
- Cholesterol: 130 mg
- Total Fat: 26 g
- Protein: 38 g

192. Fiesta Chicken Skillet

Serving: 4 | Prep: 25mins | Cook: | Ready in: 25mins

Ingredients

- 4 small boneless skinless chicken breasts (1 lb.)
- 1 tsp. chili powder
- 1 pkg. (16 oz.) frozen bell pepper and onion strips, thawed
- 3/4 cup TACO BELL® Thick & Chunky Salsa
- 2 cups hot cooked long-grain brown rice
- 1/2 cup KRAFT Mexican Style 2% Milk Finely Shredded Four Cheese
- 1/4 cup BREAKSTONE'S or KNUDSEN Sour Cream

Direction

- Sprinkle chicken with chili powder; cook in large nonstick skillet on medium heat 6 to 8 min. on each side or until done (165°F). Transfer to plate; cover to keep warm.
- Add vegetables and salsa to same skillet; cook and stir 4 min. or until heated through.

- Spoon rice onto platter; top with chicken, vegetable mixture, cheese and sour cream.

Nutrition Information

- Calories: 350
- Cholesterol: 80 mg
- Total Carbohydrate: 35 g
- Sodium: 520 mg
- Sugar: 5 g
- Protein: 33 g
- Total Fat: 8 g
- Saturated Fat: 3.5 g
- Fiber: 4 g

193. Foil Pack Bruschetta Chicken Bake

Serving: 6 | Prep: 15mins | Cook: 35mins | Ready in: 50mins

Ingredients

- 1 pkg. (6 oz.) STOVE TOP Stuffing Mix for Chicken
- 1 can (28 oz.) diced tomatoes, drained
- 2 cloves garlic, minced
- 6 small boneless skinless chicken breasts (1-1/2 lb.)
- 1 tsp. dried basil leaves
- 1 cup KRAFT 2% Milk Shredded Mozzarella Cheese

Direction

- Heat oven to 400°F.
- Combine stuffing mix, tomatoes and garlic just until stuffing mix is moistened.
- Place 1 chicken breast on center of each of 6 large sheets heavy-duty foil sprayed with cooking spray; sprinkle with basil. Top with stuffing mixture and cheese. Fold foil to make 6 packets. Place in single layer on rimmed baking sheet.
- Bake 30 to 35 min. or until chicken is done (165°F). Cut slits in foil to release steam before carefully opening packets.

Nutrition Information

- Calories: 300
- Saturated Fat: 2.5 g
- Cholesterol: 75 mg
- Total Fat: 7 g
- Total Carbohydrate: 0 g
- Fiber: 2 g
- Protein: 33 g
- Sugar: 0 g
- Sodium: 660 mg

194. Foil Pack Chicken & Broccoli Dinner

Serving: 6 | Prep: 10mins | Cook: 35mins | Ready in: 45mins

Ingredients

- 1 pkg. (6 oz.) STOVE TOP Stuffing Mix for Chicken
- 1-1/2 cups water
- 6 small boneless skinless chicken breasts (1-1/2 lb.), 1/2 inch thick
- 4 cups broccoli florets
- 1-1/2 cups KRAFT Shredded Cheddar Cheese
- 1/4 cup OSCAR MAYER Real Bacon Bits
- 1/2 cup KRAFT Classic Ranch Dressing

Direction

- Heat oven to 400°F.
- Combine stuffing mix and water; spoon onto centers of 6 large sheets heavy-duty foil. Top with remaining ingredients; fold to make 6 packets.
- Place in single layer on rimmed baking sheet.
- Bake 30 to 35 min. or until chicken is done (165°F). Remove packets from oven; let stand 5

min. Cut slits in foil to release steam before opening packets.

Nutrition Information

- Calories: 450
- Total Carbohydrate: 26 g
- Protein: 37 g
- Fiber: 3 g
- Sugar: 4 g
- Total Fat: 22 g
- Saturated Fat: 8 g
- Cholesterol: 100 mg
- Sodium: 970 mg

195. Four Cheese Bacon Chicken Pizza

Serving: 6 | Prep: 20mins | Cook: 10mins | Ready in: 30mins

Ingredients

- 1 can (13.8 oz.) refrigerated pizza crust
- 1/4 cup KRAFT Mayo with Olive Oil Reduced Fat Mayonnaise
- 1/2 cup KRAFT Ranch with Bacon Dressing, divided
- 1-1/2 cups KRAFT Shredded Four Cheese, divided
- 1-1/2 cups finely chopped cooked chicken
- 8 slices OSCAR MAYER Bacon, cooked, crumbled
- 1-1/2 cups finely shredded lettuce
- 1 tomato, finely chopped

Direction

- Heat oven to 400°F.
- Unroll pizza dough on baking sheet sprayed with cooking spray; press into 15x10-inch rectangle. Bake 10 min.
- Mix mayo and 1/3 cup dressing until blended; spread onto crust. Top with half the cheese, chicken, remaining cheese and bacon.
- Bake 5 min. or until crust is golden brown and cheese is melted. Top with lettuce and tomatoes; drizzle with remaining dressing.

Nutrition Information

- Calories: 500
- Cholesterol: 70 mg
- Sodium: 1170 mg
- Fiber: 1 g
- Protein: 26 g
- Sugar: 7 g
- Total Fat: 28 g
- Saturated Fat: 8 g
- Total Carbohydrate: 36 g

196. French Country Chicken Casserole

Serving: 8 | Prep: 15mins | Cook: 40mins | Ready in: 55mins

Ingredients

- 8 small boneless skinless chicken breasts (2 lb.)
- 2 Tbsp. KRAFT Zesty Italian Dressing
- 2 large carrots, thinly sliced
- 1/2 lb. sliced fresh mushrooms
- 1 can (10-3/4 oz.) condensed cream of chicken soup
- 1 cup hot water
- 1 pkg. (6 oz.) STOVE TOP Stuffing Mix for Chicken
- 3/4 cup KRAFT Shredded Cheddar Cheese
- 1 tsp. dried thyme leaves

Direction

- Heat oven to 350°F.
- Place chicken in 13x9-inch baking dish sprayed with cooking spray; brush with

dressing. Add carrots and mushrooms; cover with soup.
- Add hot water to stuffing mix; stir just until moistened. Spoon over chicken; sprinkle with cheese and thyme.
- Bake 40 min. or until chicken is done (165°F).

Nutrition Information

- Calories: 310
- Sodium: 750 mg
- Cholesterol: 80 mg
- Total Fat: 10 g
- Saturated Fat: 4 g
- Total Carbohydrate: 23 g
- Sugar: 4 g
- Fiber: 2 g
- Protein: 31 g

197. Fresh Chopped Salad

Serving: 0 | Prep: 20mins | Cook: | Ready in: 20mins

Ingredients

- 6 cups tightly packed chopped mixed salad greens
- 2 cups chopped cooked chicken
- 1 navel orange, sectioned, chopped
- 1 avocado, chopped
- 1 small red onion, chopped
- 1/2 cup KRAFT Balsamic Vinaigrette Dressing

Direction

- Combine all ingredients except dressing in large bowl.
- Add dressing just before serving; toss to coat.

Nutrition Information

- Calories: 270
- Sodium: 360 mg
- Sugar: 0 g
- Saturated Fat: 2.5 g
- Fiber: 6 g
- Total Fat: 12 g
- Cholesterol: 60 mg
- Total Carbohydrate: 0 g
- Protein: 22 g

198. Garden Herb Chicken

Serving: 4 | Prep: 10mins | Cook: 45mins | Ready in: 55mins

Ingredients

- 2 cups fresh parsley
- 1 clove garlic
- 1 tsp. fresh thyme leaves
- 1 tsp. lemon zest
- 1/2 cup KRAFT Zesty Italian Dressing
- 4 small boneless skinless chicken breasts (1 lb.)

Direction

- Use pulsing action to process first 4 ingredients in food processor just until coarsely chopped. Add dressing; pulse just until blended. (Do not overprocess.) Pour over chicken in shallow dish; turn to coat both sides of each breast. Refrigerate 30 min. to marinate.
- Heat grill to medium heat. Remove chicken from marinade; discard marinade.
- Grill chicken 6 to 8 min. on each side or until done (165°F).

Nutrition Information

- Calories: 180
- Fiber: 1 g
- Saturated Fat: 1.5 g
- Total Fat: 7 g
- Total Carbohydrate: 0 g
- Protein: 25 g
- Sodium: 230 mg
- Sugar: 0 g

- Cholesterol: 65 mg

199. Garlic Chicken Primavera

Serving: 0 | Prep: 5mins | Cook: 30mins | Ready in: 35mins

Ingredients

- 4 small boneless skinless chicken breasts (about 1 lb.)
- 1 Tbsp. oil
- 1 pkg. (14 oz.) KRAFT Deluxe Macaroni & Sharp Cheddar Cheese Sauce
- 2 cups frozen vegetable blend, thawed
- 1/2 tsp. garlic powder

Direction

- Cook chicken in hot oil in large skillet on medium-high heat for 3 to 4 minutes on each side or until browned on both sides.
- Add 2-1/2 cups water and Macaroni. Bring to boil; cover. Reduce heat to medium-low; simmer 15 to 17 minutes or until macaroni is tender, stirring occasionally. (Do not drain.)
- Stir in Cheese Sauce, vegetable blend and garlic powder; cook until heated through, stirring occasionally.

Nutrition Information

- Calories: 510
- Cholesterol: 85 mg
- Protein: 38 g
- Saturated Fat: 4.5 g
- Sodium: 980 mg
- Total Carbohydrate: 0 g
- Total Fat: 16 g
- Sugar: 0 g
- Fiber: 4 g

200. Gorgonzola Waldorf Sandwiches

Serving: 0 | Prep: 10mins | Cook: | Ready in: 10mins

Ingredients

- 1 lb. boneless skinless chicken breasts, cooked, chopped
- 1 cup each: seedless green and red grapes, halved
- 1/2 cup ATHENOS Crumbled Gorgonzola Cheese
- 1/2 cup PLANTERS Walnut Pieces, toasted
- 1 apple, chopped
- 4 green onions, sliced
- 1 Tbsp. lemon juice
- 6 whole grain rolls, split

Direction

- Combine all ingredients except rolls.
- Fill rolls with chicken mixture.

Nutrition Information

- Calories: 370
- Total Fat: 15 g
- Saturated Fat: 4 g
- Total Carbohydrate: 0 g
- Sodium: 420 mg
- Cholesterol: 60 mg
- Protein: 24 g
- Fiber: 4 g
- Sugar: 0 g

201. Grecian Pizza Bowl Salad

Serving: 0 | Prep: 15mins | Cook: | Ready in: 15mins

Ingredients

- 1 ready-to-use baked pizza crust (12 inch)

- 1/2 cup plus 2 Tbsp. KRAFT Zesty Italian Dressing, divided
- 1 cup KRAFT Shredded Mozzarella Cheese
- 1 pkg. (5 oz.) torn salad greens
- 1 pkg. (6 oz.) OSCAR MAYER CARVING BOARD Flame Grilled Chicken Breast Strips
- 1 tomato, coarsely chopped
- 1/2 cup quartered sliced cucumbers
- 1/2 cup ATHENOS Traditional Crumbled Feta Cheese
- 2 Tbsp. sliced black olives

Direction

- Heat oven to 425°F.
- Place pizza crust on baking sheet; brush with 2 Tbsp. dressing. Top with mozzarella. Bake 7 to 8 min. or until cheese is melted.
- Toss greens with chicken, tomatoes and cucumbers. Add remaining dressing; mix lightly.
- Cut pizza into wedges; top with salad and remaining ingredients.

Nutrition Information

- Calories: 340
- Sugar: 0 g
- Saturated Fat: 6 g
- Sodium: 1010 mg
- Protein: 18 g
- Cholesterol: 40 mg
- Total Carbohydrate: 0 g
- Fiber: 2 g
- Total Fat: 17 g

202. Greek Style Skillet Chicken

Serving: 4 | Prep: 30mins | Cook: | Ready in: 30mins

Ingredients

- 1/4 cup KRAFT Greek Vinaigrette with Feta Cheese and Oregano Dressing made with Extra Virgin Olive Oil, divided
- 4 small boneless skinless chicken breasts (1 lb.)
- 1 small zucchini, sliced
- 1 small onion, sliced, separated into rings
- 1/2 cup chopped red peppers
- 2 cloves garlic, minced
- 1-1/4 cups fat-free reduced-sodium chicken broth
- 1 Tbsp. fresh lemon juice
- 1 cup couscous, uncooked
- 1/2 cup ATHENOS Traditional Crumbled Feta Cheese
- 1/2 cup halved grape tomatoes

Direction

- Heat 2 Tbsp. dressing in large skillet on medium heat. Add chicken; cook 6 to 7 min. on each side until done (165°F). Remove chicken from skillet; cover to keep warm.
- Heat remaining dressing in same skillet. Add zucchini, onions, peppers and garlic; cook 3 min., stirring frequently. Stir in broth and lemon juice; bring to boil, stirring frequently.
- Add couscous; stir. Top with chicken. Remove from heat. Cover; let stand 5 min.
- Move chicken to one side of skillet; fluff couscous mixture with fork. Serve couscous mixture topped with chicken; sprinkle with cheese and tomatoes.

Nutrition Information

- Calories: 420
- Total Carbohydrate: 0 g
- Sugar: 0 g
- Fiber: 4 g
- Cholesterol: 80 mg
- Protein: 35 g
- Saturated Fat: 4 g
- Sodium: 540 mg
- Total Fat: 12 g

203. Greek Style Stuffed Chicken Breasts

Serving: 4 | Prep: 15mins | Cook: 55mins | Ready in: 1hours10mins

Ingredients

- 4 small boneless skinless chicken breasts (1 lb.)
- 1/2 cup KRAFT Greek Vinaigrette with Feta Cheese and Oregano Dressing made with Extra Virgin Olive Oil, divided
- 1/3 cup chopped fresh parsley, divided
- 1 tsp. dried oregano leaves
- 20 round buttery crackers, crushed
- 2 cloves garlic, minced
- 1/4 cup ATHENOS Traditional Crumbled Feta Cheese
- 1 can (14-1/2 oz.) diced tomatoes with basil, garlic and oregano

Direction

- Make 3-inch-long cut in one long side of each chicken breast to form pocket, being careful to not cut all the way though to opposite side of chicken. Place chicken in shallow dish; drizzle with 1/4 cup dressing. Refrigerate 30 min. to marinate.
- Heat oven to 375°F. Combine parsley and oregano. Mix cracker crumbs, garlic, 1/4 cup parsley mixture and remaining dressing. Remove chicken from marinade; discard marinade. Spoon about 3 Tbsp. crumb mixture into pocket in each chicken breast; place on rimmed baking sheet sprayed with cooking spray.
- Bake 25 min. or until chicken is done (165°F). Meanwhile, combine cheese and remaining parsley mixture. About 5 min. before chicken is done, cook tomatoes in saucepan on medium heat until heated through, stirring occasionally.
- Drain tomatoes. Serve chicken topped with tomatoes and cheese mixture.

Nutrition Information

- Calories: 350
- Total Carbohydrate: 20 g
- Protein: 28 g
- Sodium: 810 mg
- Sugar: 6 g
- Saturated Fat: 4 g
- Cholesterol: 75 mg
- Fiber: 3 g
- Total Fat: 16 g

204. Green Salad With Skillet BBQ Chicken

Serving: 0 | Prep: 20mins | Cook: | Ready in: 20mins

Ingredients

- 2 pkg. (6 oz. each) OSCAR MAYER CARVING BOARD Flame Grilled Chicken Breast Strips, coarsely chopped
- 1/2 cup BULL'S-EYE Original Barbecue Sauce
- 1 pkg. (10 oz.) torn mixed salad greens
- 1 large tomato, cut into wedges
- 1/2 cup sliced red onions
- 1/2 cup KRAFT Buttermilk Ranch Dressing
- 1/2 cup KRAFT Natural Sharp Cheddar Cheese Crumbles

Direction

- Cook chicken and barbecue sauce in large skillet on medium-high heat until heated through, stirring occasionally.
- Toss greens with chicken, tomatoes and onions in large bowl.
- Top with dressing and cheese; mix lightly.

Nutrition Information

- Calories: 250
- Sodium: 860 mg
- Sugar: 0 g

- Cholesterol: 60 mg
- Total Carbohydrate: 0 g
- Saturated Fat: 3.5 g
- Fiber: 2 g
- Protein: 18 g
- Total Fat: 13 g

- Sodium: 260 mg
- Cholesterol: 65 mg
- Total Carbohydrate: 8 g

205. Grilled BBQ Chicken Breasts

Serving: 4 | Prep: 30mins | Cook: | Ready in: 30mins

Ingredients

- 1/4 cup KRAFT Original Barbecue Sauce
- 2 Tbsp. finely chopped onion s
- 1 Tbsp. HEINZ Apple Cider Vinegar
- 1 clove garlic, minced
- 2 tsp. HEINZ Yellow Mustard
- 1/4 tsp. cumin seed
- 4 small boneless skinless chicken breasts (1 lb.)
- 1/2 tsp. ground red pepper (cayenne)

Direction

- Heat grill to medium heat.
- Bring first 6 ingredients to boil in saucepan on medium heat, stirring frequently. Remove from heat.
- Sprinkle chicken with pepper.
- Grill chicken 6 min. on each side. Brush with half the barbecue sauce mixture; grill 1 to 2 min. or until chicken is done (165ºF), turning and brushing occasionally with remaining barbecue sauce mixture.

Nutrition Information

- Calories: 160
- Saturated Fat: 1 g
- Fiber: 0 g
- Protein: 25 g
- Total Fat: 3 g
- Sugar: 7 g

206. Grilled BBQ Chicken Thighs

Serving: 8 | Prep: 15mins | Cook: 30mins | Ready in: 45mins

Ingredients

- 3 Tbsp. brown sugar
- 2 Tbsp. finely chopped onions
- 2 Tbsp. HEINZ Apple Cider Vinegar
- 1 clove garlic, minced
- 1 Tbsp. HEINZ Yellow Mustard
- 1/4 tsp. cumin seed
- 1/2 tsp. smoked paprika
- 1/2 tsp. dried thyme leaves
- 1/4 tsp. ground red pepper (cayenne)
- 8 bone-in skinless chicken thighs (about 3 lb.)

Direction

- Heat grill to medium heat.
- Bring sugar, onions, vinegar, garlic, mustard, and cumin to boil in small saucepan on medium heat, stirring frequently. Stir until sugar dissolves. Remove from heat; set aside.
- Combine paprika, thyme and pepper; rub onto chicken.
- Grill chicken 15 min. on each side. Brush with sauce mixture; grill 3 to 5 min. or until done (165°F), turning and brushing occasionally with remaining sauce mixture.

Nutrition Information

- Calories: 170
- Protein: 21 g
- Cholesterol: 120 mg
- Fiber: 0 g
- Saturated Fat: 2 g

- Total Carbohydrate: 0 g
- Sugar: 0 g
- Sodium: 90 mg
- Total Fat: 7 g

207. Grilled Bruschetta Chicken

Serving: 4 | Prep: 25mins | Cook: 10mins | Ready in: 35mins

Ingredients

- 4 small boneless skinless chicken breasts (1 lb.)
- 1/4 cup KRAFT Sun Dried Tomato Vinaigrette Dressing, divided
- 1 tomato, finely chopped
- 1/2 cup KRAFT Shredded Low-Moisture Part-Skim Mozzarella Cheese
- 1/4 cup chopped fresh basil

Direction

- Heat grill to medium heat.
- Place chicken in large resealable plastic bag. Add 2 Tbsp. dressing; seal bag. Turn bag over several times to evenly coat chicken with dressing. Refrigerate 10 min. Remove chicken from bag; discard bag and dressing.
- Cover half the grill grate with sheet of heavy-duty foil. Place chicken on uncovered side of grill grate; grill 6 min. Meanwhile, combine remaining dressing, tomatoes, cheese and basil.
- Turn chicken over; place on foil. Top with tomato mixture. Grill 8 min. or until chicken is done (165°F).

Nutrition Information

- Calories: 210
- Total Carbohydrate: 0 g
- Fiber: 1 g
- Sugar: 0 g

- Protein: 28 g
- Cholesterol: 75 mg
- Sodium: 340 mg
- Total Fat: 8 g
- Saturated Fat: 2.5 g

208. Grilled Chicken Caesar Salad

Serving: 0 | Prep: 15mins | Cook: | Ready in: 15mins

Ingredients

- 1/2 cup KRAFT Zesty Italian Dressing
- 1 chipotle pepper in adobo sauce
- 1/4 cup cilantro leaves
- 2 anchovies
- 8 cups torn romaine lettuce
- 1 lb. boneless skinless chicken breasts, grilled, cut into strips
- 1 cup seasoned croutons
- 1/2 cup KRAFT Shredded Parmesan Cheese

Direction

- Place dressing, chipotle pepper, cilantro and anchovies in blender container; cover. Blend on medium speed until smooth.
- Toss lettuce with chicken, croutons and cheese in large bowl.
- Add dressing mixture; mix lightly. Serve immediately.

Nutrition Information

- Calories: 330
- Protein: 31 g
- Total Carbohydrate: 12 g
- Saturated Fat: 4.5 g
- Cholesterol: 80 mg
- Sodium: 1090 mg
- Fiber: 2 g
- Sugar: 3 g
- Total Fat: 17 g

209. Grilled Chicken Rolls With Spicy Sauce

Serving: 4 | Prep: 10mins | Cook: 15mins | Ready in: 25mins

Ingredients

- 4 boneless skinless chicken breasts (1 lb.), butterflied
- 4 slices OSCAR MAYER Boiled Ham
- 1/2 cup sliced roasted red pepper
- 4 scallions, cut in half
- 1/4 cup KRAFT Real Mayo Mayonnaise
- 1/4 tsp. ground red pepper (cayenne)

Direction

- Preheat grill to medium heat. Place chicken, smooth-sides down, on cutting board. Top each evenly with 1 ham slice, red pepper slices and scallions. Roll up tightly.
- Cut each roll into 4 slices. Skewer each slice onto wooden skewer, leaving some space in between for even grilling. Mix mayo and ground red pepper in small bowl; reserve 2 Tbsp. for dipping. Brush chicken with remaining mayo mixture.
- Grill chicken 12 to 15 min. or until chicken is cooked through (170°F), turning every 4 min. Serve with reserved 2 Tbsp. dipping sauce.

Nutrition Information

- Calories: 260
- Sugar: 1 g
- Protein: 28 g
- Cholesterol: 80 mg
- Total Carbohydrate: 3 g
- Saturated Fat: 3 g
- Total Fat: 15 g
- Sodium: 480 mg
- Fiber: 1 g

210. Grilled Chicken Salad On Crispy Tortillas

Serving: 0 | Prep: 20mins | Cook: 14mins | Ready in: 34mins

Ingredients

- 4 flour tortillas (10 inch)
- 1/2 cup KRAFT Italian Dressing, divided
- 1 medium red pepper, cut into thin strips
- 2 medium tomatoes, chopped
- 1 cup chopped fresh pineapple
- 1 pkg. (6 oz.) OSCAR MAYER CARVING BOARD Flame Grilled Chicken Breast Strips
- 1 bag (10 oz.) mixed salad greens

Direction

- Preheat oven to 375°F. Place tortillas in single layer on baking sheets; brush evenly with 1 Tbsp. of the dressing. Bake 6 to 8 min. or until tortillas are crisp and lightly browned.
- Heat 3 Tbsp. of the remaining dressing in large skillet on medium-high heat. Add peppers; cook and stir 3 min. or until crisp-tender. Add tomatoes, pineapple and chicken; cook and stir 3 min. or until heated through.
- Toss greens with remaining 1/4 cup dressing in large bowl. Place tortillas on salad plates. Spoon greens mixture evenly onto tortillas; top with the chicken mixture.

Nutrition Information

- Calories: 450
- Total Fat: 18 g
- Cholesterol: 30 mg
- Total Carbohydrate: 0 g
- Sugar: 0 g
- Protein: 18 g
- Fiber: 6 g
- Saturated Fat: 3.5 g

- Sodium: 980 mg

211. Grilled Chicken Salad With Avocado Dressing

Serving: 8 | Prep: 35mins | Cook: 2hours | Ready in: 2hours35mins

Ingredients

- 1/2 cup oil
- 1/3 cup GREY POUPON Dijon Mustard
- 1/4 cup HEINZ Red Wine Vinegar
- 2 Tbsp. lime juice
- 2 Tbsp. chopped fresh cilantro
- 1/4 tsp. dried oregano leaves
- 1/8 tsp. ground red pepper (cayenne)
- 8 small boneless skinless chicken breasts (2 lb.)
- 1/2 cup chopped avocados
- 10 cups tightly packed torn salad greens
- 2 large tomatoes, cut into wedges

Direction

- Whisk first 7 ingredients until blended. Reserve 1/2 cup mustard mixture; refrigerate for later use. Pour remaining mustard mixture over chicken in shallow dish; turn to evenly coat both sides of each breast. Refrigerate 2 hours to marinate.
- Meanwhile, blend avocados and 1/3 cup of the reserved mustard mixture in blender until smooth. Refrigerate until ready to serve with salad.
- Heat grill to medium heat. Remove chicken from marinade; discard marinade. Grill chicken 6 to 8 min. on each side or until done (165°F), brushing with remaining mustard mixture for the last few minutes.
- Slice chicken. Cover platter with salad greens; top with chicken and tomatoes. Drizzle with avocado dressing just before serving.

Nutrition Information

- Calories: 270
- Fiber: 3 g
- Sugar: 0 g
- Saturated Fat: 2.5 g
- Total Fat: 16 g
- Sodium: 260 mg
- Total Carbohydrate: 0 g
- Cholesterol: 65 mg
- Protein: 26 g

212. Grilled Chicken With Mushroom Pasta

Serving: 4 | Prep: 30mins | Cook: 30mins | Ready in: 1hours

Ingredients

- 1/4 cup KRAFT Zesty Italian Dressing
- 4 small boneless skinless chicken breasts (1 lb.)
- 1/2 lb. linguine, uncooked
- 1/4 cup butter
- 1/2 lb. sliced fresh mushrooms
- 1/2 cup chopped onions
- 1 cup water
- 1 tsp. WYLER'S Instant Bouillon Chicken Flavored Granules
- 1 jar (15 oz.) CLASSICO Roasted Garlic Alfredo Pasta Sauce
- 2 Tbsp. chopped fresh chives
- 2 tsp. each chopped fresh parsley and thyme

Direction

- Pour dressing over chicken in shallow dish; turn to evenly coat both sides of chicken with dressing. Refrigerate 30 min. to marinate.
- Heat grill to medium-high heat. Remove chicken from marinade; discard marinade. Grill chicken 6 to 8 min. on each side or until done (165°F).
- Meanwhile, cook pasta as directed on package, omitting salt. While pasta is cooking, melt butter in large skillet on medium heat. Add mushrooms and onions; cook 5 min., stirring

frequently. Add water and bouillon; stir. Bring to boil; simmer on medium-low heat 5 min. or until liquid is reduced by half, stirring occasionally. Stir in remaining ingredients; simmer 4 to 5 min. or until heated through, stirring occasionally.
- Drain pasta; place in large bowl. Add pasta sauce mixture; mix lightly. Serve with chicken.

Nutrition Information

- Calories: 570
- Cholesterol: 130 mg
- Fiber: 3 g
- Total Carbohydrate: 53 g
- Protein: 37 g
- Sugar: 6 g
- Saturated Fat: 12 g
- Sodium: 1040 mg
- Total Fat: 24 g

213. Grilled Chicken With Strawberry Salsa

Serving: 4 | Prep: 25mins | Cook: 30mins | Ready in: 55mins

Ingredients

- 1/2 cup KRAFT Balsamic Vinaigrette Dressing, divided
- 4 small boneless skinless chicken breasts (1 lb.)
- 2 cups small strawberries, chopped
- 1/2 cup ATHENOS Traditional Crumbled Feta Cheese
- 2 Tbsp. chopped fresh basil

Direction

- Pour 1/4 cup dressing over chicken in shallow dish; turn to evenly coat both sides of each breast with dressing. Refrigerate 30 min. to marinate. Meanwhile, combine strawberries

and remaining dressing. Refrigerate until ready to use.
- Heat grill to medium heat. Remove chicken from marinade; discard marinade. Grill chicken 6 to 8 min. on each side or until done (165ºF).
- Transfer chicken to platter; sprinkle with cheese and basil. Serve with strawberry salsa.

Nutrition Information

- Calories: 250
- Total Fat: 10 g
- Protein: 28 g
- Saturated Fat: 3.5 g
- Fiber: 2 g
- Total Carbohydrate: 0 g
- Sodium: 370 mg
- Sugar: 0 g
- Cholesterol: 80 mg

214. Grilled Chicken, Veggie And Pasta Salad

Serving: 6 | Prep: 25mins | Cook: 30mins | Ready in: 55mins

Ingredients

- 4 small boneless skinless chicken breasts (1 lb.)
- 2 tsp. A.1. Dry Rub Bold Original
- 2-2/3 cups rotini pasta, cooked, cooled
- 2 cups chopped spring lettuce mix
- 1 pkg. (10 oz.) grape tomatoes
- 1 red pepper, chopped
- 1 cup frozen peas, thawed
- 2 carrots, thinly sliced
- 2 green onions, sliced
- 1/4 cup chopped fresh cilantro
- 1/2 cup KRAFT Classic Ranch Dressing

Direction

- Heat grill to medium heat.

- Rub chicken with Dry Rub; grill 6 to 8 min. on each side or until done (165°F). Cool completely.
- Cut chicken into bite-size pieces; place in large bowl.
- Add remaining ingredients; mix lightly.

Nutrition Information

- Calories: 350
- Saturated Fat: 2 g
- Cholesterol: 50 mg
- Sodium: 350 mg
- Total Fat: 10 g
- Sugar: 0 g
- Fiber: 4 g
- Total Carbohydrate: 0 g
- Protein: 24 g

215. Grilled Hot Chicken Sausage Sandwich

Serving: 4 | Prep: 25mins | Cook: | Ready in: 25mins

Ingredients

- 1 each green and red pepper, cut in half
- 1 onion, cut to 4 slices
- 1/4 cup KRAFT Lite House Italian Dressing
- 4 whole wheat submarine rolls, partially split

Direction

- Heat grill to medium heat.
- Toss peppers and onions with dressing to coat.
- Grill sausage and vegetables 13 to 15 min. or until sausage is done (165°F) and vegetables are tender, turning occasionally. Slice peppers.
- Fill rolls with sausage; top with peppers and onions.

Nutrition Information

- Calories: 380
- Total Carbohydrate: 0 g
- Protein: 30 g
- Fiber: 6 g
- Saturated Fat: 3 g
- Sodium: 1150 mg
- Total Fat: 11 g
- Cholesterol: 80 mg
- Sugar: 0 g

216. Grilled Italian Chicken Tacos

Serving: 0 | Prep: 4hours | Cook: 15mins | Ready in: 4hours15mins

Ingredients

- 1 pkt. GOOD SEASONS Italian Dressing Mix
- 3 boneless skinless chicken breasts
- 1/2 cup KRAFT Shredded Mozzarella Cheese
- 1 cup shredded lettuce
- 1 cup diced tomatoes
- 6-8 flour tortillas

Direction

- Prepare Italian dressing as directed on packaging.
- In a large plastic bag, mix Italian dressing with raw chicken, seal and refrigerate for 4 hours or overnight.
- Remove chicken from dressing. Discard plastic bag and dressing.
- Grill chicken for 4-6 minutes on each side, until chicken is cooked through.
- Slice chicken into 1/2 inch slices.
- Grill tortillas for a minute until each side until warm and golden brown.
- Serve warm tortillas with sliced chicken, cheese, lettuce and tomatoes.

Nutrition Information

- Calories: 0 g

- Sodium: 0 g
- Fiber: 0 g
- Saturated Fat: 0 g
- Sugar: 0 g
- Protein: 0 g
- Total Carbohydrate: 0 g
- Total Fat: 0 g
- Cholesterol: 0 g

217. Grilled Spicy Teriyaki Drumsticks

Serving: 8 | Prep: 10mins | Cook: 35mins | Ready in: 45mins

Ingredients

- 1/3 cup KRAFT Classic CATALINA Dressing
- 1/3 cup teriyaki sauce
- 4 cloves garlic, minced
- 1 tsp. ground ginger
- 1 tsp. sesame oil
- 16 chicken drumsticks (3 lb.)
- 1/4 cup BULL'S-EYE Texas Style Barbecue Sauce

Direction

- Heat greased grill to medium heat.
- Mix first 5 ingredients until well blended; pour 1/2 cup over chicken in shallow dish. Turn drumsticks to evenly coat both sides of each. Refrigerate 10 min. Meanwhile, stir barbecue sauce into remaining dressing mixture.
- Remove chicken from dressing mixture; discard dressing mixture.
- Place chicken on grill grate. Turn off burners directly below chicken; cover grill with lid. Grill chicken 25 min. or until done (165°F), turning occasionally and brushing with barbecue sauce mixture for the last 10 min.

Nutrition Information

- Calories: 270
- Protein: 29 g
- Cholesterol: 95 mg
- Sugar: 6 g
- Sodium: 570 mg
- Saturated Fat: 3.5 g
- Fiber: 0 g
- Total Carbohydrate: 7 g
- Total Fat: 13 g

218. HEALTHY LIVING Easy Chicken BLT Salad

Serving: 0 | Prep: 15mins | Cook: | Ready in: 15mins

Ingredients

- 8 cups loosely packed torn romaine lettuce
- 3 cups cooked chicken breast strips (3/4 lb.)
- 2 cups cherry tomatoes, halved
- 1/2 cup slivered red onions
- 1 cup KRAFT Natural 2% Milk Colby & Monterey Jack Cheese Crumbles, divided
- 1/4 cup KRAFT Lite Ranch Dressing
- 2 slices OSCAR MAYER Turkey Bacon, cooked, cut into 1-inch pieces

Direction

- Combine lettuce, chicken, tomatoes, onions and 1/2 cup cheese in large bowl.
- Add dressing; mix lightly.
- Top with remaining cheese and bacon.

Nutrition Information

- Calories: 300
- Saturated Fat: 5 g
- Total Fat: 12 g
- Protein: 36 g
- Total Carbohydrate: 0 g
- Sugar: 0 g
- Cholesterol: 100 mg
- Sodium: 570 mg

- Fiber: 3 g

219. Hearty Mexican Chicken Soup

Serving: 0 | Prep: 30mins | Cook: | Ready in: 30mins

Ingredients

- 1 large yellow onion, chopped
- 1 Tbsp. oil
- 1 clove garlic, minced
- 1/2 tsp. ground cumin
- 1 qt. (4 cups) fat-free reduced-sodium chicken broth
- 1 can (15.5 oz.) cannellini beans, rinsed
- 1 cup TACO BELL® Thick & Chunky Salsa
- 2 cups shredded rotisserie chicken
- 1 cup frozen corn
- 2 green onions, chopped
- 1/4 cup chopped fresh cilantro
- 1 cup KRAFT Mexican Style Finely Shredded Four Cheese

Direction

- Cook yellow onions in hot oil in large saucepan on medium heat 6 to 7 min. or until tender, stirring frequently. Add garlic and cumin; cook and stir 1 min.
- Add broth, beans and salsa; stir. Bring to boil. Stir in chicken and corn. Return to boil; simmer 5 min., stirring occasionally. Remove from heat.
- Stir in green onions and cilantro. Serve topped with cheese.

Nutrition Information

- Calories: 230
- Cholesterol: 50 mg
- Fiber: 5 g
- Sodium: 690 mg
- Total Carbohydrate: 0 g
- Sugar: 0 g
- Saturated Fat: 4.5 g
- Protein: 15 g
- Total Fat: 11 g

220. Herb Crusted Creamy Jalapeño Stuffed Chicken

Serving: 4 | Prep: 25mins | Cook: 35mins | Ready in: 1hours

Ingredients

- 4 small boneless skinless chicken breasts (1 lb.), pounded to 1/4-inch thickness
- 1/2 cup (1/2 of 8-oz. tub) PHILADELPHIA Spicy Jalapeño Cream Cheese Spread
- 1/2 cup panko bread crumbs
- 1 tsp. lemon zest
- 1 Tbsp. minced fresh chives
- 1 Tbsp. extra virgin olive oil

Direction

- Heat oven to 375ºF.
- Place chicken, top sides down, on work surface; spread with cream cheese spread. Roll up tightly, starting at one short end of each breast.
- Place, seam sides down, in single layer in shallow pan sprayed with cooking spray.
- Combine remaining ingredients; press on tops and sides of roll-ups.
- Bake 35 min. or until chicken is done (165ºF).

Nutrition Information

- Calories: 240
- Sodium: 230 mg
- Protein: 27 g
- Saturated Fat: 4.5 g
- Total Carbohydrate: 7 g
- Total Fat: 11 g
- Sugar: 2 g

- Cholesterol: 85 mg
- Fiber: 0 g

221. Homestyle Chicken Fajitas

Serving: 4 | Prep: 25mins | Cook: | Ready in: 25mins

Ingredients

- 1/4 cup KRAFT Zesty Lime Vinaigrette Dressing, divided
- 1 lb. boneless skinless chicken breasts, cut into strips
- 1 each red and yellow bell pepper, cut into strips
- 1/2 cup red onion slices
- 1 tomato, chopped
- 1 jalapeño pepper, seeded, finely chopped
- 1/4 cup chopped fresh parsley
- 1-1/2 cups chopped iceberg lettuce
- 1 cup KRAFT Shredded Cheddar Cheese
- 8 flour tortillas (6 inch)

Direction

- Heat 1 Tbsp. dressing in large nonstick skillet on medium heat. Add chicken; cook and stir 4 min. or until done.
- Add bell peppers, onions and 1 Tbsp. of the remaining dressing; cook 3 to 5 min. or until vegetables are crisp-tender, stirring occasionally.
- Meanwhile, combine tomatoes, jalapeños, parsley and remaining dressing.
- Serve chicken mixture with tomato mixture, lettuce, cheese and tortillas.

Nutrition Information

- Calories: 530
- Cholesterol: 95 mg
- Saturated Fat: 8 g
- Sugar: 0 g
- Protein: 38 g
- Sodium: 900 mg
- Total Carbohydrate: 0 g
- Fiber: 4 g
- Total Fat: 20 g

222. Honey Mustard Pear Salad

Serving: 0 | Prep: 20mins | Cook: | Ready in: 20mins

Ingredients

- 1 pkg. (10 oz.) torn mixed salad greens
- 1 lb. boneless skinless chicken breasts, cooked, sliced
- 1 fresh pear, sliced
- 1/2 cup chopped dates
- 1/4 cup chopped PLANTERS Walnuts, toasted
- 1/2 cup KRAFT Honey Mustard Dressing

Direction

- Toss greens with all remaining ingredients except dressing.
- Add dressing just before serving; mix lightly.

Nutrition Information

- Calories: 130
- Cholesterol: 55 mg
- Sodium: 35 mg
- Total Fat: 2 g
- Fiber: 0.9803 g
- Protein: 17 g
- Total Carbohydrate: 0 g
- Saturated Fat: 0 g
- Sugar: 0 g

223. Hot & Spicy Crispy Chicken Sandwich

Serving: 4 | Prep: 10mins | Cook: 20mins | Ready in: 30mins

Ingredients

- 4 small boneless skinless chicken breasts (1 lb.)
- 1 pkt. SHAKE 'N BAKE Hot & Spicy Seasoned Coating Mix
- 4 KRAFT Slim Cut Colby Jack Cheese Slices
- 4 ciabatta sandwich rolls, partially split
- 1/4 cup KRAFT Real Mayo Mayonnaise
- 4 lettuce leaves
- 1 large tomato, cut into 4 slices

Direction

- Heat oven to 400°F.
- Coat chicken with coating mix as directed on package; place on foil-covered baking sheet.
- Bake 20 min. or until done (165°F). Top with cheese; bake 2 min. or until melted.
- Spread cut sides of rolls with mayo; fill with chicken, lettuce and tomatoes.

Nutrition Information

- Calories: 600
- Sodium: 1010 mg
- Sugar: 0 g
- Total Carbohydrate: 0 g
- Saturated Fat: 5 g
- Cholesterol: 80 mg
- Protein: 38 g
- Fiber: 4 g
- Total Fat: 24 g

224. Hot And Spicy Grilled Chicken Wings

Serving: 8 | Prep: 10mins | Cook: 35mins | Ready in: 45mins

Ingredients

- 12 chicken wings (2 lb.), split at joints, tips removed
- 3/4 cup KRAFT Real Mayo Mayonnaise
- 3 Tbsp. Buffalo wing sauce
- 1 tsp. garlic powder
- 1/4 cup KRAFT Classic Ranch Dressing

Direction

- Heat grill for indirect grilling: Light one side of grill, leaving other side unlit. Close lid; heat grill to 400°F.
- Place wings in single layer in shallow foil pan. Place pan on grate over unlit area; close lid. Grill 20 min. or until wings are lightly browned, monitoring for consistent temperature.
- Meanwhile, mix mayo, hot pepper sauce and garlic powder until blended. Reserve 1/2 cup mayo mixture; mix remaining mayo mixture with ranch dressing.
- Brush both sides of wings generously with reserved mayo mixture. Grill 15 min. or until wings are done. Serve with dressing mixture.

Nutrition Information

- Calories: 320
- Total Fat: 29 g
- Saturated Fat: 6 g
- Sodium: 370 mg
- Total Carbohydrate: 0.8553 g
- Fiber: 0 g
- Protein: 13 g
- Sugar: 0 g
- Cholesterol: 85 mg

225. Indian Baked Chicken

Serving: 4 | Prep: 10mins | Cook: 35mins | Ready in: 45mins

Ingredients

- 1/4 cup MIRACLE WHIP Dressing
- 2 tsp. curry powder
- 1/2 tsp. garlic powder
- 2 bone-in chicken breast (1-1/4 lb.), cut crosswise in half

Direction

- Heat oven to 400°F.
- Mix dressing and seasonings until blended; spread onto chicken.
- Place on foil-covered rimmed baking sheet.
- Bake 35 min. or until chicken is done (165°F).

Nutrition Information

- Calories: 190
- Fiber: 0 g
- Protein: 23 g
- Total Carbohydrate: 0 g
- Saturated Fat: 2 g
- Cholesterol: 65 mg
- Sugar: 0 g
- Total Fat: 9 g
- Sodium: 150 mg

226. Indian Chicken Curry

Serving: 4 | Prep: 40mins | Cook: | Ready in: 40mins

Ingredients

- 2 Tbsp. olive oil
- 1 lb. boneless skinless chicken breasts, cut into bite-size pieces
- 2 cloves garlic, minced
- 1 red pepper, cut into strips
- 1 cup frozen peas
- 2 green onions, sliced
- 1/2 cup MIRACLE WHIP Dressing
- 1 Tbsp. curry powder
- 3/4 cup fat-free reduced-sodium chicken broth
- 2 cups hot cooked long-grain white rice

Direction

- Heat oil in large skillet on medium heat. Add chicken and garlic; cook and stir 8 to 10 min. or until chicken is done. Remove from pan; cover to keep warm. Add remaining oil, peppers, peas and green onions; cook and stir 3 to 4 min. or until peppers are tender.
- Mix dressing and curry powder until blended. Add to vegetable mixture in skillet; mix well. Stir in chicken. Add broth; cook 3 to 4 min. or until mixture is heated through and sauce is well blended.
- Serve over rice.

Nutrition Information

- Calories: 450
- Protein: 29 g
- Cholesterol: 75 mg
- Fiber: 4 g
- Sodium: 380 mg
- Saturated Fat: 3.5 g
- Sugar: 0 g
- Total Carbohydrate: 0 g
- Total Fat: 20 g

227. Indian Chicken Curry Recipe

Serving: 0 | Prep: 35mins | Cook: | Ready in: 35mins

Ingredients

- 1 sweet potato (8 oz.), peeled, cut into 3/4-inch pieces
- 1/3 cup KRAFT Zesty Lime Vinaigrette Dressing, divided
- 1 lb. boneless skinless chicken thighs, cut into bite-size pieces
- 1 small onion, finely chopped
- 1 Tbsp. grated fresh ginger

- 2 tsp. curry powder
- 1 Tbsp. flour
- 1 cup lite coconut milk
- 1 apple, chopped
- 1/4 cup PLANTERS Cashew Halves with Pieces
- 3 cups hot cooked basmati rice

Direction

- Cook potatoes in pan of boiling water 5 min.; drain. Rinse under cold water to cool.
- Heat 1 Tbsp. dressing in large skillet on medium-high heat. Add chicken; cook and stir 4 min. or until lightly browned. Remove from skillet; cover to keep warm.
- Add 2 Tbsp. of the remaining dressing, onions, ginger, curry powder and potatoes to skillet; cook and stir 5 min. or until vegetables are tender.
- Whisk flour and remaining dressing in medium bowl until blended. Gradually whisk in coconut milk. Add to potato mixture in skillet along with the apples and chicken; stir. Simmer on medium heat 3 to 5 min. or until chicken is done and sauce is thickened, stirring occasionally. Sprinkle with nuts. Serve with rice.

Nutrition Information

- Calories: 360
- Fiber: 3 g
- Total Fat: 13 g
- Saturated Fat: 4 g
- Protein: 18 g
- Sodium: 220 mg
- Cholesterol: 65 mg
- Total Carbohydrate: 0 g
- Sugar: 0 g

228. Italian Chicken & Tomato Pasta Toss

Serving: 0 | Prep: 10mins | Cook: 10mins | Ready in: 20mins

Ingredients

- 3 cups curly egg noodles, uncooked
- 1 Tbsp. olive oil
- 1 lb. boneless skinless chicken breasts, cut into 1-1/2-inch pieces
- 2 cups grape or cherry tomatoes, halved
- 1/4 cup KRAFT Balsamic Vinaigrette Dressing
- 3 cloves garlic, minced
- 1/2 cup chopped fresh basil
- 1/4 cup KRAFT Grated Parmesan Cheese

Direction

- Cook pasta as directed on package, omitting salt.
- Meanwhile, heat oil in large nonstick skillet on medium-high heat. Add chicken; cook 6 min. or until done, stirring occasionally. Add tomatoes, dressing and garlic; cook and stir 3 min. or until heated through.
- Drain pasta. Toss with chicken mixture and basil; sprinkle with Parmesan.

Nutrition Information

- Calories: 370
- Total Fat: 14 g
- Total Carbohydrate: 0 g
- Sodium: 360 mg
- Cholesterol: 100 mg
- Sugar: 0 g
- Protein: 33 g
- Saturated Fat: 3.5 g
- Fiber: 2 g

229. Italian Chicken Sausage & Brown And Wild Rice

Serving: 6 | Prep: 30mins | Cook: | Ready in: 30mins

Ingredients

- 1/4 cup KRAFT Lite Zesty Italian Dressing
- 1 each green and red pepper, cut into strips
- 1 can (14-1/2 oz.) no-salt-added diced tomatoes with basil, garlic and oregano, undrained
- 3 cups cooked wild and brown rice blend
- 2 Tbsp. KRAFT Grated Parmesan Cheese

Direction

- Heat dressing in large deep skillet on medium heat. Add sausage; cook 5 min., stirring frequently.
- Add peppers and tomatoes; stir. Simmer on low heat 6 to 8 min. or until sausage is done and peppers are tender, stirring occasionally.
- Stir in rice; cook 2 min. or until heated through, stirring frequently. Sprinkle with cheese.

Nutrition Information

- Calories: 290
- Sodium: 720 mg
- Fiber: 4 g
- Saturated Fat: 2.5 g
- Total Carbohydrate: 0 g
- Sugar: 0 g
- Cholesterol: 60 mg
- Protein: 20 g
- Total Fat: 8 g

230. Italian Chicken Sausage With Pasta

Serving: 6 | Prep: 20mins | Cook: | Ready in: 20mins

Ingredients

- 1/2 lb. linguine, uncooked
- 1 Tbsp. olive oil
- 1 onion, chopped
- 2 cloves garlic, minced
- 2 cups CLASSICO Vodka Sauce Pasta Sauce
- 1 can (14-1/2 oz.) diced tomatoes with basil, garlic and oregano, undrained
- 1/4 cup KRAFT Shredded Parmesan Cheese

Direction

- Cook pasta as directed on package, omitting salt.
- Meanwhile, heat oil in large skillet on medium heat. Add onions; cook 2 min., stirring frequently. Add garlic; cook and stir 30 sec. Add all remaining ingredients except cheese; mix well. Simmer on low heat 8 to 10 min. or until heated through, stirring occasionally.
- Drain pasta. Serve topped with pasta sauce mixture and cheese.

Nutrition Information

- Calories: 360
- Sugar: 0 g
- Saturated Fat: 3.5 g
- Cholesterol: 55 mg
- Sodium: 940 mg
- Fiber: 4 g
- Total Fat: 11 g
- Protein: 20 g
- Total Carbohydrate: 0 g

231. Italian Chicken And Ham Sandwiches

Serving: 2 | Prep: 20mins | Cook: | Ready in: 20mins

Ingredients

- 1/2 cup roasted red pepper strips

- 1/4 cup sliced black olives
- 2 Tbsp. KRAFT Zesty Italian Dressing
- 2 focaccia bread pieces (1-1/2 oz. each), split
- 1 boneless skinless chicken breast (6 oz.), cooked, cut in half
- 6 slices OSCAR MAYER Deli Fresh Smoked Ham
- 2 KRAFT Slim Cut Mozzarella Cheese Slices

Direction

- Combine peppers, olives and dressing.
- Fill bread with pepper mixture, chicken, ham and cheese to make 2 sandwiches.

Nutrition Information

- Calories: 320
- Cholesterol: 70 mg
- Saturated Fat: 3 g
- Sugar: 0 g
- Total Carbohydrate: 0 g
- Fiber: 2 g
- Total Fat: 11 g
- Protein: 30 g
- Sodium: 1150 mg

232. Italian Style Chicken Enchiladas

Serving: 6 | Prep: 30mins | Cook: 12mins | Ready in: 42mins

Ingredients

- 2 cups chopped cooked chicken
- 1 cup KRAFT Shredded Mozzarella Cheese, divided
- 6 fresh basil leaves, chopped
- 1 jar (14 oz.) CLASSICO Tomato and Basil Pasta Sauce
- 1/4 cup CLASSICO Traditional Basil Pesto Sauce and Spread
- 6 flour tortillas (6 inch)

Direction

- Heat oven to 450°F.
- Combine chicken, 1/2 cup cheese and basil.
- Mix sauces; spread 2 Tbsp. sauce mixture onto bottom of 13x9-inch baking dish sprayed with cooking spray. Spoon about 1/3 cup chicken mixture down center of each tortilla; roll up. Place, seam sides down, in dish; top with remaining sauce mixture and cheese.
- Bake 10 to 12 min. or until heated through.

Nutrition Information

- Calories: 300
- Saturated Fat: 4 g
- Protein: 22 g
- Sugar: 3 g
- Total Fat: 13 g
- Cholesterol: 55 mg
- Total Carbohydrate: 22 g
- Fiber: 2 g
- Sodium: 720 mg

233. Jamaican Jerk Chicken Breasts

Serving: 6 | Prep: 25mins | Cook: 1hours | Ready in: 1hours25mins

Ingredients

- 1 env. (0.7 oz.) GOOD SEASONS Italian Dressing Mix
- 2 Tbsp. brown sugar
- 2 Tbsp. oil
- 2 Tbsp. lite soy sauce
- 1 tsp. ground cinnamon
- 1 tsp. ground thyme
- 1/2 tsp. ground red pepper (cayenne)
- 6 small boneless skinless chicken breasts (1-1/2 lb.)
- 4 cups hot cooked brown rice

Direction

- Mix all ingredients except chicken and rice until blended. Pour over chicken in shallow dish; turn to evenly coat both sides of each breast. Refrigerate 1 hour to marinate.
- Heat greased grill to medium-high heat. Remove chicken from marinade; discard marinade. Grill chicken 6 to 8 min. on each side or until done (165°F).
- Serve with rice.

Nutrition Information

- Calories: 330
- Protein: 28 g
- Total Carbohydrate: 0 g
- Fiber: 3 g
- Cholesterol: 65 mg
- Total Fat: 8 g
- Saturated Fat: 1.5 g
- Sodium: 670 mg
- Sugar: 0 g

234. Jerk BBQ Chicken Salad

Serving: 6 | Prep: 30mins | Cook: | Ready in: 30mins

Ingredients

- 3/4 cup KRAFT Buttermilk Ranch Dressing
- 1 tsp. jerk seasoning, divided
- 1 can (20 oz.) pineapple chunks in juice, undrained
- 1/2 cup KRAFT Sweet Brown Sugar Barbecue Sauce
- 2 Tbsp. A.1. Original Sauce
- 6 small boneless skinless chicken breasts (1-1/2 lb.)
- 1 Tbsp. olive oil
- 4 cups loosely packed torn romaine lettuce
- 1 can (15 oz.) baby corn, drained
- 1 can (15 oz.) black beans, rinsed
- 1-1/2 cups chopped red peppers
- 1 can (2.8 oz.) french-fried onions

Direction

- Heat grill to medium-high heat.
- Mix dressing and 3/4 tsp. seasoning; refrigerate until ready to use. Drain pineapple, reserving 2 Tbsp. juice. Refrigerate pineapple chunks for later use.
- Combine barbecue sauce, reserved pineapple juice, A.1. and remaining seasoning in saucepan; cook on medium-low heat 3 to 5 min. or until heated through, stirring frequently.
- Brush chicken with oil; grill 5 min. on each side. Brush with barbecue sauce mixture; grill 4 to 6 min. or until done (165°F), turning and brushing occasionally with remaining barbecue sauce mixture.
- Toss lettuce with pineapple chunks, corn, beans and peppers. Slice chicken; place on salad. Drizzle dressing mixture; top with onions.

Nutrition Information

- Calories: 580
- Cholesterol: 95 mg
- Total Carbohydrate: 0 g
- Total Fat: 25 g
- Sodium: 880 mg
- Protein: 31 g
- Saturated Fat: 7 g
- Fiber: 6 g
- Sugar: 0 g

235. Kicked Up BBQ Chicken Chili With Beans

Serving: 0 | Prep: 30mins | Cook: | Ready in: 30mins

Ingredients

- 1 can (28 oz.) diced tomatoes, undrained

- 1 lb. cooked boneless skinless chicken breasts, cut into bite-size pieces
- 1 can (15 oz.) black beans, rinsed
- 1 can (15 oz.) great Northern beans, rinsed
- 1 cup KRAFT Hickory Smoke Barbecue Sauce
- 1 onion, chopped
- 1 tsp. chili powder
- 1 tsp. ground cumin
- 1/2 tsp. ground red pepper (cayenne)

Direction

- Combine ingredients in saucepan; bring to boil on medium-high heat.
- Simmer on low heat 10 min. or until heated through, stirring occasionally.

Nutrition Information

- Calories: 260
- Total Fat: 2.5 g
- Sugar: 0 g
- Protein: 25 g
- Sodium: 730 mg
- Saturated Fat: 0.5 g
- Cholesterol: 50 mg
- Total Carbohydrate: 0 g
- Fiber: 8 g

236. Kickin' Chicken Spread

Serving: 0 | Prep: 10mins | Cook: 14mins | Ready in: 24mins

Ingredients

- 1 pkg. (8 oz.) PHILADELPHIA Cream Cheese, softened
- 1 cup finely chopped cooked chicken
- 1/2 cup BULL'S-EYE Original Barbecue Sauce
- 2 canned chipotle peppers in adobo sauce, finely chopped
- 1/2 cup KRAFT Shredded Cheddar & Monterey Jack Cheeses
- 2 green onions, sliced
- 1 tomato, chopped
- large thin wheat snack crackers

Direction

- Heat oven to 350°F.
- Spread cream cheese onto bottom of 9-inch pie plate sprayed with cooking spray. Combine chicken, barbecue sauce and peppers; spoon over cream cheese. Top with shredded cheese, onions and tomatoes.
- Bake 15 to 20 min. or until hot and bubbly.
- Serve spread with crackers.

Nutrition Information

- Calories: 210
- Sugar: 7 g
- Total Fat: 9 g
- Protein: 5 g
- Cholesterol: 20 mg
- Fiber: 2 g
- Total Carbohydrate: 25 g
- Saturated Fat: 3 g
- Sodium: 360 mg

237. Kung Pao Chicken Wings

Serving: 8 | Prep: 30mins | Cook: 30mins | Ready in: 1hours

Ingredients

- 1/3 cup lime juice
- 2 Tbsp. lite soy sauce
- 1 Tbsp. chopped garlic
- 1 tsp. ground red pepper (cayenne)
- 2 lb. chicken wings, split at joints, tips removed
- 3/4 cup HEINZ Ketchup Blended with Sriracha Flavor
- 1 green onion, cut into thin slices

- 1 Tbsp. PLANTERS Lightly Salted COCKTAIL Peanuts, finely chopped
- 1 tsp. crushed red pepper

Direction

- Mix first 4 ingredients until blended; pour over wings in shallow dish. Turn to even coat both sides of wings. Refrigerate 30 min. to marinate.
- Heat grill to medium-high heat. Remove wings from marinade; discard marinade. Grill wings 15 to 20 min. or until done, turning occasionally.
- Place wings in large bowl. Add ketchup; toss until wings are evenly coated.
- Place wings on platter; top with remaining ingredients.

Nutrition Information

- Calories: 150
- Protein: 13 g
- Total Carbohydrate: 3 g
- Fiber: 0 g
- Saturated Fat: 2.5 g
- Cholesterol: 75 mg
- Total Fat: 10 g
- Sodium: 135 mg
- Sugar: 0.79 g

238. Layered Chicken Taco Salad

Serving: 4 | Prep: 25mins | Cook: | Ready in: 25mins

Ingredients

- 4 small boneless skinless chicken breasts (1 lb.)
- 1/2 tsp. each ground cumin, garlic powder, ground red pepper (cayenne)
- 1/2 cup BREAKSTONE'S Reduced Fat or KNUDSEN Light Sour Cream
- 1/2 cup TACO BELL® Thick & Chunky Mild Salsa
- 1 pkg. (10 oz.) torn romaine lettuce
- 1 large tomato, chopped
- 1/2 cup KRAFT Mexican Style 2% Milk Finely Shredded Taco Cheese
- 4 green onions, sliced

Direction

- Sprinkle chicken with combined seasonings. Cook in nonstick skillet on medium heat 6 to 8 min. on each side or until done (165°F).
- Meanwhile, mix sour cream and salsa until blended.
- Cut chicken into thin strips. Cover platter with lettuce; top with chicken, tomatoes, cheese and onions. Serve with sour cream mixture.

Nutrition Information

- Calories: 250
- Cholesterol: 85 mg
- Sodium: 410 mg
- Protein: 32 g
- Total Carbohydrate: 0 g
- Saturated Fat: 4 g
- Sugar: 0 g
- Total Fat: 9 g
- Fiber: 3 g

239. Layered Chicken, Bacon & Avocado Salad

Serving: 4 | Prep: 15mins | Cook: | Ready in: 15mins

Ingredients

- 6 cups chopped romaine lettuce
- 2 cups chopped cooked chicken breasts
- 6 slices cooked OSCAR MAYER Bacon, crumbled
- 1 avocado, peeled, chopped
- 1/4 cup chopped red onions

- 1 cup KRAFT Natural Three Cheese Crumbles
- 1/2 cup KRAFT Balsamic Vinaigrette Dressing

Direction

- Place lettuce on platter.
- Top with rows of chicken, bacon, avocados, onions and cheese.
- Drizzle with dressing just before serving.

Nutrition Information

- Calories: 460
- Saturated Fat: 9 g
- Protein: 33 g
- Total Carbohydrate: 0 g
- Fiber: 5 g
- Sugar: 0 g
- Total Fat: 31 g
- Sodium: 780 mg
- Cholesterol: 100 mg

240. Layered Egg, Chicken And Pea Salad

Serving: 0 | Prep: 10mins | Cook: 1hours | Ready in: 1hours10mins

Ingredients

- 6 cups shredded iceberg lettuce
- 2 cups chopped cooked chicken
- 2 hard-cooked eggs, chopped
- 1 cup frozen peas
- 1/4 cup KRAFT Lite Ranch Dressing

Direction

- Layer lettuce, chicken, eggs and peas in large bowl. Pour dressing evenly over salad; spread to cover peas.
- Refrigerate 1 hour.
- Toss before serving.

Nutrition Information

- Calories: 250
- Saturated Fat: 2.5 g
- Total Fat: 10 g
- Cholesterol: 160 mg
- Sodium: 320 mg
- Total Carbohydrate: 0 g
- Fiber: 3 g
- Sugar: 0 g
- Protein: 26 g

241. Lemon Garlic Chicken And Pasta

Serving: 4 | Prep: 25mins | Cook: | Ready in: 25mins

Ingredients

- 1/2 lb. thin spaghetti, uncooked
- 1 tsp. zest and 1/4 cup juice from 2 lemons
- 1/4 cup water
- 1 Tbsp. WYLER'S Instant Bouillon Chicken Flavored Granules
- 5 cloves garlic, minced
- 4 small boneless skinless chicken breasts (1 lb.)
- 2 Tbsp. KRAFT Grated Parmesan Cheese
- 2 Tbsp. chopped fresh parsley

Direction

- Cook spaghetti as directed on package, omitting salt.
- Meanwhile, combine lemon zest, lemon juice, water, bouillon and garlic. Cook chicken in large nonstick skillet on medium heat 3 to 4 min. on each side or until evenly browned on both sides. Stir lemon juice mixture; pour over chicken. Bring to boil; simmer on medium-low heat 5 to 6 min. or until chicken is done (165°F).
- Drain spaghetti; place on platter. Top with chicken and sauce; sprinkle with cheese and parsley.

Nutrition Information

- Calories: 360
- Protein: 33 g
- Total Fat: 5 g
- Fiber: 2 g
- Saturated Fat: 1.5 g
- Cholesterol: 70 mg
- Total Carbohydrate: 0 g
- Sugar: 0 g
- Sodium: 680 mg

242. Lemon Rosemary Chicken Salad Spread

Serving: 0 | Prep: 10mins | Cook: 1hours | Ready in: 1hours10mins

Ingredients

- 1 cup finely chopped cooked chicken
- 1/4 cup KRAFT Light Mayo Reduced Fat Mayonnaise
- 1 green onion, finely chopped
- 1 Tbsp. KRAFT Grated Parmesan Cheese
- 1 tsp. zest and 2 tsp. juice from 1 lemon
- 3/4 tsp. chopped fresh rosemary
- 1/4 tsp. pepper

Direction

- Combine ingredients.
- Refrigerate 1 hour.

Nutrition Information

- Calories: 60
- Sugar: 0 g
- Protein: 5 g
- Total Fat: 3.5 g
- Sodium: 80 mg
- Total Carbohydrate: 0 g
- Cholesterol: 20 mg
- Fiber: 0 g
- Saturated Fat: 1 g

243. Lemon Rosemary Chicken Salad Topper

Serving: 0 | Prep: 15mins | Cook: 1hours | Ready in: 1hours15mins

Ingredients

- 1 small boneless skinless chicken breast half (4 oz.), cooked, finely chopped (about 1 cup)
- 1/4 cup finely chopped celery
- 1/4 KRAFT Light Mayo Reduced Fat Mayonnaise
- 1 tsp. lemon zest
- 1/2 tsp. chopped fresh rosemary
- 1/4 tsp. pepper
- 2 large leaf lettuce leaves
- 24 whole wheat saltine crackers

Direction

- Combine all ingredients except lettuce and crackers.
- Refrigerate 1 hour.
- Tear each lettuce leaf into 12 small pieces; place on crackers. Top with chicken mixture.

Nutrition Information

- Calories: 90
- Cholesterol: 10 mg
- Total Carbohydrate: 0 g
- Sugar: 0 g
- Protein: 4 g
- Saturated Fat: 1 g
- Sodium: 180 mg
- Fiber: 1 g
- Total Fat: 5 g

244. Lime Chicken Salad Wrap

Serving: 0 | Prep: 20mins | Cook: | Ready in: 20mins

Ingredients

- 2 small boneless skinless chicken breasts (1/2 lb.), cooked, chopped
- 1/2 cup drained canned corn
- 1/4 cup chopped fresh cilantro
- Zest and juice from 1 lime
- 1/8 tsp. ground red pepper (cayenne)
- 1/4 cup KRAFT Classic Ranch Dressing
- 2 flour tortillas (6 inch)
- 1/2 cup KRAFT 2% Milk Shredded Colby & Monterey Jack Cheeses
- 2 lettuce leaves

Direction

- Mix chicken, corn, cilantro, lime zest and juice, pepper and dressing in medium bowl. Refrigerate until ready to serve.
- Top tortillas with chicken mixture, cheese and lettuce.
- Fold in opposite sides of each tortilla, then roll up burrito style.

Nutrition Information

- Calories: 470
- Protein: 35 g
- Sodium: 830 mg
- Total Carbohydrate: 0 g
- Sugar: 0 g
- Total Fat: 25 g
- Saturated Fat: 8 g
- Cholesterol: 100 mg
- Fiber: 2 g

245. MIRACLE WHIP Awesome Waldorf Salad

Serving: 4 | Prep: 15mins | Cook: 1hours | Ready in: 1hours15mins

Ingredients

- 2 cups coarsely chopped cooked chicken
- 1 small apple, coarsely chopped
- 1 stalk celery, sliced
- 1/3 cup MIRACLE WHIP Light Dressing
- 1/4 cup coarsely chopped PLANTERS Walnuts
- 2 Tbsp. raisins

Direction

- Combine ingredients.
- Refrigerate 1 hour.

Nutrition Information

- Calories: 230
- Sugar: 6 g
- Total Carbohydrate: 9 g
- Protein: 22 g
- Saturated Fat: 2 g
- Sodium: 240 mg
- Fiber: 1 g
- Total Fat: 12 g
- Cholesterol: 65 mg

246. Madras Curry Chicken

Serving: 0 | Prep: 15mins | Cook: 20mins | Ready in: 35mins

Ingredients

- 1 Tbsp. butter or margarine
- 1/2 cup chopped green peppers
- 1/2 cup chopped onions
- 1 clove garlic, minced
- 2 tsp. curry powder

- 1-1/2 lb. boneless skinless chicken breasts, cut into bite-size pieces
- 1 can (14-1/2 oz.) diced tomatoes, drained
- 1 tsp. lemon juice
- 1/2 tsp. dried thyme leaves
- 1/8 tsp. black pepper
- 1/2 lb. (8 oz.) VELVEETA, cut into 1/2-inch cubes
- 3 cups cooked long-grain white rice

Direction

- Melt butter in large saucepan on medium heat. Add green peppers, onions, garlic and curry powder; cook and stir until vegetables are crisp-tender. Add chicken; cook and stir 5 min. or until no longer pink.
- Stir in tomatoes, lemon juice, thyme and black pepper; simmer on low heat 5 min. or until chicken is done, stirring occasionally.
- Add VELVEETA; cook until melted, stirring frequently. Serve over rice.

Nutrition Information

- Calories: 330
- Protein: 26 g
- Sodium: 640 mg
- Sugar: 4 g
- Total Fat: 10 g
- Total Carbohydrate: 30 g
- Cholesterol: 80 mg
- Saturated Fat: 5 g
- Fiber: 2 g

247. Mango Chicken Salad Sandwiches

Serving: 4 | Prep: 15mins | Cook: 30mins | Ready in: 45mins

Ingredients

- 1 pkg. (7 oz.) OSCAR MAYER CARVING BOARD Flame Grilled Chicken Breast Strips, coarsely chopped
- 3/4 cup chopped fresh mangos
- 2 Tbsp. chopped red onions
- 2 Tbsp. KRAFT Real Mayo Mayonnaise
- 2 Tbsp. KRAFT Mango Chipotle Vinaigrette Dressing
- 1 Tbsp. GREY POUPON Savory Honey Mustard
- 2 ciabatta sandwich rolls (6 oz. each), split
- 2 lettuce leaves

Direction

- Combine chicken, mangos and onions in medium bowl.
- Mix mayo, dressing and mustard until blended. Add to chicken mixture; mix lightly.
- Refrigerate 30 min.
- Fill rolls with lettuce and chicken salad. Cut diagonally in half.

Nutrition Information

- Calories: 400
- Fiber: 3 g
- Sugar: 0 g
- Protein: 22 g
- Sodium: 840 mg
- Total Carbohydrate: 0 g
- Total Fat: 14 g
- Saturated Fat: 2.5 g
- Cholesterol: 40 mg

248. Maple Mustard Roast Chicken Dinner

Serving: 6 | Prep: 15mins | Cook: 50mins | Ready in: 1hours5mins

Ingredients

- 1/4 cup maple-flavored or pancake syrup

- 1/4 cup KRAFT Balsamic Vinaigrette Dressing
- 2 Tbsp. GREY POUPON Harvest Coarse Ground Mustard
- 6 chicken leg quarters (2 lb.)
- 1 lb. carrots, peeled
- 1 lb. red new potatoes, halved
- 2 Tbsp. MIRACLE WHIP Light Dressing

Direction

- Heat oven to 400°F.
- Whisk syrup, vinaigrette and mustard until blended. Reserve half for later use.
- Place chicken in single layer on half of parchment-covered baking sheet; spread vegetables onto other side of baking sheet. Brush chicken with remaining syrup mixture; brush vegetables with MIRACLE WHIP.
- Bake 30 min. Turn vegetables. Bake chicken and vegetables an additional 20 min. or until chicken is done (165°F), brushing chicken occasionally with reserved syrup mixture.

Nutrition Information

- Calories: 390
- Total Carbohydrate: 0 g
- Protein: 30 g
- Sodium: 440 mg
- Fiber: 4 g
- Saturated Fat: 3 g
- Cholesterol: 145 mg
- Sugar: 0 g
- Total Fat: 14 g

249. Marinated Italian Chicken Skewers

Serving: 6 | Prep: 30mins | Cook: 1hours | Ready in: 1hours30mins

Ingredients

- 2 red onions, each cut into 8 wedges, divided
- 1-1/4 cups KRAFT Italian Vinaigrette Dressing made with Extra Virgin Olive Oil
- 2 cloves garlic, minced
- 1 Tbsp. chopped fresh basil
- 6 small boneless skinless chicken breasts (1-1/2 lb.), each cut into 4 pieces
- 2 small zucchini, cut into 1-1/2-inch pieces

Direction

- Chop 4 onion wedges finely; mix with dressing, garlic and basil until blended.
- Thread chicken onto 6 skewers alternately with zucchini and remaining onion wedges; place in shallow dish. Pour 1 cup dressing mixture over kabobs; turn to evenly coat kabobs. Refrigerate 1 hour to marinate, turning occasionally.
- Heat grill to medium heat. Remove kabobs from marinade; discard marinade. Grill kabobs 12 to 15 min. or until chicken is done and vegetables are crisp-tender, turning occasionally and brushing with remaining dressing mixture.

Nutrition Information

- Calories: 190
- Sodium: 370 mg
- Total Carbohydrate: 0 g
- Total Fat: 6 g
- Saturated Fat: 1 g
- Fiber: 1 g
- Sugar: 0 g
- Protein: 25 g
- Cholesterol: 65 mg

250. Marinated Zesty Chicken

Serving: 4 | Prep: 15mins | Cook: 1hours30mins | Ready in: 1hours45mins

Ingredients

- 1/2 cup KRAFT Zesty Italian Dressing
- 4 small boneless skinless chicken breasts (1 lb.)
- 1/4 cup KRAFT Reduced Fat Parmesan Style Grated Topping
- 1 cup sliced fresh mushrooms
- 2 Tbsp. chopped fresh basil
- 1/4 cup KRAFT 2% Milk Shredded Colby & Monterey Jack Cheeses

Direction

- Heat oven to 350°F.
- Pour dressing over chicken in shallow glass dish; turn to evenly coat chicken. Refrigerate 1 hour to marinate.
- Remove chicken from marinade; discard marinade. Place grated topping in shallow dish. Add chicken; turn to evenly coat both sides of each breast. Place in single layer in shallow pan sprayed with cooking spray.
- Bake 30 min. Meanwhile, cook mushrooms in skillet sprayed with cooking spray on high heat 3 min. or until tender, stirring frequently. Stir in basil.
- Top chicken with mushrooms and shredded cheese; bake 5 min. or until cheese is melted.

Nutrition Information

- Calories: 240
- Total Carbohydrate: 0 g
- Protein: 28 g
- Fiber: 0 g
- Sugar: 0 g
- Cholesterol: 80 mg
- Total Fat: 10 g
- Saturated Fat: 3 g
- Sodium: 540 mg

251. Mediterranean Chicken & Hummus Wraps

Serving: 6 | Prep: 25mins | Cook: | Ready in: 25mins

Ingredients

- 4 small boneless skinless chicken breasts (1 lb.)
- 1/4 cup KRAFT Greek Vinaigrette Dressing
- 6 flour tortillas (10 inch)
- 1 container (7 oz.) ATHENOS Original Hummus
- 6 romaine lettuce leaves
- 1 large tomato, cut into thin slices
- 1/3 cup ATHENOS Traditional Crumbled Feta Cheese

Direction

- Heat greased grill to medium heat.
- Grill chicken 6 to 8 min. on each side or until done (165°F).
- Cut chicken into thin strips; place in medium bowl. Add dressing; toss to evenly coat.
- Spread tortillas with hummus. Top with lettuce, tomatoes, chicken and cheese; roll up.

Nutrition Information

- Calories: 430
- Sodium: 910 mg
- Sugar: 0 g
- Fiber: 4 g
- Total Fat: 16 g
- Protein: 25 g
- Total Carbohydrate: 0 g
- Saturated Fat: 4 g
- Cholesterol: 50 mg

252. Mediterranean Chicken Pasta

Serving: 0 | Prep: 30mins | Cook: | Ready in: 30mins

Ingredients

- 1 Tbsp. oil
- 4 small boneless skinless chicken breasts (1 lb.)
- 1 pkg. (6.4 oz.) KRAFT Italian Pasta Salad

- 2 cups water
- 1/3 cup KRAFT Zesty Italian Dressing
- 1 tomato, chopped
- 1 small red onion, sliced
- 1 pkg. (4 oz.) ATHENOS Traditional Crumbled Feta Cheese
- 1/2 tsp. dried oregano leaves

Direction

- Heat oil in large nonstick skillet on medium heat. Add chicken; cook 3 to 4 min. on each side or until browned on both sides.
- Stir in contents of Pasta and Seasoning pouches and water. Reduce heat to medium; cover. Cook 7 to 9 min. or until pasta is tender.
- Remove chicken from skillet. Add dressing, tomatoes and onions to skillet; stir. Top with chicken; cover. Cook 5 min. or until heated through. Sprinkle with Parmesan, feta and oregano.

Nutrition Information

- Calories: 460
- Protein: 37 g
- Total Carbohydrate: 38 g
- Sugar: 7 g
- Cholesterol: 90 mg
- Sodium: 920 mg
- Total Fat: 18 g
- Saturated Fat: 6 g
- Fiber: 3 g

253. Mediterranean Chicken Recipe

Serving: 0 | Prep: 5mins | Cook: 20mins | Ready in: 25mins

Ingredients

- 4 small boneless skinless chicken breasts (1 lb.)

- 1 can (14-1/2 oz.) Italian-style diced tomatoes, undrained
- 1/2 cup black olives, chopped
- 1 Tbsp. lemon zest
- 1 cup KRAFT Finely Shredded Italian* Five Cheese Blend
- 3 cups hot cooked rotini pasta

Direction

- Heat large nonstick skillet on medium-high heat. Add chicken; cover. Cook 5 to 7 min. on each side or until done (165ºF). Remove chicken from skillet.
- Add tomatoes, olives and lemon zest to skillet. Cook 4 min. or until hot, stirring frequently.
- Return chicken to skillet; cook 1 min. or until hot. Top with cheese. Serve over pasta.

Nutrition Information

- Calories: 410
- Fiber: 3 g
- Total Carbohydrate: 0 g
- Sugar: 0 g
- Total Fat: 11 g
- Saturated Fat: 5 g
- Cholesterol: 85 mg
- Protein: 38 g
- Sodium: 970 mg

254. Mediterranean Chicken Skillet

Serving: 4 | Prep: 40mins | Cook: | Ready in: 40mins

Ingredients

- 4 small boneless skinless chicken breasts (1 lb.)
- 1/2 tsp. ground black pepper, divided
- 2 Tbsp. olive oil, divided
- 1 yellow squash, sliced
- 1 red pepper, chopped
- 1 onion, sliced, separated into rings

- 2 cloves garlic, minced
- 1 can (10-3/4 oz.) reduced-sodium condensed tomato soup
- 1/4 cup water
- 2 cups hot cooked couscous
- 1/2 cup ATHENOS Traditional Crumbled Feta Cheese

Direction

- Sprinkle chicken with 1/4 tsp. black pepper. Heat 1 Tbsp. oil in large skillet on medium heat. Add chicken; cook 6 to 7 min. on each side or until done (165°F). Remove chicken from skillet; cover to keep warm.
- Heat remaining oil in same skillet. Add squash, red peppers, onions, garlic and remaining black pepper; cook 3 min. or until vegetables are crisp-tender, stirring frequently. Stir in soup and water. Bring to boil; cover. Simmer on low heat 5 min., stirring occasionally.
- Serve couscous topped with chicken, vegetable mixture and cheese.

Nutrition Information

- Calories: 400
- Sugar: 11 g
- Total Fat: 14 g
- Saturated Fat: 4 g
- Sodium: 280 mg
- Total Carbohydrate: 36 g
- Cholesterol: 80 mg
- Protein: 33 g
- Fiber: 4 g

255. Mediterranean Chicken With Orzo And Feta

Serving: 6 | Prep: 20mins | Cook: 30mins | Ready in: 50mins

Ingredients

- 6 slices OSCAR MAYER Bacon, chopped
- 6 bone-in skinless chicken thighs (2-1/4 lb.)
- 1 jar (24 oz.) CLASSICO Florentine Spinach & Cheese Pasta Sauce
- 1 can (14.5 oz.) fat-free reduced-sodium chicken broth
- 1 cup orzo pasta, uncooked
- 2 cloves garlic, minced
- 1/2 tsp. dried oregano leaves
- 12 pitted Kalamata olives, halved
- 1 pkg. (4 oz.) ATHENOS Traditional Crumbled Feta Cheese

Direction

- Cook and stir bacon in Dutch oven or large deep skillet on medium heat until crisp. Remove bacon from skillet with slotted spoon, reserving 2 Tbsp. drippings in Dutch oven. Drain bacon on paper towels.
- Add chicken to reserved drippings; cook 5 min. on each side or until lightly browned. Drain fat. Add pasta sauce, broth, pasta, garlic and oregano; mix well. Bring to boil; cover.
- Cook on low heat 25 to 30 min. or until chicken is done (165°F) and orzo is tender. Stir in reserved bacon and olives. Serve sprinkled with cheese.

Nutrition Information

- Calories: 460
- Cholesterol: 140 mg
- Protein: 33 g
- Total Carbohydrate: 0 g
- Saturated Fat: 7 g
- Sugar: 0 g
- Total Fat: 23 g
- Sodium: 1110 mg
- Fiber: 3 g

256. Mexican Chicken Casserole

Serving: 4 | Prep: 25mins | Cook: 20mins | Ready in: 45mins

Ingredients

- 3/4 lb. boneless skinless chicken breasts, cut into bite-size pieces
- 1 tsp. ground cumin
- 1 green pepper, chopped
- 1-1/2 cups TACO BELL® Thick & Chunky Salsa
- 2 oz. (1/4 of 8-oz. pkg.) PHILADELPHIA Neufchatel Cheese, cubed
- 1 can (15.5 oz.) no-salt-added black beans, rinsed
- 1 tomato, chopped
- 2 whole wheat tortillas (6 inch)
- 1/2 cup KRAFT Mexican Style 2% Milk Finely Shredded Four Cheese, divided

Direction

- Heat oven to 375°F.
- Cook and stir chicken and cumin in nonstick skillet on medium heat 2 min. Add peppers; cook 2 min., stirring occasionally. Stir in salsa; cook 2 min. Add Neufchatel; cook and stir 2 min. or until melted. Stir in beans and tomatoes.
- Spread 1/3 of the chicken mixture onto bottom of 8-inch square baking dish sprayed with cooking spray; cover with 1 tortilla and half each of the remaining chicken mixture and shredded cheese. Top with remaining tortilla and chicken mixture; cover.
- Bake 20 min. or until heated through. Sprinkle with remaining shredded cheese; bake, uncovered, 5 min. or until melted.

Nutrition Information

- Calories: 140
- Saturated Fat: 2.5 g
- Total Carbohydrate: 0 g
- Protein: 20 g
- Cholesterol: 70 mg
- Sugar: 0 g
- Fiber: 0 g
- Sodium: 100 mg
- Total Fat: 5 g

257. Mexican Marinated & Broiled Chicken Breasts

Serving: 0 | Prep: 20mins | Cook: 33mins | Ready in: 53mins

Ingredients

- 4 boneless skinless chicken breasts (1 lb.)
- 1 cup TACO BELL® Thick & Chunky Salsa, divided
- 4 KRAFT Singles
- 4 cups hot cooked long-grain white rice

Direction

- Coat chicken with 1/2 cup of the salsa in shallow dish or resealable plastic bag; cover. Refrigerate 15 minutes to marinate.
- Preheat broiler. Drain chicken; discard marinade. Place chicken on rack of broiler pan. Broil, 4 to 6 inches from heat, for 7 to 9 minutes on each side or until chicken is cooked through, turning and brushing occasionally with the remaining 1/2 cup salsa and topping with the Singles during the last few minutes of the chicken broiling time.
- Serve with rice.

Nutrition Information

- Calories: 380
- Cholesterol: 70 mg
- Total Carbohydrate: 51 g
- Saturated Fat: 3 g
- Sodium: 700 mg
- Protein: 25 g

- Sugar: 4 g
- Fiber: 3 g
- Total Fat: 7 g

- Sugar: 3 g
- Total Fat: 8 g
- Sodium: 870 mg
- Fiber: 8 g
- Total Carbohydrate: 34 g
- Cholesterol: 30 mg

258. Mexican Taco Soup With Chicken

Serving: 0 | Prep: 25mins | Cook: |Ready in: 25mins

Ingredients

- 1 lb. lean ground chicken
- 1 onion, chopped
- 3 cans (15.5 oz. each) mild chili beans, undrained
- 1 can (14.5 oz.) no-salt-added diced tomatoes and green chiles, undrained
- 1 can (14.25 oz.) no-salt-added corn, drained
- 1-1/2 cups water
- 1 can (8 oz.) no-salt-added tomato sauce
- 1 pkg. (1 oz.) TACO BELL® Reduced Sodium Taco Seasoning Mix
- 1-1/2 cups KRAFT 2% Milk Shredded Cheddar Cheese
- 1/4 cup chopped fresh cilantro
- 6 cups baked tortilla chips

Direction

- Cook chicken with onions in large saucepan until chicken is done; drain. Return chicken mixture to pan.
- Add all remaining ingredients except cheese, cilantro and chips; stir, breaking up tomatoes with spoon. Bring to boil; simmer on medium-low heat 5 min., stirring occasionally.
- Top with cheese and cilantro. Serve with chips.

Nutrition Information

- Calories: 250
- Protein: 15 g
- Saturated Fat: 2 g

259. Mini Butter Chicken Pies

Serving: 6 | Prep: 30mins | Cook: 25mins |Ready in: 55mins

Ingredients

- 3 Tbsp. butter
- 2 cups chopped onions
- 1 tsp. garam masala
- 1 jar (24 oz.) CLASSICO Marinara with Plum Tomatoes & Olive Oil Pasta Sauce
- 4 oz. (1/2 of 8-oz. pkg.) PHILADELPHIA Cream Cheese, cubed
- 3 cups chopped cooked chicken
- 2 cups frozen peas and carrots
- 1/2 Easy Homemade Pie Dough

Direction

- Melt butter in large skillet on medium heat. Add onions; cook 7 min. or until tender and lightly browned, stirring occasionally. Stir in garam masala; cook and stir 1 min.
- Add pasta sauce and cream cheese; stir. Cook on medium-low heat 5 min. or until cream cheese is completely melted and sauce is well blended, stirring frequently. Remove from heat. Add chicken and vegetables; mix well.
- Spoon into 6 (1-cup) ovenproof ramekins or soup crocks sprayed with cooking spray.
- Heat oven to 400°F. Roll out Easy Homemade Pie Dough on lightly floured surface to 1/8-inch thickness. Cut into 6 (4-incn) rounds with biscuit cutter, rerolling scraps as necessary. Place over chicken mixture; seal and flute edges. Cut several small slits in top of each crust to permit steam to escape.

- Bake 20 to 25 min. or until filling is hot and bubbly, and crusts are golden brown.

Nutrition Information

- Calories: 500
- Saturated Fat: 15 g
- Total Carbohydrate: 0 g
- Sugar: 0 g
- Cholesterol: 130 mg
- Sodium: 850 mg
- Fiber: 5 g
- Total Fat: 29 g
- Protein: 28 g

260. Mini Chicken Patties With Spring Green Salad

Serving: 4 | Prep: 15mins | Cook: 20mins | Ready in: 35mins

Ingredients

- 1 lb. ground chicken
- 1 pkg. (6 oz.) STOVE TOP Lower Sodium Stuffing Mix for Chicken
- 2 cloves garlic, minced
- 2 egg whites
- 6 cups loosely packed arugula
- 2-1/2 cups snow peas
- 4 small green onions, quartered
- 1/4 cup KRAFT Tuscan House Italian Dressing

Direction

- Heat oven to 400°F.
- Mix chicken, stuffing mix, garlic and egg whites just until blended. Roll into 20 balls; flatten to 1/4-inch thickness. Place on baking sheet sprayed with cooking spray.
- Bake 20 min. or until done.
- Toss arugula with peas and onions; place on 4 plates. Top with chicken patties. Drizzle with dressing.

Nutrition Information

- Calories: 450
- Protein: 31 g
- Sugar: 0 g
- Cholesterol: 90 mg
- Fiber: 5 g
- Saturated Fat: 4 g
- Total Carbohydrate: 0 g
- Sodium: 610 mg
- Total Fat: 18 g

261. Miracle Whip Chicken Skillet

Serving: 4 | Prep: 10mins | Cook: 35mins | Ready in: 45mins

Ingredients

- 1-1/2 cups instant white rice, uncooked
- 1-1/2 cups fat-free reduced-sodium chicken broth
- 1/4 cup MIRACLE WHIP Dressing
- 1 Tbsp. chili powder
- 4 small boneless skinless chicken breasts (1 lb.)
- 1 tomato, chopped
- 1/2 cup KRAFT Shredded Cheddar Cheese

Direction

- Mix first 4 ingredients in large skillet. Top with chicken.
- Bring to boil; cover. Simmer on low heat 25 min.
- Top with remaining ingredients. Cook 10 min. or until chicken is done (165°F).

Nutrition Information

- Calories: 360
- Sugar: 2 g
- Protein: 31 g
- Saturated Fat: 4.5 g
- Total Carbohydrate: 32 g
- Cholesterol: 85 mg
- Sodium: 450 mg
- Total Fat: 11 g
- Fiber: 2 g

262. Mulligatawny Soup

Serving: 8 | Prep: 15mins | Cook: 20mins | Ready in: 35mins

Ingredients

- 1 Tbsp. oil
- 2 large onions, chopped
- 2 cloves garlic, minced
- 1 Tbsp. curry powder
- 1/2 tsp. ground red pepper (cayenne)
- 1/2 tsp. ground turmeric
- 2 pkg. (9 oz. each) frozen lentils, rinsed
- 4 cups fat-free reduced-sodium chicken broth
- 1 Tbsp. HEINZ Apple Cider Vinegar
- 1 cup chopped cooked boneless skinless chicken breasts
- 1 cup coconut milk
- 2 Granny Smith apples, chopped
- 8 dashes LEA & PERRINS Worcestershire Sauce

Direction

- Heat oil in 4-qt. Dutch oven on medium-high heat. Add onions and garlic; cook 3 to 4 min. or until golden brown, stirring occasionally. Add curry powder, pepper and turmeric. Stir in lentils until coated. Add broth and vinegar; bring to boil.
- Simmer on medium-low heat 10 to 15 min or until lentils are tender. Stir in chicken, coconut milk and apples.
- Top each serving with a dash of Worcestershire sauce.

Nutrition Information

- Calories: 200
- Saturated Fat: 5 g
- Sugar: 0 g
- Total Carbohydrate: 0 g
- Total Fat: 8 g
- Sodium: 250 mg
- Fiber: 7 g
- Protein: 12 g
- Cholesterol: 15 mg

263. Mushroom Smothered Chicken & Green Bean Skillet

Serving: 4 | Prep: 25mins | Cook: | Ready in: 25mins

Ingredients

- 4 small boneless skinless chicken breasts (1 lb.)
- 2 cups frozen green beans
- 1 can (10-3/4 oz.) reduced-fat reduced-sodium condensed cream of mushroom soup
- 1/2 cup water
- 1/4 tsp. dried thyme leaves
- 1 cup KRAFT Shredded Colby & Monterey Jack Cheeses

Direction

- Cook chicken in nonstick skillet on medium-high heat 6 to 7 min. on each side or until done (165°F). Remove from skillet; cover to keep warm.
- Add beans, soup, water and thyme to skillet; stir. Cover; simmer on medium heat 6 min. or until heated through, stirring frequently.
- Return chicken to skillet; spoon sauce over chicken. Cook, uncovered, 1 min. or until heated through. Top with cheese.

Nutrition Information

- Calories: 300
- Cholesterol: 95 mg
- Sodium: 540 mg
- Sugar: 3 g
- Protein: 33 g
- Saturated Fat: 6 g
- Total Fat: 12 g
- Fiber: 2 g
- Total Carbohydrate: 12 g

264. Mushroom Stuffing Chicken Roll Ups

Serving: 6 | Prep: 20mins | Cook: 40mins | Ready in: 1hours

Ingredients

- 1/3 cup MIRACLE WHIP Dressing
- 2 Tbsp. flour
- 1 cup fat-free milk
- 1 pkg. (6 oz.) STOVE TOP Stuffing Mix for Chicken
- 1/2 lb. sliced fresh mushrooms
- 1 Tbsp. butter
- 6 small boneless skinless chicken breasts (1-1/2 lb.), pounded to 1/4-inch thickness
- 1/2 cup KRAFT 2% Milk Shredded Colby & Monterey Jack Cheeses

Direction

- Heat oven to 400ºF.
- Whisk dressing and flour in medium microwaveable bowl until blended. Gradually stir in milk. Microwave on HIGH 3 to 4 min. or until thickened, stirring every 2 min.
- Prepare stuffing as directed on package; set aside. Cook and stir mushrooms in butter in skillet until tender. Add to stuffing; mix well.
- Place chicken, top sides down, on work surface; spread with stuffing to within 1/2 inch of edges. Starting at one short end, roll up each breast; place, seam side down, in 13x9-inch baking dish sprayed with cooking spray. Top with sauce and cheese; cover.
- Bake 35 to 40 min. or until chicken is done (165ºF), uncovering for the last 5 min.

Nutrition Information

- Calories: 350
- Total Carbohydrate: 0 g
- Saturated Fat: 4 g
- Total Fat: 11 g
- Sugar: 0 g
- Sodium: 650 mg
- Cholesterol: 80 mg
- Protein: 33 g
- Fiber: 1 g

265. Nana's Smothered Chicken Skillet With Cheese

Serving: 4 | Prep: 25mins | Cook: | Ready in: 25mins

Ingredients

- 4 small boneless skinless chicken breasts (1 lb.)
- 2 cups frozen green beans
- 1 can (10-3/4 oz.) reduced-fat reduced-sodium condensed cream of mushroom soup
- 1/2 cup water
- 1/4 tsp. dried thyme leaves
- 1 cup KRAFT Shredded Four Cheese

Direction

- Cook chicken in nonstick skillet on medium-high heat 6 to 7 min. on each side or until done (165ºF). Remove from skillet; cover to keep warm.
- Add beans, soup, water and thyme to skillet; stir. Cover; simmer on medium heat 6 min. or until heated through, stirring frequently.

- Return chicken to skillet; spoon sauce over chicken. Cook, uncovered, 1 min. or until heated through. Top with cheese.

Nutrition Information

- Calories: 290
- Total Fat: 11 g
- Saturated Fat: 5 g
- Sugar: 3 g
- Sodium: 580 mg
- Fiber: 2 g
- Protein: 34 g
- Total Carbohydrate: 12 g
- Cholesterol: 90 mg

266. One Pan Chicken 'N Noodles

Serving: 4 | Prep: 30mins | Cook: | Ready in: 30mins

Ingredients

- 4 slices OSCAR MAYER Bacon, cut into 1-inch pieces
- 4 small boneless skinless chicken breasts (1 lb.)
- 2 cups sliced fresh mushrooms
- 1 small onion, chopped
- 2 Tbsp. flour
- 1 can (14-1/2 oz.) fat-free reduced-sodium chicken broth
- 1/4 cup water
- 2 cups egg noodles, uncooked
- 1/2 cup (1/2 of 8-oz. tub) PHILADELPHIA Cream Cheese Spread
- 1/2 tsp. zest and 1 Tbsp. juice from 1 lemon
- 1/4 tsp. garlic powder
- 1/8 tsp. black pepper

Direction

- Cook and stir bacon in large skillet on medium heat until crisp. Remove bacon from skillet with slotted spoon; drain on paper towels. Discard all but 1 Tbsp. drippings from skillet.
- Add chicken to reserved drippings; cook 2 min. on each side or until each breast is lightly browned on both sides. Remove from skillet; set aside. Add vegetables to skillet; cook 3 min. or until tender, stirring frequently. Add flour; cook and stir 1 min. Stir in broth and water; bring to boil, stirring frequently.
- Spoon vegetables to edge of skillet. Add noodles to center of skillet; press with back of spoon to completely cover noodles with broth. Top with chicken; cover. Simmer 7 to 8 min. or until chicken is done (165ºF), noodles are tender and sauce is thickened, stirring after 4 min. to combine sauce ingredients.
- Mix cream cheese spread, lemon zest, juice, garlic powder and pepper in medium bowl until blended. Add to ingredients in skillet; cook and stir 2 to 3 min. or until heated through. Sprinkle with bacon.

Nutrition Information

- Calories: 370
- Fiber: 2 g
- Sugar: 2 g
- Saturated Fat: 7 g
- Sodium: 520 mg
- Total Carbohydrate: 21 g
- Protein: 33 g
- Cholesterol: 110 mg
- Total Fat: 17 g

267. One Pan Chicken, Tomato And Pepper Pasta

Serving: 0 | Prep: 10mins | Cook: 25mins | Ready in: 35mins

Ingredients

- 1 lb. boneless skinless chicken breasts, cut into thin strips
- 1 Tbsp. oil
- 2 cups chicken broth
- 1 Tbsp. grated lemon zest
- 4 cups rotini pasta, uncooked
- 1 cup halved cherry tomatoes
- 1 small green pepper, cut into thin strips
- 2 Tbsp. KRAFT Grated Parmesan Cheese

Direction

- Cook and stir chicken in hot oil in large skillet on medium-high heat for 5 minutes or until chicken is lightly browned.
- Add 3 cups water, chicken broth and lemon peel; mix well. Stir in pasta; cover. Bring to boil. Reduce heat to low; simmer 15 minutes or until pasta is tender.
- Stir in tomatoes and pepper strips; cook an additional 5 minutes or until chicken is cooked through and vegetables are crisp-tender. Add cheese; toss lightly.

Nutrition Information

- Calories: 400
- Total Fat: 7 g
- Protein: 28 g
- Sodium: 340 mg
- Fiber: 2 g
- Saturated Fat: 1.5 g
- Total Carbohydrate: 0 g
- Cholesterol: 45 mg
- Sugar: 0 g

---

268. Onion & Feta Greek BBQ Chicken Pizza

Serving: 6 | Prep: 10mins | Cook: 12mins | Ready in: 22mins

Ingredients

- 1 ready-to-use baked pizza crust (12 inch)
- 1 cup KRAFT Shredded Four Cheese, divided
- 1 pkg. (6 oz.) OSCAR MAYER CARVING BOARD Flame Grilled Chicken Breast Strips, coarsely chopped
- 1/4 cup KRAFT Hickory Smoke Barbecue Sauce
- 1 pkg. (4 oz.) ATHENOS Traditional Crumbled Feta Cheese
- 1 small red onion, halved, sliced and separated into rings

Direction

- Heat oven to 450°F.
- Place pizza crust on baking sheet; sprinkle with 1/2 cup shredded cheese.
- Toss chicken with barbecue sauce; spoon onto crust. Top with feta, onions and remaining shredded cheese.
- Bake 10 to 12 min. or until shredded cheese is melted and crust is golden brown. Let stand 5 min. before cutting to serve.

Nutrition Information

- Calories: 310
- Saturated Fat: 6 g
- Fiber: 1 g
- Total Fat: 12 g
- Cholesterol: 50 mg
- Total Carbohydrate: 31 g
- Sodium: 970 mg
- Sugar: 5 g
- Protein: 20 g

---

269. Orange Chicken Rice Bowl

Serving: 0 | Prep: 30mins | Cook: | Ready in: 30mins

Ingredients

- 1 lb. boneless skinless chicken breasts, cut into thin strips
- 1/4 cup KRAFT Asian Toasted Sesame Dressing
- 1/4 cup orange juice
- 3 cups frozen stir-fry vegetables (broccoli, yellow, red and green peppers, onions)
- 3 cups hot cooked long-grain white rice
- 1/4 cup chopped PLANTERS COCKTAIL Peanuts

Direction

- Cook chicken in large nonstick skillet on medium heat 5 min. or until done, stirring frequently.
- Stir in dressing and juice. Bring to boil. Add vegetables; cook 5 to 7 min. or until heated through, stirring occasionally.
- Serve over rice; top with nuts.

Nutrition Information

- Calories: 410
- Total Fat: 11 g
- Sodium: 290 mg
- Cholesterol: 65 mg
- Sugar: 0 g
- Protein: 31 g
- Total Carbohydrate: 0 g
- Fiber: 3 g
- Saturated Fat: 2 g

270. PHILLY Chicken Pot Pie Minis

Serving: 6 | Prep: 25mins | Cook: 30mins | Ready in: 55mins

Ingredients

- 1 recipe Foolproof PHILLY Pie Crust Recipe
- 1 tub (8 oz.) PHILADELPHIA Cream Cheese Spread
- 1/2 cup milk
- 1 tsp. garlic powder
- 1/4 tsp. dried thyme leaves
- 3 cups chopped cooked chicken
- 3 cups frozen mixed vegetables (broccoli, carrots, cauliflower), thawed, drained

Direction

- Prepare Foolproof PHILLY Pie Crust dough and roll into 11-inch round. Use 3-1/2-inch round cutter to cut dough into 6 rounds; discard dough trimmings or reserve for another use. (See tip.)
- Heat oven to 400°F. Whisk cream cheese spread, milk and seasonings in large bowl until blended; stir in chicken and vegetables. Spoon into 6 (6 to 8 oz.) ramekins.
- Place pastry rounds over ingredients in ramekins; press edges of pastry to edges of ramekins to seal. Cut several slits in each crust to permit steam to escape. Place ramekins on baking sheet.
- Bake 25 to 30 min. or until crusts are golden brown.

Nutrition Information

- Calories: 540
- Fiber: 2 g
- Cholesterol: 155 mg
- Sugar: 3 g
- Protein: 28 g
- Total Carbohydrate: 24 g
- Total Fat: 37 g
- Saturated Fat: 21 g
- Sodium: 450 mg

271. PLANTERS Chicken Piccata Skillet Simmer

Serving: 4 | Prep: 15mins | Cook: 15mins | Ready in: 30mins

Ingredients

- 4 small boneless skinless chicken breasts (1 lb.)
- 1/4 cup flour
- 2 Tbsp. olive oil
- 2/3 cup fat-free reduced-sodium chicken broth
- 1/2 cup dry white wine
- 3 Tbsp. lemon juice
- 1/2 cup chopped toasted PLANTERS Walnuts

Direction

- Coat chicken with flour; shake off excess.
- Heat oil in large skillet on medium heat. Add chicken; cook 3 min. on each side. (Chicken will not be done.)
- Mix broth, wine and lemon juice until blended; pour over chicken. Bring to boil; simmer on low heat 12 to 15 min. or until chicken is done (165°F), sprinkling with nuts for the last few minutes.

Nutrition Information

- Calories: 350
- Cholesterol: 65 mg
- Protein: 28 g
- Total Fat: 19 g
- Sugar: 1 g
- Saturated Fat: 2.5 g
- Sodium: 135 mg
- Total Carbohydrate: 10 g
- Fiber: 1 g

---

272. Parmesan, Chicken And Pasta Toss

Serving: 4 | Prep: 20mins | Cook: | Ready in: 20mins

Ingredients

- 1/2 lb. spaghetti, uncooked
- 3 cups broccoli florets
- 2 cups chopped cooked chicken
- 1/4 cup KRAFT Zesty Italian Dressing
- 2 tsp. garlic powder
- 2 Tbsp. KRAFT Grated Parmesan Cheese

Direction

- Cook pasta in a large saucepan as directed on package, omitting salt and adding broccoli to the boiling water for the last 4 min.; drain.
- Stir in chicken, dressing and garlic powder.
- Sprinkle with cheese.

Nutrition Information

- Calories: 410
- Protein: 31 g
- Total Fat: 10 g
- Cholesterol: 65 mg
- Total Carbohydrate: 0 g
- Fiber: 4 g
- Saturated Fat: 2.5 g
- Sodium: 300 mg
- Sugar: 0 g

---

273. Parmesan, Chicken And Tomato Salad

Serving: 4 | Prep: 10mins | Cook: | Ready in: 10mins

Ingredients

- 1/2 cup KRAFT Shredded Parmesan Cheese
- 1/4 cup KRAFT Tuscan House Italian Dressing
- 2 Tbsp. water
- 2 cups shredded cooked chicken
- 1 can (15.5 oz.) kidney beans, rinsed
- 1 cup halved cherry tomatoes
- 6 cups loosely packed arugula

Direction

- Combine first 3 ingredients; spoon into 4 salad bowls.
- Top with remaining ingredients.

- Mix lightly just before serving.

Nutrition Information

- Calories: 370
- Sodium: 520 mg
- Cholesterol: 75 mg
- Protein: 34 g
- Saturated Fat: 4.5 g
- Total Carbohydrate: 0 g
- Total Fat: 16 g
- Fiber: 6 g
- Sugar: 0 g

274. Pecan Crusted Chicken With Citrus Tomato Topping

Serving: 8 | Prep: 30mins | Cook: | Ready in: 30mins

Ingredients

- 4 navel oranges (about 1-1/4 lb.)
- 1/3 cup KRAFT Real Mayo Mayonnaise
- 35 RITZ Crackers, finely crushed (about 1-1/2 cups)
- 3/4 cup finely chopped PLANTERS Pecans
- 8 small boneless skinless chicken breasts (2 lb.), pounded to 1/4-inch thickness
- 2 Tbsp. oil, divided
- 8 cherry tomatoes, quartered
- 3 green onions, sliced

Direction

- Peel oranges; cut into segments over medium bowl, reserving juice in bowl. Mix 2 Tbsp. orange juice and mayo in pie plate. Combine cracker crumbs and nuts in second pie plate. Discard remaining orange juice; place orange segments in bowl.
- Dip chicken in mayo mixture, then crumb mixture, turning to evenly coat both sides of each breast. Heat 1 Tbsp. oil in large skillet. Add half the chicken; cook 8 to 10 min. or until golden brown on both sides and done (165°F), turning after 5 min. Remove chicken from skillet; carefully wipe skillet with paper towel. Repeat with remaining oil and chicken.
- Add tomatoes and onions to oranges; mix lightly. Serve spooned over chicken.

Nutrition Information

- Calories: 380
- Total Carbohydrate: 0 g
- Protein: 27 g
- Fiber: 3 g
- Sugar: 0 g
- Cholesterol: 70 mg
- Sodium: 180 mg
- Total Fat: 22 g
- Saturated Fat: 3.5 g

275. Pepper Chicken Macaroni And Cheese

Serving: 0 | Prep: 25mins | Cook: 15mins | Ready in: 40mins

Ingredients

- 1 pkg. (14 oz.) KRAFT Deluxe Four Cheese Macaroni & Cheese Dinner
- 1 lb. cooked boneless skinless chicken breasts, cut into bite-size pieces
- 1 cup milk
- 1 red pepper, chopped
- 1/2 cup KRAFT Shredded Mozzarella Cheese
- 4 slices cooked OSCAR MAYER Bacon, crumbled

Direction

- Heat oven to 375°F.
- Prepare Dinner as directed on package. Stir in chicken, milk and peppers.

- Spoon into 8-inch square baking dish sprayed with cooking spray. Top with cheese and bacon.
- Bake 15 min.

Nutrition Information

- Calories: 380
- Sodium: 810 mg
- Protein: 29 g
- Sugar: 5 g
- Fiber: 1 g
- Total Carbohydrate: 33 g
- Total Fat: 13 g
- Saturated Fat: 5 g
- Cholesterol: 70 mg

276. Pesto Chicken Spirals

Serving: 0 | Prep: 30mins | Cook: 15mins | Ready in: 45mins

Ingredients

- 2 cups chopped fresh parsley
- 6 Tbsp. GREY POUPON Dijon Mustard, divided
- 2 Tbsp. KRAFT Grated Parmesan Cheese
- 3 cloves garlic, minced
- 2 tsp. dried basil leaves
- 2/3 cup cholesterol-free egg product, divided
- 1-1/2 cups plain dry bread crumbs, divided
- 8 small boneless skinless chicken breasts (2 lb.), pounded to 1/4 inch thickness
- 8 wooden skewers
- 2 Tbsp. margarine or butter, melted
- 4 cups hot cooked rice

Direction

- Preheat broiler. Mix parsley, 4 Tbsp. (1/4 cup) of the mustard, the cheese, garlic, basil and 1/4 cup of the egg product in small bowl until well blended. Stir in 1/2 cup of the bread crumbs; mix well. Spread evenly onto chicken breasts; roll up each breast starting from one of the short ends.
- Blend remaining egg product and remaining 2 Tbsp. mustard. Dip chicken rolls in egg mixture, then in remaining 1 cup bread crumbs, turning to evenly coat all sides. Cut each roll-up crosswise into 4 equal pieces, then thread onto skewer. (Each skewer will hold 4 spirals.)
- Broil, 6 inches from heat, 10 to 15 min. or until chicken is cooked through, turning occasionally and brushing with the melted margarine. Serve with rice.

Nutrition Information

- Calories: 380
- Total Carbohydrate: 0 g
- Protein: 34 g
- Saturated Fat: 2 g
- Sodium: 580 mg
- Fiber: 2 g
- Total Fat: 9 g
- Cholesterol: 70 mg
- Sugar: 0 g

277. Pesto Chicken Pasta

Serving: 6 | Prep: 20mins | Cook: | Ready in: 20mins

Ingredients

- 2 pkg. (9 oz. each) refrigerated cheese tortellini, uncooked
- 1/2 cup KRAFT Italian Vinaigrette Dressing made with Extra Virgin Olive Oil
- 1-1/2 lb. boneless skinless chicken breasts, cut into thin strips
- 1 large red peppers, cut into strips
- 1-1/2 cups CLASSICO Traditional Basil Pesto Sauce and Spread

Direction

- Cook pasta as directed on package, omitting salt.
- Meanwhile, heat dressing in large skillet on medium heat. Add chicken and peppers; cook and stir 5 min. or until chicken is done.
- Drain pasta, reserving 1/4 cup cooking water. Add pasta and pesto sauce to chicken mixture; mix lightly. Stir in reserved cooking water, 1 Tbsp. at a time, until sauce is of desired consistency.

Nutrition Information

- Calories: 670
- Total Carbohydrate: 0 g
- Saturated Fat: 7 g
- Protein: 37 g
- Sodium: 1400 mg
- Fiber: 6 g
- Cholesterol: 100 mg
- Sugar: 0 g
- Total Fat: 34 g

278. Poppyseed & Pine Nut Chicken Salad

Serving: 0 | Prep: 10mins | Cook: | Ready in: 10mins

Ingredients

- 8 cups torn salad greens
- 2 pkg. (6 oz. each) OSCAR MAYER CARVING BOARD Flame Grilled Chicken Breast Strips, coarsely chopped
- 2 cups halved seedless red grapes
- 1 red pepper, cut into strips
- 2 green onions, chopped
- 1 pkg. (2 oz.) pine nuts (about 1/3 cup), toasted
- 3/4 cup KRAFT Creamy Poppyseed Dressing

Direction

- Combine all ingredients except dressing in large bowl.
- Add dressing just before serving; toss to coat.

Nutrition Information

- Calories: 200
- Cholesterol: 45 mg
- Total Fat: 10 g
- Sugar: 0 g
- Saturated Fat: 1.5 g
- Protein: 19 g
- Total Carbohydrate: 0 g
- Sodium: 580 mg
- Fiber: 3 g

279. Pork Medallions With Cranberry Stuffing

Serving: 6 | Prep: 20mins | Cook: | Ready in: 20mins

Ingredients

- 2 pork tenderloins (1-1/2 lb.)
- 1/4 cup KRAFT Sun Dried Tomato Vinaigrette Dressing
- 1 Tbsp. GREY POUPON Dijon Mustard
- 1 pkg. (6 oz.) STOVE TOP Stuffing Mix for Chicken
- 1/3 cup dried cranberries

Direction

- Cut each tenderloin crosswise into 6 slices; pound to 1/2-inch thickness. Cook in large skillet sprayed with cooking spray on medium-high heat 3 min. on each side or until browned on both sides.
- Mix dressing and mustard; pour over meat. Cook on low heat 3 min. on each side or until meat is done and sauce is thickened. Meanwhile, prepare stuffing as directed on package, but reducing spread to 1 Tbsp. and

adding cranberries to water along with stuffing mix.
- Spoon stuffing onto serving plates. Add meat; top with sauce.

Nutrition Information

- Calories: 290
- Protein: 25 g
- Total Fat: 7 g
- Sodium: 640 mg
- Sugar: 0 g
- Saturated Fat: 2 g
- Cholesterol: 60 mg
- Total Carbohydrate: 0 g
- Fiber: 1 g

280. Potato Chicken Pie

Serving: 4 | Prep: 20mins | Cook: 15mins | Ready in: 35mins

Ingredients

- 1 pkt. (1/2 of 11.75-oz. pkg.) VELVEETA Cheesy Mashed Potatoes
- 1/2 tsp. garlic powder
- 1 lb. lean ground chicken
- 1 onion, chopped
- 1/3 cup A.1. Bold & Spicy Sauce

Direction

- Heat oven to 350°F.
- Prepare Potatoes as directed on package, adding garlic powder with the water.
- Brown chicken with onions in large skillet; drain. Stir in A.1. Sauce. Spoon into 1-1/2-qt. casserole; cover with potatoes.
- Bake 15 min. or until heated through.

Nutrition Information

- Calories: 320
- Total Carbohydrate: 29 g
- Saturated Fat: 3 g
- Fiber: 2 g
- Cholesterol: 60 mg
- Sodium: 910 mg
- Protein: 25 g
- Sugar: 9 g
- Total Fat: 12 g

281. Pretzel Chicken Dippers

Serving: 12 | Prep: 10mins | Cook: 20mins | Ready in: 30mins

Ingredients

- 1-1/2 lb. boneless skinless chicken breasts, cut into 1-1/2- to 2-inch pieces
- 1 pkt. SHAKE 'N BAKE Crunchy Pretzel Flavor Seasoned Coating Mix
- 1/4 lb. (4 oz.) VELVEETA, cut into 1/2-inch cubes
- 3 Tbsp. milk
- 1 tsp. GREY POUPON Dijon Mustard

Direction

- Heat oven to 400°F.
- Coat chicken with coating mix and bake as directed on package.
- Microwave remaining ingredients in microwaveable bowl on HIGH 1 to 1-1/2 min. or until VELVEETA is completely melted and sauce is well blended, stirring after 1 min.
- Serve chicken with sauce.

Nutrition Information

- Calories: 110
- Total Carbohydrate: 5 g
- Protein: 14 g
- Saturated Fat: 1.5 g
- Sugar: 1 g
- Cholesterol: 40 mg

- Sodium: 350 mg
- Fiber: 0 g
- Total Fat: 3.5 g

- Sodium: 670 mg
- Total Carbohydrate: 0 g

282. Quick & Easy Lemon Chicken & Rice

Serving: 0 | Prep: 15mins | Cook: 20mins | Ready in: 35mins

Ingredients

- 1/2 cup KRAFT Tuscan House Italian Dressing
- 1 lb. boneless skinless chicken breasts, cut into strips
- 1 cup chicken broth
- 1 cup small broccoli florets
- 1 red pepper, cut into strips
- 1 cup thinly sliced carrots
- 2 cups instant brown rice, uncooked
- 1 tsp. lemon pepper seasoning
- 2 Tbsp. KRAFT Grated Parmesan Cheese

Direction

- Heat dressing in large skillet on medium-high heat. Add chicken; cook and stir 1 min.
- Add broth, broccoli, red pepper and carrots. Bring to boil.
- Stir in rice. Return to boil. Reduce heat to low; cover. Simmer 5 min. Remove from heat. Let stand 5 min. Stir in lemon pepper seasoning; sprinkle with cheese.

Nutrition Information

- Calories: 460
- Protein: 33 g
- Cholesterol: 75 mg
- Fiber: 4 g
- Sugar: 0 g
- Total Fat: 17 g
- Saturated Fat: 3.5 g

283. Quick 'n' Easy Italian Chicken & Pasta For Two

Serving: 0 | Prep: 30mins | Cook: | Ready in: 30mins

Ingredients

- 1-1/2 cups whole wheat penne pasta, uncooked
- 1/4 cup KRAFT Lite House Italian Dressing, divided
- 1/2 lb. boneless skinless chicken breasts, cut into strips
- 1/2 cup fat-free reduced-sodium chicken broth
- 1 cup small broccoli florets
- 1 small red pepper, cut into strips
- 1 cup sliced fresh mushrooms
- 1/2 cup thin carrot slices
- 1/2 tsp. dried Italian seasoning
- 2 Tbsp. KRAFT Grated Parmesan Cheese

Direction

- Cook pasta as directed on package, omitting salt.
- Meanwhile, heat 2 Tbsp. dressing in large nonstick skillet on medium-high heat. Add chicken; cook and stir 1 min. Add broth and vegetables; stir. Bring to boil; cover. Simmer on low heat 5 min.
- Drain pasta. Add to chicken mixture along with the remaining dressing and Italian seasoning; mix lightly. Simmer 2 to 3 min. or until heated through, stirring occasionally. Sprinkle with cheese.

Nutrition Information

- Calories: 500
- Fiber: 9 g
- Sodium: 690 mg

- Saturated Fat: 2.5 g
- Total Fat: 6 g
- Cholesterol: 75 mg
- Total Carbohydrate: 0 g
- Sugar: 0 g
- Protein: 41 g

- Calories: 520
- Fiber: 4 g
- Total Fat: 18 g
- Sugar: 0 g
- Protein: 37 g
- Cholesterol: 100 mg
- Sodium: 1170 mg
- Saturated Fat: 8 g
- Total Carbohydrate: 0 g

284. Quick Chicken & Peppers BBQ Fajitas

Serving: 4 | Prep: 20mins | Cook: 20mins | Ready in: 40mins

Ingredients

- 1 lb. boneless skinless chicken breasts, cut into strips
- 1 each green and red pepper, cut into strips
- 1 onion, cut into thin wedges
- 1/2 cup KRAFT Hickory Smoke Barbecue Sauce
- 8 flour tortillas (6 inch), warmed
- 1 cup KRAFT Mexican Style Finely Shredded Four Cheese
- 1/2 cup TACO BELL® Thick & Chunky Salsa
- 1/4 cup BREAKSTONE'S or KNUDSEN Sour Cream

Direction

- Heat grill to medium-high heat.
- Combine chicken, vegetables and barbecue sauce. Let stand 5 min. Poke holes evenly in bottom of 13x9-inch disposable foil roasting pan with fork or skewer. Spoon chicken mixture into pan; place pan on grill grate. Cover grill with lid.
- Grill 20 min. or until chicken is done and vegetables are crisp-tender, stirring occasionally.
- Spoon onto tortillas; top with remaining ingredients. Roll up.

Nutrition Information

285. Quick Indian Karhai Chicken

Serving: 4 | Prep: 35mins | Cook: | Ready in: 35mins

Ingredients

- 1 Tbsp. oil
- 1/2 tsp. cumin seed
- 1 onion, finely chopped
- 1 yellow pepper, coarsely chopped
- 2 cloves garlic, minced
- 1 tsp. minced gingerroot
- 1 tomato, chopped
- 1 tsp. each dried fenugreek leaves, ground coriander, ground cumin
- 1/2 tsp. each garam masala and ground turmeric
- 1/4 tsp. ground red pepper (cayenne)
- 1 lb. boneless skinless chicken breasts, cut into bite-size pieces
- 1/4 cup KRAFT Sun Dried Tomato Vinaigrette Dressing
- 2 Tbsp. chopped fresh cilantro
- 1 Tbsp. lemon juice

Direction

- Heat oil in large skillet on medium-high heat. Add cumin seed; cook and stir 30 sec. Stir in onions, peppers, garlic and ginger; cook and stir 5 min. or until vegetables are crisp-tender.
- Stir in tomatoes and seasonings; cook 5 min., stirring frequently.

- Add chicken and dressing; stir. Cook 10 min. or until chicken is done, stirring occasionally. Stir in cilantro and lemon juice.

Nutrition Information

- Calories: 230
- Sugar: 5 g
- Sodium: 340 mg
- Protein: 26 g
- Cholesterol: 65 mg
- Total Carbohydrate: 10 g
- Fiber: 2 g
- Total Fat: 9 g
- Saturated Fat: 1.5 g

286. Quick Salsa Chicken Skillet

Serving: 0 | Prep: 10mins | Cook: 20mins | Ready in: 30mins

Ingredients

- 6 slices OSCAR MAYER Bacon, chopped
- 6 small boneless skinless chicken breasts (1-1/2 lb.)
- 1 onion, chopped
- 1 each green and red pepper, chopped
- 1 jalapeño pepper, seeded, chopped
- 1 can (14.5 oz.) diced tomatoes
- 3 cups hot cooked long-grain white rice
- 1 cup KRAFT Shredded Pepper Jack Cheese

Direction

- Cook and stir bacon in large skillet on medium heat until crisp. Remove bacon from skillet with slotted spoon, reserving 1 Tbsp. drippings in skillet. Drain bacon on paper towels.
- Add chicken to drippings in skillet; cook 4 to 5 min. on each side or until done (165°F). Remove from skillet; cover to keep warm. Add onions and peppers to skillet; cook 5 min. or until crisp-tender, stirring frequently. Stir in tomatoes and bacon.
- Spoon rice onto serving plates; top with chicken, vegetable mixture and cheese.

Nutrition Information

- Calories: 390
- Cholesterol: 95 mg
- Sugar: 0 g
- Total Fat: 14 g
- Total Carbohydrate: 0 g
- Fiber: 3 g
- Sodium: 420 mg
- Protein: 34 g
- Saturated Fat: 6 g

287. Quick Thai Style Chicken Kabobs

Serving: 4 | Prep: 20mins | Cook: 10mins | Ready in: 30mins

Ingredients

- 1/4 cup KRAFT Zesty CATALINA Dressing
- 3 Tbsp. creamy peanut butter
- 1 Tbsp. lite soy sauce
- 1 lb. boneless skinless chicken breasts, cut lengthwise into strips
- 2 Tbsp. PLANTERS Dry Roasted Peanuts, chopped
- 1 green onion, chopped

Direction

- Mix first 3 ingredients until blended. Pour over chicken in medium bowl; toss to evenly coat. Refrigerate 10 min.
- Heat broiler. Remove chicken from dressing mixture; discard dressing mixture. Thread chicken onto 8 skewers. Place on rack of broiler pan.

- Broil, 6 inches from heat, 4 min. on each side or until chicken is done. Top with nuts and onions.

Nutrition Information

- Calories: 280
- Cholesterol: 65 mg
- Sugar: 0 g
- Sodium: 470 mg
- Fiber: 1 g
- Total Carbohydrate: 0 g
- Total Fat: 16 g
- Protein: 28 g
- Saturated Fat: 3 g

288. Ranch Chicken & Rice Skillet

Serving: 4 | Prep: 5mins | Cook: 23mins | Ready in: 28mins

Ingredients

- 1 tsp. oil
- 4 small boneless skinless chicken breasts (1 lb.)
- 1 can (14-1/2 oz.) fat-free reduced-sodium chicken broth
- 1/4 cup KRAFT Classic Ranch Dressing
- 2 oz. (1/4 of 8-oz. pkg.) PHILADELPHIA Cream Cheese, cubed
- 1-1/2 cups instant white rice, uncooked
- 2 cups snow peas
- 1 cup julienne carrot strips

Direction

- Heat oil in large nonstick skillet on medium-high heat. Add chicken; cook 5 min. on each side or until browned on both sides.
- Add broth and dressing. Bring to boil. Reduce heat to medium-low; simmer 3 min.
- Stir in cream cheese, rice, snow peas and carrots; cover. Simmer 5 min. or until chicken is cooked through (170°F.) Remove from heat. Cover and let stand 5 min.

Nutrition Information

- Calories: 420
- Total Fat: 15 g
- Cholesterol: 85 mg
- Total Carbohydrate: 36 g
- Sugar: 5 g
- Protein: 34 g
- Sodium: 540 mg
- Fiber: 4 g
- Saturated Fat: 5 g

289. Ranch Honey Chicken For Two

Serving: 2 | Prep: 25mins | Cook: | Ready in: 25mins

Ingredients

- 2 small boneless skinless chicken breasts (1/2 lb.)
- 1 tsp. oil
- 1/2 cup fat-free reduced-sodium chicken broth
- 2 Tbsp. KRAFT Classic Ranch Dressing
- 1 Tbsp. honey
- 2 cloves garlic, minced
- 1 cup frozen peas

Direction

- Cook chicken in hot oil in large nonstick skillet on medium-high heat 5 min. on each side or until chicken is evenly browned on both sides.
- Mix broth, dressing, honey and garlic until blended; pour over chicken. Bring just to boil; cover. Simmer on medium-low heat 3 min.
- Stir in peas; cook, covered, 3 to 4 min. or until chicken is done (165°F) and peas are heated through.

Nutrition Information

- Calories: 300
- Sodium: 400 mg
- Cholesterol: 70 mg
- Total Fat: 11 g
- Saturated Fat: 2 g
- Sugar: 0 g
- Protein: 29 g
- Total Carbohydrate: 0 g
- Fiber: 3 g

290. Recipe For Chicken Enchiladas

Serving: 0 | Prep: 20mins | Cook: 15mins | Ready in: 35mins

Ingredients

- 2 Tbsp. butter or margarine
- 1/2 cup chopped onion
- 6 oz. Mexican VELVEETA, cut up
- 1/2 cup milk
- 2 cups chopped cooked chicken
- 1/2 cup sliced pitted black olives
- 8 flour tortillas (6 inch)
- 1/2 cup TACO BELL® Thick & Chunky Salsa

Direction

- Preheat oven to 350°F. Melt butter in large saucepan on medium heat. Add onion; cook and stir until crisp-tender. Reduce heat to low. Add VELVEETA and milk; cook until VELVEETA is completely melted, stirring frequently. Add chicken and olives; mix well. Remove from heat.
- Spoon 1/4 cup of the chicken mixture down center of each tortilla; roll up. Place, seam sides down, in 12x8-inch baking dish; top with salsa.
- Bake 15 minutes or until heated through.

Nutrition Information

- Calories: 560
- Saturated Fat: 11 g
- Sodium: 1600 mg
- Sugar: 8 g
- Fiber: 2 g
- Protein: 33 g
- Cholesterol: 115 mg
- Total Carbohydrate: 46 g
- Total Fat: 27 g

291. Roasted Sweet Potato And Chicken Salad

Serving: 4 | Prep: 20mins | Cook: 1hours | Ready in: 1hours20mins

Ingredients

- 1 lb. sweet potatoes (about 2), cut into 2-inch-thick wedges
- 1 Tbsp. oil
- 8 cups tightly packed torn romaine lettuce
- 2 cups shredded rotisserie chicken
- 1 cup cut-up fresh green beans (2 inch lengths), cooked, cooled
- 1 cup halved cherry tomatoes
- 1 avocado, chopped
- 4 slices OSCAR MAYER Bacon, cooked, crumbled
- 1/2 cup KRAFT Classic Ranch Dressing
- 1/4 cup pumpkin seeds

Direction

- Heat oven to 400°F.
- Toss potatoes with oil; spread onto foil-covered rimmed baking sheet sprayed with cooking spray.
- Bake 25 to 30 min. or until tender, turning after 15 min.
- Combine potatoes with all remaining ingredients except dressing and pumpkin seeds in large bowl. Add dressing; mix lightly.

- Sprinkle with pumpkin seeds.

Nutrition Information

- Calories: 550
- Cholesterol: 85 mg
- Fiber: 10 g
- Total Fat: 36 g
- Sugar: 12 g
- Saturated Fat: 8 g
- Sodium: 740 mg
- Total Carbohydrate: 37 g
- Protein: 23 g

292. Rosemary Garlic Pasta Primavera

Serving: 0 | Prep: 20mins | Cook: |Ready in: 20mins

Ingredients

- 2-2/3 cups penne pasta, uncooked
- 2 Tbsp. olive oil
- 1 lb. boneless skinless chicken breasts, cut into bite-size pieces
- 2 cups tightly packed baby spinach leaves
- 1 red pepper, cut into thin strips
- 1/2 cup thin zucchini slices
- 1/3 cup KRAFT Seasoned Grated Parmesan Cheese Rosemary & Garlic

Direction

- Cook pasta as directed on package, omitting salt.
- Meanwhile, heat oil in large skillet on medium heat. Add chicken; cook and stir 5 to 7 min. or until no longer pink. Add next 3 ingredients; cook and stir 4 min. or until chicken is done.
- Drain pasta. Add to chicken mixture in skillet along with the cheese; mix lightly.

Nutrition Information

- Calories: 330
- Total Fat: 9 g
- Sodium: 160 mg
- Protein: 25 g
- Fiber: 2 g
- Total Carbohydrate: 0 g
- Sugar: 0 g
- Cholesterol: 50 mg
- Saturated Fat: 2.5 g

293. SHAKE 'N BAKE Chicken Nugget Kabobs

Serving: 0 | Prep: 15mins | Cook: 15mins |Ready in: 30mins

Ingredients

- 1-1/2 lb. boneless skinless chicken breasts, cut into 1-1/2 to 2-inch pieces
- 1 pkt. SHAKE 'N BAKE Extra Crispy Seasoned Coating Mix
- 2 cups KRAFT Cheddar Cheese Cubes
- 1-1/2 cups cherry tomatoes
- 1 can (8 oz.) pineapple chunks in juice, drained

Direction

- Heat oven to 400°F.
- Moisten chicken with water; shake off excess water. Add 3 or 4 chicken pieces at a time to coating mix in shaker bag; shake to evenly coat. Place chicken in 15x10x1-inch pan. Discard any remaining coating mix.
- Bake chicken 15 min. or until done.
- Arrange 3 cooked chicken nuggets, 3 cheese cubes, 2 tomatoes and 1 pineapple chunk on each of 12 (9-inch) wooden skewers.

Nutrition Information

- Calories: 380
- Saturated Fat: 10 g
- Sugar: 6 g

- Total Fat: 19 g
- Sodium: 730 mg
- Protein: 36 g
- Cholesterol: 110 mg
- Total Carbohydrate: 16 g
- Fiber: 1 g

294. STOVE TOP Easy Chicken Bake

Serving: 0 | Prep: 10mins | Cook: 30mins | Ready in: 40mins

Ingredients

- 1 pkg. (6 oz.) STOVE TOP Stuffing Mix for Chicken
- 1-1/2 lb. boneless skinless chicken breasts, cut into bite-size pieces
- 1 pkg. (16 oz.) frozen mixed vegetables (carrots, corn, green beans, peas), thawed, drained
- 1 can (10-3/4 oz.) condensed cream of chicken soup
- 1/3 cup BREAKSTONE'S or KNUDSEN Sour Cream

Direction

- Heat oven to 400°F.
- Prepare stuffing as directed on package.
- Combine remaining ingredients in 13x9-inch baking dish sprayed with cooking spray; top with stuffing.
- Bake 30 min. or until chicken is done.

Nutrition Information

- Calories: 410
- Fiber: 3 g
- Total Carbohydrate: 0 g
- Protein: 31 g
- Sugar: 0 g
- Sodium: 910 mg

- Saturated Fat: 4.5 g
- Cholesterol: 80 mg
- Total Fat: 15 g

295. STOVE TOP Spicy Chicken Sausage Stuffing

Serving: 6 | Prep: 30mins | Cook: | Ready in: 30mins

Ingredients

- 1/2 lb. chicken sausage links, casing removed
- 1/2 cup chopped onions
- 2 cloves garlic, minced
- 1 cup water
- 1/2 tsp. crushed red pepper
- 1 pkg. (6 oz.) STOVE TOP Savory Herbs Stuffing Mix

Direction

- Crumble sausage into medium saucepan; cook on medium-high heat until done, stirring frequently. Remove from pan; drain.
- Add onions and garlic to pan; cook on medium heat 2 to 3 min. or until onions are crisp-tender. Stir in water and crushed pepper; bring to boil. Add stuffing mix and sausage; mix well. Cover.
- Remove from heat. Let stand 5 min. Fluff with fork.

Nutrition Information

- Calories: 150
- Total Carbohydrate: 0 g
- Cholesterol: 15 mg
- Sodium: 640 mg
- Fiber: 1 g
- Sugar: 0 g
- Total Fat: 3 g
- Saturated Fat: 1 g
- Protein: 8 g

296. Salsa Chicken Wrap With Pineapple Pico De Gallo

Serving: 4 | Prep: 20mins | Cook: | Ready in: 20mins

Ingredients

- 2 cups finely chopped fresh pineapple
- 1/4 cup finely chopped red onions
- 2 Tbsp. chopped fresh cilantro
- 1 Tbsp. finely chopped jalapeño peppers
- 1 Tbsp. lime juice
- 2 cups shredded cooked chicken
- 1/4 cup KRAFT Zesty Italian Dressing
- 1/2 cup (1/2 of 8-oz. tub) PHILADELPHIA Cream Cheese Spread
- 2 Tbsp. TACO BELL® Thick & Chunky Salsa
- 4 flour tortillas (10 inch)
- 4 leaf lettuce leaves
- 1 large tomato, cut into 8 thin slices, halved

Direction

- Combine first 5 ingredients.
- Toss chicken with dressing. Mix cream cheese spread and salsa until blended; spread onto tortillas. Top with lettuce, tomatoes, chicken mixture and half the pineapple mixture; roll up, tucking in both sides of each tortilla as it is rolled. Secure with toothpicks; cut in half.
- Serve with remaining pineapple mixture.

Nutrition Information

- Calories: 510
- Total Fat: 20 g
- Fiber: 4 g
- Cholesterol: 80 mg
- Sugar: 0 g
- Protein: 29 g
- Sodium: 880 mg
- Saturated Fat: 7 g
- Total Carbohydrate: 0 g

297. Salsa Chicken Tostadas

Serving: 4 | Prep: 20mins | Cook: | Ready in: 20mins

Ingredients

- 1 lb. boneless skinless chicken breasts, cut into 1/2-inch pieces
- 1/2 cup water
- 1 pkg. (1 oz.) TACO BELL® Taco Seasoning Mix
- 1 cup TACO BELL® Refried Beans, warmed
- 4 tostada shells (6 inch)
- 1/2 cup KRAFT Mexican Style Finely Shredded Four Cheese
- 1 cup shredded lettuce
- 1 avocado, chopped
- 1/4 cup TACO BELL® Thick & Chunky Medium Salsa
- 1/4 cup BREAKSTONE'S or KNUDSEN Sour Cream

Direction

- Cook and stir chicken in large nonstick skillet on medium-high heat 3 min. or until no longer pink.
- Add water and seasoning mix; simmer on medium-low heat 5 min. or until chicken is done and sauce is thickened, stirring occasionally.
- Spread beans onto tostada shells; top with layers of chicken mixture and remaining ingredients.

Nutrition Information

- Calories: 480
- Fiber: 7 g
- Total Fat: 22 g
- Saturated Fat: 7 g
- Protein: 35 g
- Cholesterol: 90 mg
- Sugar: 3 g
- Total Carbohydrate: 36 g

- Sodium: 1020 mg

298. Sarah's Super Baked Chicken & Carrots

Serving: 6 | Prep: 15mins | Cook: 50mins | Ready in: 1hours5mins

Ingredients

- 1 broiler-fryer chicken (3-1/2 lb.), cut up
- 5 carrots, peeled, cut into 1/2-inch-thick slices
- 1/2 cup KRAFT Zesty Italian Dressing

Direction

- Heat oven to 350°F.
- Place chicken pieces and carrots in large roasting pan; drizzle with dressing.
- BAKE 45 to 50 min. or until chicken is done (165°F) and carrots are tender.

Nutrition Information

- Calories: 310
- Protein: 29 g
- Total Carbohydrate: 0 g
- Fiber: 2 g
- Sodium: 320 mg
- Sugar: 0 g
- Saturated Fat: 4.5 g
- Total Fat: 18 g
- Cholesterol: 90 mg

299. Saucy Chicken Stir Fry

Serving: 0 | Prep: 40mins | Cook: | Ready in: 40mins

Ingredients

- 1 cup long-grain white rice, uncooked
- 1 tsp. cornstarch
- 1/2 tsp. ground ginger
- 2 Tbsp. lite soy sauce
- 1/4 cup KRAFT Asian Toasted Sesame Dressing
- 1 lb. boneless skinless chicken breasts, cut into thin strips
- 1 small red pepper, cut into thin strips
- 1/2 lb. sugar snap peas, trimmed
- 2 green onions, diagonally sliced

Direction

- Cook rice as directed on package, omitting salt. Meanwhile, mix cornstarch, ginger and soy sauce until blended.
- Heat dressing in wok or large skillet on medium heat. Add chicken; stir-fry 2 min. Add peppers and peas; stir-fry 3 min. Add onions and rice; stir-fry 1 min. or until chicken is done.
- Stir cornstarch mixture. Add to chicken mixture; stir-fry 1 min. or until sauce is thickened.

Nutrition Information

- Calories: 390
- Saturated Fat: 1.5 g
- Protein: 30 g
- Sodium: 510 mg
- Fiber: 3 g
- Total Fat: 6 g
- Total Carbohydrate: 0 g
- Sugar: 0 g
- Cholesterol: 65 mg

300. Savory Chicken Pie Recipe

Serving: 6 | Prep: 20mins | Cook: 30mins | Ready in: 50mins

Ingredients

- 1 pkg. (8 oz.) PHILADELPHIA Cream Cheese, cubed
- 1/2 cup fat-free reduced-sodium chicken broth
- 3 cups chopped cooked chicken
- 1 pkg. (16 oz.) frozen mixed vegetables (carrots, corn, green beans, peas), thawed, drained
- 1/4 tsp. garlic powder
- 1 egg
- 1/2 cup milk
- 1 cup all-purpose baking mix

Direction

- Heat oven to 400°F.
- Cook cream cheese and broth in large saucepan on low heat until cream cheese is completely melted and mixture is well blended, stirring frequently with whisk. Stir in chicken, vegetables and garlic powder.
- Spoon into 9-inch pie plate. Whisk egg and milk in medium bowl until blended. Add baking mix; stir just until moistened. Spread over chicken mixture. Place pie plate on baking sheet.
- Bake 25 to 30 min. or until golden brown.

Nutrition Information

- Calories: 380
- Protein: 23 g
- Fiber: 3 g
- Cholesterol: 120 mg
- Sodium: 690 mg
- Total Fat: 23 g
- Saturated Fat: 11 g
- Total Carbohydrate: 0 g
- Sugar: 0 g

301.   Senorita Fajita Sandwich

Serving: 0 | Prep: 10mins | Cook: | Ready in: 10mins

Ingredients

- 1/2 cup thin green pepper strips
- 1/4 cup slivered onions
- 2 oz. OSCAR MAYER CARVING BOARD Rotisserie Seasoned Chicken Breast
- 1 whole wheat tortilla (8 inch)
- 1 Tbsp. KRAFT Chipotle Aioli
- 1 KRAFT Big Slice Pepper Jack Cheese Slice, cut in half

Direction

- Cook and stir vegetables in medium nonstick skillet on medium-high heat 4 min. or until crisp-tender; spoon to one side of skillet.
- Add meat to other side of skillet; cook 2 min. or until heated through, turning after 1 min.
- Spread tortilla with aioli; top with cheese, meat and vegetables. Roll up.

Nutrition Information

- Calories: 400
- Cholesterol: 60 mg
- Fiber: 2 g
- Total Fat: 22 g
- Total Carbohydrate: 0 g
- Saturated Fat: 6 g
- Protein: 23 g
- Sugar: 0 g
- Sodium: 1010 mg

302.   Shortcut Salsa Chicken

Serving: 0 | Prep: 5mins | Cook: 25mins | Ready in: 30mins

Ingredients

- 4 frozen breaded chicken breasts (1 lb.)
- 1/2 cup TACO BELL® Thick & Chunky Salsa
- 1/2 cup KRAFT Mexican Style Finely Shredded Four Cheese

Direction

- Preheat oven to 400°F. Place chicken in 13x9-inch baking dish.
- Spread salsa over chicken; sprinkle with cheese.
- Bake 25 min. or until chicken is cooked through (165°F) and cheese is melted.

Nutrition Information

- Calories: 340
- Protein: 19 g
- Total Fat: 21 g
- Saturated Fat: 7 g
- Cholesterol: 50 mg
- Sodium: 770 mg
- Sugar: 3 g
- Total Carbohydrate: 22 g
- Fiber: 2 g

303. Simple Chicken Enchiladas

Serving: 6 | Prep: 15mins | Cook: 20mins | Ready in: 35mins

Ingredients

- 3 cups shredded cooked chicken breasts
- 1 jar (16 oz.) TACO BELL® Thick & Chunky Mild Salsa, divided
- 1-1/2 cups KRAFT 2% Milk Shredded Mild Cheddar Cheese, divided
- 12 flour tortillas (6 inch)

Direction

- Heat oven to 350°F.
- Mix chicken and 1/2 cup each salsa and cheese in bowl.
- Spread 1/2 cup of the remaining salsa onto bottom of 13x9-inch baking dish. Spoon chicken mixture down centers of tortillas; roll up. Place, seam sides down, in baking dish. Top with remaining salsa and cheese.
- Bake 20 min. or until heated through.

Nutrition Information

- Calories: 400
- Fiber: 2 g
- Sodium: 1170 mg
- Total Fat: 12 g
- Total Carbohydrate: 0 g
- Cholesterol: 80 mg
- Saturated Fat: 5 g
- Protein: 34 g
- Sugar: 0 g

304. Simply Amazing Greek Chicken Recipe

Serving: 8 | Prep: 20mins | Cook: 50mins | Ready in: 1hours10mins

Ingredients

- 1/4 cup lemon juice
- 1/4 cup olive oil
- 2 Tbsp. water
- 1 pkt. (1.25 oz.) A.1. Savory Garlic & Herb Marinade Mix
- 8 small boneless skinless chicken breasts (2 lb.)
- 1 cup grape tomatoes
- 1 cucumber, chopped
- 1/2 cup ATHENOS Traditional Crumbled Feta Cheese
- 1/2 cup chopped Kalamata olives
- 1/2 cup chopped red onions
- 1/4 cup chopped pepperoncini peppers

Direction

- Whisk first 4 ingredients until blended. Reserve 1/4 cup; pour remaining marinade over chicken in shallow dish. Turn to evenly coat both sides of each breast. Refrigerate 30 min., turning after 15 min.

- Meanwhile, combine remaining ingredients and reserved marinade. Refrigerate until ready to serve.
- Heat grill to medium-high heat. Lightly grease grill grates. Remove chicken from marinade; discard marinade. Grill chicken 10 min. on each side or until done (165°F). Serve with vegetable mixture.

Nutrition Information

- Calories: 250
- Sugar: 3 g
- Sodium: 670 mg
- Protein: 27 g
- Fiber: 2 g
- Cholesterol: 70 mg
- Total Fat: 12 g
- Total Carbohydrate: 7 g
- Saturated Fat: 2.5 g

305. Sizzlin' Marinated Chicken Kabobs

Serving: 4 | Prep: 20mins | Cook: 2hours | Ready in: 2hours20mins

Ingredients

- 1/3 cup hot water
- 1/4 cup KRAFT Mesquite Smoke Barbecue Sauce
- 1/4 cup lite soy sauce
- 1/4 cup creamy peanut butter
- 2 Tbsp. chopped fresh parsley
- 2 Tbsp. GREY POUPON Savory Honey Mustard
- 2 Tbsp. apricot preserves
- 1/2 tsp. coriander seed
- 1 lb. boneless skinless chicken thighs, cut into 12 thin strips

Direction

- Whisk all ingredients except chicken in large bowl until blended. Pour half into serving bowl; refrigerate for later use. Add chicken to remaining sauce; stir to evenly coat. Refrigerate 2 hours to marinate.
- Heat grill to medium-high heat. Remove chicken from marinade; discard marinade. Thread chicken, in accordion fashion, onto 12 skewers
- Grill 5 to 7 min. or until done, turning after 4 min. Serve with reserved sauce.

Nutrition Information

- Calories: 270
- Cholesterol: 100 mg
- Sodium: 790 mg
- Fiber: 1 g
- Sugar: 11 g
- Protein: 23 g
- Total Carbohydrate: 16 g
- Total Fat: 13 g
- Saturated Fat: 3 g

306. Skillet Chicken & Dumplings

Serving: 6 | Prep: 25mins | Cook: 15mins | Ready in: 40mins

Ingredients

- 1 Tbsp. oil
- 1 lb. boneless skinless chicken breasts, cut into bite-size pieces
- 1 can (14 oz.) fat-free reduced-sodium chicken broth
- 1/4 cup flour
- 1/2 cup (1/2 of 8-oz. tub) PHILADELPHIA Chive & Onion Cream Cheese Spread
- 1 pkg. (10 oz.) frozen peas and carrots
- 1 cup all-purpose baking mix
- 1/4 cup BREAKSTONE'S or KNUDSEN Sour Cream

- 1/4 cup milk
- 2 Tbsp. KRAFT Grated Parmesan Cheese
- 2 Tbsp. chopped fresh parsley

Direction

- Heat oil in large deep skillet on medium-high heat. Add chicken; cook and stir 4 min. or until no longer pink. Transfer to bowl.
- Add broth gradually to flour in small bowl, whisking constantly until blended. Add to skillet; cook and stir on medium heat 2 min. or until thickened. Add cream cheese spread; cook and stir 3 min. or until melted. Remove from heat; stir in chicken and vegetables.
- Stir baking mix, sour cream and milk just until baking mix is moistened. Spoon into 6 mounds over mixture in skillet; cook on medium-high heat 2 min. Cover skillet; cook on low heat 15 min. or until chicken is done and toothpick inserted in dumplings comes out clean.
- Top with Parmesan and parsley.

Nutrition Information

- Calories: 320
- Saturated Fat: 6 g
- Sugar: 0 g
- Protein: 23 g
- Cholesterol: 70 mg
- Sodium: 590 mg
- Total Carbohydrate: 0 g
- Total Fat: 15 g
- Fiber: 2 g

307. Skillet Chicken Breasts With Corn Sauce

Serving: 6 | Prep: 25mins | Cook: 30mins | Ready in: 55mins

Ingredients

- 6 slices OSCAR MAYER Bacon
- 1 tsp. dried basil leaves
- 1/4 tsp. pepper
- 6 small bone-in chicken breasts (2-1/4 lb.), skin removed
- 4 green onions, thinly sliced
- 1 container (8 oz.) BREAKSTONE'S or KNUDSEN Sour Cream
- 2 Tbsp. flour
- 2/3 cup milk
- 1 cup frozen corn, thawed

Direction

- Cook bacon in large skillet until crisp. Remove bacon from skillet, reserve 2 Tbsp. dripping in skillet. Drain bacon on paper towels. Combine basil and pepper; rub on chicken.
- Add chicken to reserved drippings; cook on medium heat 5 min. on each side or until browned. Add onions; cover. Cook on low heat 30 min. or until chicken is done (165°F).
- Combine sour cream and flour in small bowl; gradually stir in milk. Remove chicken from skillet; drain. Add sour cream mixture to skillet. Cook 1 to 2 min. or until thickened and bubbly, stirring constantly. Stir in corn. Return chicken to skillet; cook 1 to 2 min. or until heated through. Crumble bacon; sprinkle over chicken.

Nutrition Information

- Calories: 370
- Sodium: 260 mg
- Sugar: 0 g
- Protein: 39 g
- Fiber: 1 g
- Total Fat: 19 g
- Saturated Fat: 8 g
- Cholesterol: 130 mg
- Total Carbohydrate: 0 g

308. Skillet Chicken Chili

Serving: 8 | Prep: 30mins | Cook: | Ready in: 30mins

Ingredients

- 1 lb. boneless skinless chicken thighs, cut into bite-size pieces
- 1 onion, chopped
- 1 can (28 oz.) diced tomatoes, drained
- 1 pkg. (1 oz.) TACO BELL® Taco Seasoning Mix
- 1 each green and red pepper, chopped
- 1 can (15-1/2 oz.) kidney beans, rinsed
- 4 cups hot cooked long-grain white rice
- 1 cup KRAFT Mexican Style Finely Shredded Four Cheese

Direction

- Cook and stir chicken and onions in large nonstick skillet on medium-high heat 6 min. Stir in tomatoes and seasoning mix. Bring to boil, stirring occasionally.
- Stir in peppers and beans; cook on medium heat 5 min. or until chicken is done and peppers are crisp-tender, stirring occasionally.
- Spoon over rice; top with cheese.

Nutrition Information

- Calories: 310
- Sugar: 0 g
- Saturated Fat: 3.5 g
- Protein: 19 g
- Fiber: 5 g
- Total Fat: 8 g
- Cholesterol: 65 mg
- Sodium: 460 mg
- Total Carbohydrate: 0 g

309. Slow Cooker 'Osso Buco' With Chicken

Serving: 6 | Prep: 20mins | Cook: 5hours | Ready in: 5hours20mins

Ingredients

- 2 Tbsp. flour
- 1/2 tsp. ground black pepper
- 6 bone-in skinless chicken thighs (2 lb.)
- 2 Tbsp. olive oil
- 1/2 cup fat-free reduced-sodium chicken broth
- 1 can (14.5-oz.) diced tomatoes, undrained
- 1 tsp. zest and 1 Tbsp. juice from 1 lemon
- 1 tsp. dried thyme leaves
- 1 cup each chopped carrots and celery
- 1 cup chopped onions
- 6 cloves garlic, minced
- 2 Tbsp. MINUTE Tapioca

Direction

- Combine flour and pepper in shallow dish. Add chicken, 1 thigh at a time, turning to evenly coat each thigh with flour mixture.
- Heat oil in large skillet on medium heat. Add chicken; cook 5 min. on each side or until evenly browned on both sides. Remove chicken from skillet; cover to keep warm.
- Add broth to skillet; cook 2 min., stirring constantly to remove browned bits from bottom of skillet. Remove from heat. Stir in tomatoes, lemon zest, lemon juice and thyme.
- Place carrots, celery, onions and garlic in slow cooker sprayed with cooking spray; sprinkle with tapioca. Top with chicken. Pour broth mixture over chicken; cover with lid.
- Cook on LOW 5 to 6 hours (or on HIGH 2-1/2 to 3 hours).

Nutrition Information

- Calories: 250
- Protein: 23 g
- Saturated Fat: 2.5 g
- Sodium: 250 mg

- Total Carbohydrate: 0 g
- Sugar: 0 g
- Cholesterol: 115 mg
- Fiber: 3 g
- Total Fat: 12 g

310. Slow Cooker BBQ Chicken Stir Fry

Serving: 8 | Prep: 15mins | Cook: 6hours | Ready in: 6hours15mins

Ingredients

- 1 can (20 oz.) pineapple chunks in juice, undrained
- 1/2 cup reduced-sodium soy sauce
- 1 tsp. ground ginger
- 2 cloves garlic, minced
- 3/4 cup KRAFT Original Barbecue Sauce, divided
- 4 lb. mixed bone-in chicken pieces
- 2 Tbsp. cornstarch
- 1/4 cup water
- 1 pkg. (16 oz.) frozen Asian-style stir-fry vegetables
- 4 cups hot cooked long-grain white rice

Direction

- Drain pineapple, reserving juice. Mix reserved juice with soy sauce, ginger, garlic and 1/2 cup barbecue sauce in slow cooker.
- Top with chicken; cover with lid.
- Cook on LOW 6 to 8 hours (or on HIGH 5 hours). About 35 min. before serving, mix cornstarch and water. Add to slow cooker with vegetables, pineapple chunks and remaining barbecue sauce; stir. Cook 30 min. or until heated through.
- Serve with rice.

Nutrition Information

- Calories: 450
- Protein: 30 g
- Saturated Fat: 3.5 g
- Cholesterol: 80 mg
- Total Fat: 13 g
- Total Carbohydrate: 0 g
- Sodium: 970 mg
- Fiber: 2 g
- Sugar: 0 g

311. Slow Cooker Mini Chicken Pot Pies

Serving: 4 | Prep: 5mins | Cook: 4hours | Ready in: 4hours5mins

Ingredients

- 1 pkt. (7.5 oz) OSCAR MAYER CARVING BOARD Rotisserie Seasoned Chicken Breast
- 1/3 cup chopped carrot
- 1/3 cup chopped celery
- 1/3 cup chopped onion
- 1 cup chicken broth
- 1/4 cup flour
- 2 Tbsp. butter
- 1/4 tsp. rosemary
- 1/4 tsp. thyme
- seasonings to taste
- 1 sheet (1/2 of 17.3-oz. pkg.), frozen puff pastry, thawed

Direction

- Combine all ingredients except dough crust into slow cooker and cook on low for about 4 hours or high for 2.
- Pour chicken pot pie filling into four separate cocottes or ramekins.
- Cut puff pastry sheet into 4 pieces. Cover each cocotte with a piece of puff sheet and pinch sides to close. Create vents with a fork.
- Bake on 350 for 20 minutes (or until pastry puff crusts are a golden brown).
- Remove from heat, let cool and enjoy!

Nutrition Information

- Calories: 0 g
- Cholesterol: 0 g
- Sodium: 0 g
- Total Fat: 0 g
- Total Carbohydrate: 0 g
- Fiber: 0 g
- Saturated Fat: 0 g
- Sugar: 0 g
- Protein: 0 g

Nutrition Information

- Calories: 470
- Fiber: 3 g
- Protein: 27 g
- Total Fat: 6 g
- Total Carbohydrate: 0 g
- Sodium: 520 mg
- Sugar: 0 g
- Cholesterol: 65 mg
- Saturated Fat: 1.5 g

312. Slow Cooker Pineapple BBQ Chicken

Serving: 8 | Prep: 15mins | Cook: 6hours | Ready in: 6hours15mins

Ingredients

- 1-1/4 cups HEINZ BBQ Sauce Hawaii Style Sweet & Smoky, divided
- 1 cup fat-free reduced-sodium chicken broth
- 1 broiler-fryer chicken (4 lb.), cut up, skin removed
- 2 large red peppers, coarsely chopped
- 1 onion, chopped
- 1 can (20 oz.) pineapple chunks in juice, drained
- 8 cups cooked long-grain white rice

Direction

- Reserve 1/4 cup barbecue sauce for later use. Mix remaining barbecue sauce with chicken broth in slow cooker sprayed with cooking spray until blended.
- Top with all remaining ingredients except rice; cover with lid.
- Cook on LOW 6 to 8 hours (or on HIGH 4 hours).
- Serve chicken mixture over rice topped with reserved barbecue sauce.

313. Smart Choice Swiss 'n Chicken Casserole

Serving: 0 | Prep: 15mins | Cook: 40mins | Ready in: 55mins

Ingredients

- 4 cups chopped cooked chicken
- 2 cups whole wheat croutons
- 1-1/2 cups KRAFT Shredded Swiss Cheese
- 2/3 cup MIRACLE WHIP Light Dressing
- 1/2 cup fat-free milk
- 4 stalks celery, sliced
- 1/4 cup chopped onions

Direction

- Heat oven to 350°F.
- Combine ingredients.
- Spoon into 2-qt. casserole sprayed with cooking spray.
- Bake 40 min. or until heated through.

Nutrition Information

- Calories: 410
- Total Fat: 20 g
- Total Carbohydrate: 0 g
- Sugar: 0 g
- Saturated Fat: 7 g

- Protein: 38 g
- Cholesterol: 115 mg
- Sodium: 570 mg
- Fiber: 3 g

314. Smothered Chicken With Brown Rice

Serving: 6 | Prep: 15mins | Cook: 30mins | Ready in: 45mins

Ingredients

- 6 slices OSCAR MAYER Bacon, chopped
- 6 small boneless skinless chicken breasts (1-1/2 lb.)
- 1 large onion, chopped
- 6 large carrot s (1-1/2 lb.), thinly sliced
- 1 can (14-1/2 oz.) fat-free reduced-sodium chicken broth, divided
- 4 oz. (1/2 of 8-oz. pkg.) PHILADELPHIA Neufchatel Cheese, cubed
- 3 cups hot cooked brown rice

Direction

- Cook and stir bacon in large nonstick skillet on medium heat 5 min. or until crisp. Remove bacon from skillet; drain on paper towels. Discard drippings from skillet. Add chicken, cook 1 to 2 min. on each side or until browned; cover. Cook 8 min. or until chicken is done (165°F). Transfer chicken to plate; cover to keep warm.
- Add onions to skillet; cook 5 min. or until tender. Stir in carrots and 3/4 cup broth; cover. Simmer 10 min. or until vegetables are tender. Reserve 1/3 cup vegetables.
- Place remaining broth, reserved 1/3 cup vegetables and Neufchatel in blender; blend until smooth. Add sauce and reserved chicken to vegetables in skillet; cover. Cook 2 min. or until heated through. Spoon rice onto serving plate; top with chicken mixture, sauce and bacon.

Nutrition Information

- Calories: 390
- Sugar: 10 g
- Cholesterol: 85 mg
- Fiber: 5 g
- Total Fat: 11 g
- Protein: 34 g
- Saturated Fat: 4.5 g
- Sodium: 530 mg
- Total Carbohydrate: 36 g

315. Soba Noodles Recipe

Serving: 0 | Prep: 15mins | Cook: 20mins | Ready in: 35mins

Ingredients

- 3.2 oz. (1/4 of 12.8-oz. pkg.) soba noodles, uncooked
- 1/3 cup . A.1. Bold & Spicy Sauce
- 1/4 cup water
- 3 Tbsp. creamy peanut butter
- 2 tsp. brown sugar
- 1/2 tsp. Sriracha sauce (hot chili sauce)
- 2 Tbsp. olive oil
- 1 lb. boneless skinless chicken breasts, cut into bite-size pieces
- 1 red pepper, cut into thin strips
- 1 cup halved pea pods
- 1 jar (7 oz.) baby corn, drained

Direction

- Cook noodles as directed on package. Meanwhile, mix next 5 ingredients until well blended. Drain noodles.
- Heat oil in large skillet on medium-high heat. Add chicken; cook 4 min., stirring frequently. Stir in peppers; cook and stir 2 min. Add pea pods and corn; cook 2 min. or until pea pods are crisp-tender, stirring frequently. Stir in

sauce; cook and stir 2 to 3 min. or until chicken is done and mixture is heated through.
- Drain noodles. Add to ingredients in skillet; toss to coat.

Nutrition Information

- Calories: 440
- Cholesterol: 65 mg
- Sugar: 0 g
- Sodium: 520 mg
- Fiber: 3 g
- Total Carbohydrate: 0 g
- Protein: 34 g
- Total Fat: 16 g
- Saturated Fat: 3 g

316. Southwest Chicken Panini

Serving: 0 | Prep: 10mins | Cook: | Ready in: 10mins

Ingredients

- 1 flour tortilla (6 inch)
- 1 Tbsp. KRAFT Chipotle Aioli
- 4 slices OSCAR MAYER Deli Fresh Rotisserie Seasoned Chicken Breast
- 1 KRAFT Big Slice Colby Jack Cheese Slice
- 1/4 cup red pepper strips
- 2 Tbsp. chopped fresh cilantro

Direction

- Heat panini grill sprayed with cooking spray.
- Spread tortilla with aioli.
- Layer remaining ingredients on half of the tortilla; fold tortilla in half.
- Grill 2 to 3 min. or until golden brown.

Nutrition Information

- Calories: 300
- Sodium: 860 mg
- Total Carbohydrate: 18 g
- Fiber: 1 g
- Protein: 14 g
- Sugar: 1 g
- Cholesterol: 45 mg
- Total Fat: 20 g
- Saturated Fat: 7 g

317. Southwest Chicken Skewers

Serving: 4 | Prep: 30mins | Cook: | Ready in: 30mins

Ingredients

- 1 lb. boneless skinless chicken breasts, cut into 1-1/2-inch cubes
- 1/2 lb. fresh mushrooms
- 1 small each zucchini and yellow squash, cut into 1-inch-thick slices
- 1 small red pepper, cut into 1-inch pieces
- 1/2 red onion, cut into 1-inch chunks
- 1 pkg. (8-oz. tub) PHILADELPHIA Cream Cheese Spread
- 2 Tbsp. milk
- 1/2 oz. (1/2 of 1-oz. pkg.) TACO BELL® Reduced Sodium Taco Seasoning Mix (1 Tbsp. plus 1-1/2 tsp.)
- 2 cups hot cooked long-grain brown rice

Direction

- Heat grill to medium heat.
- Thread chicken onto 4 skewers alternately with vegetables.
- Grill 10 to 15 min. or until chicken is done, turning occasionally. Meanwhile, cook and stir cream cheese spread, milk and seasoning mix in saucepan on medium heat 2 to 3 min. or until heated through and well blended.
- Spoon rice onto plates; top with kabobs and sauce.

Nutrition Information

- Calories: 430
- Fiber: 4 g
- Sugar: 0 g
- Sodium: 480 mg
- Protein: 33 g
- Total Fat: 18 g
- Saturated Fat: 9 g
- Total Carbohydrate: 0 g
- Cholesterol: 105 mg

318. Southwest Chicken With Corn & Rice

Serving: 0 | Prep: 15mins | Cook: 35mins | Ready in: 50mins

Ingredients

- 2 cups instant white rice, uncooked
- 1 can (14-1/2-oz.) chicken broth
- 1 can (11 oz.) corn with sweet peppers, undrained
- 1/2 cup water
- 1 tsp. chili powder, divided
- 1/3 cup SHAKE 'N BAKE Chicken Coating Mix
- 4 boneless skinless chicken breasts (1-1/4 lb.)
- 1/2 cup KRAFT Shredded Cheddar Cheese

Direction

- Preheat oven to 375°F. Mix rice, broth, corn, water and 1/2 tsp. of the chili powder in 13x9-inch baking dish.
- Measure 1/3 cup coating mix and place in plastic bag with remaining 1/2 tsp. chili powder; use to evenly coat chicken as directed on package. Place chicken over rice mixture.
- Bake 30 min. Sprinkle with cheese; bake an additional 5 min. or until cheese is melted and chicken is cooked through (170°F).

Nutrition Information

- Calories: 480
- Sodium: 1070 mg
- Protein: 42 g
- Sugar: 0 g
- Saturated Fat: 3.5 g
- Cholesterol: 90 mg
- Total Fat: 9 g
- Fiber: 2 g
- Total Carbohydrate: 0 g

319. Southwestern Chicken With Black Beans & Rice

Serving: 0 | Prep: 25mins | Cook: | Ready in: 25mins

Ingredients

- 2 Tbsp. KRAFT Zesty Italian Dressing
- 2 small boneless skinless chicken breasts (1/2 lb.)
- 1/2 cup chopped onions
- 1 can (14.5 oz.) stewed tomatoes, undrained
- 1 cup rinsed canned black beans
- 3 slices OSCAR MAYER Deli Fresh Honey Ham, chopped
- 1/2 tsp. hot pepper sauce
- 1 cup instant brown rice, cooked

Direction

- Heat dressing in large skillet on medium-high heat. Add chicken and onions; cook 4 min., turning chicken and stirring onions after 2 min.
- Add tomatoes, beans, ham and hot sauce; stir. Simmer on low heat 10 min. or until chicken is done (165°F), turning chicken after 5 min.
- Serve over hot rice.

Nutrition Information

- Calories: 530
- Sodium: 980 mg
- Saturated Fat: 2 g

- Total Fat: 9 g
- Cholesterol: 75 mg
- Sugar: 0 g
- Protein: 40 g
- Total Carbohydrate: 0 g
- Fiber: 12 g

- Calories: 0 g
- Cholesterol: 0 g
- Fiber: 0 g
- Total Carbohydrate: 0 g
- Total Fat: 0 g
- Saturated Fat: 0 g
- Protein: 0 g
- Sugar: 0 g
- Sodium: 0 g

320. Southwestern Corn Bread Chicken

Serving: 6 | Prep: 10mins | Cook: 20mins | Ready in: 30mins

Ingredients

- 1 Tbsp. canola oil
- 1 lb. ground chicken
- 1/2 cup chopped onion (1 small onion)
- 1 red bell pepper, chopped
- 1/2 cup canned corn
- 1/3 cup black beans, drained and rinsed
- 1 Roma tomato, chopped
- 1-1/2 cups water
- 1/4 cup butter
- 1 pkg. (6 oz.) STOVE TOP Cornbread Stuffing Mix

Direction

- In a large skillet, heat canola oil over medium heat. Add chicken and onion and cook until onion is translucent. Stir with a large spatula breaking up the ground chicken.
- Add bell pepper, corn, black beans and tomato and stir, cooking for 8 minutes. Remove from heat and set aside.
- In a separate large saucepan, boil 1 ½ cups water and butter. Stir in stuffing mix and cover.
- Remove from heat. Let stand 5 minutes and add to the chicken mixture. Stir to combine ingredients and serve.

Nutrition Information

321. Southwestern Ranch Chicken Salad

Serving: 0 | Prep: 15mins | Cook: | Ready in: 15mins

Ingredients

- 1 whole wheat tortilla (6 inch), cut in half, then into 1/4-inch-wide strips
- 1/4 cup KRAFT Lite Ranch Dressing
- dash ground cumin
- 1 pkg. (10 oz.) salad greens
- 1 pkg. (6 oz.) OSCAR MAYER CARVING BOARD Southwestern Seasoned Chicken Breast Strips
- 1/2 cup chopped tomato es
- 1/4 cup KRAFT Mexican Style 2% Milk Finely Shredded Four Cheese

Direction

- Place tortilla strips on microwaveable plate sprayed with cooking spray. Microwave on HIGH 1 min. Meanwhile, mix dressing and cumin.
- Toss greens with chicken, tomatoes, cheese and dressing mixture in large bowl; top with tortilla strips.

Nutrition Information

- Calories: 140
- Sodium: 580 mg
- Fiber: 2 g

- Sugar: 1 g
- Total Fat: 6 g
- Cholesterol: 40 mg
- Saturated Fat: 1.5 g
- Total Carbohydrate: 10 g
- Protein: 13 g

322. Spatchcock BBQ Chicken With Grilled Green Bean Salad

Serving: 8 | Prep: 35mins | Cook: 35mins | Ready in: 1hours10mins

Ingredients

- 1 whole chicken (4 lb.)
- 1/4 cup oil, divided
- 1 Tbsp. smoked paprika, divided
- 1 cup HEINZ BBQ Sauce Kentucky Bourbon Style Rich & Savory, divided
- 1/2 lb. fresh green beans, trimmed
- 1 small red onion, sliced, separated into rings
- 1 tomato, seeded, chopped
- 1 cup frozen corn, thawed
- 1 Tbsp. HEINZ Apple Cider Vinegar

Direction

- Heat greased grill to medium heat.
- Place chicken, breast side down, on cutting board with legs toward you. Use kitchen shears to cut along each side of backbone; remove and discard bone. Open up chicken like a book; turn over. Press firmly between breasts to flatten.
- Reserve 2 Tbsp. oil for later use; brush remaining oil, then rub 2 tsp. paprika evenly onto both sides of chicken.
- Place chicken, breast side down, on grill grate; top with weight. (See tip.) Grill 5 min. Remove weight; turn chicken. Grill (without weight) 35 min. or until chicken is done. Brush chicken with 1/2 cup barbecue sauce; grill 5 min. Remove from grill, brush with 1/4 cup of the remaining barbecue sauce. Cover with foil to keep warm.
- Toss beans and onions with remaining oil and paprika in disposable foil pan sprayed with cooking spray. Grill 5 min. or until vegetables are crisp-tender. Remove from grill.
- Cut beans and onions in half; place in medium bowl. Add remaining ingredients, including remaining barbecue sauce; mix lightly. Serve with chicken.

Nutrition Information

- Calories: 400
- Saturated Fat: 4.5 g
- Cholesterol: 95 mg
- Sodium: 480 mg
- Protein: 31 g
- Fiber: 3 g
- Sugar: 0 g
- Total Carbohydrate: 0 g
- Total Fat: 22 g

323. Speedy Sweet & Spicy Chicken Stir Fry

Serving: 4 | Prep: 25mins | Cook: | Ready in: 25mins

Ingredients

- 1/4 cup KRAFT Classic CATALINA Dressing
- 1 Tbsp. soy sauce
- 1/4 tsp. crushed red pepper
- 1 lb. boneless skinless chicken breasts, cut into strips
- 1 cup snow peas
- 1 red bell pepper, cut into strips
- 1 Tbsp. oil
- 2 cups hot cooked long-grain white rice

Direction

- Mix first 3 ingredients. Add 1 Tbsp. dressing mixture to chicken; toss to coat. Let stand 5 min.
- Stir-fry chicken and vegetables in hot oil in nonstick wok or large skillet on medium-high heat 4 min. or until chicken is done.
- Add remaining dressing mixture; mix well. Simmer on medium-low heat 2 min. Serve over rice.

Nutrition Information

- Calories: 330
- Protein: 28 g
- Cholesterol: 65 mg
- Fiber: 2 g
- Sugar: 0 g
- Total Carbohydrate: 0 g
- Total Fat: 10 g
- Sodium: 510 mg
- Saturated Fat: 2 g

324. Spicy BBQ Chicken Wings Recipe

Serving: 8 | Prep: 30mins | Cook: | Ready in: 30mins

Ingredients

- 2 lb. chicken wings, split at joints, tips removed
- 2 tsp. garlic powder
- 1/2 cup KRAFT Hot 'n Spicy Wing Barbecue Sauce
- 1 green onion, sliced

Direction

- Heat grill to medium-high heat.
- Season chicken with garlic powder.
- Grill 15 min., turning occasionally. Brush lightly with some of the barbecue sauce. Continue grilling 4 to 5 min. or until chicken is done, turning and brushing frequently with remaining barbecue sauce.
- Place chicken on platter; top with onions.

Nutrition Information

- Calories: 160
- Saturated Fat: 2.5 g
- Total Carbohydrate: 6 g
- Sugar: 5 g
- Total Fat: 9 g
- Sodium: 220 mg
- Cholesterol: 75 mg
- Fiber: 0 g
- Protein: 13 g

325. Spicy Bacon Pizza

Serving: 6 | Prep: 20mins | Cook: 10mins | Ready in: 30mins

Ingredients

- 1 can (13.8 oz.) refrigerated pizza crust
- 1/4 cup KRAFT Light Mayo Reduced Fat Mayonnaise
- 1/2 cup KRAFT Three Cheese Ranch Dressing, divided
- 1-1/2 cups KRAFT Shredded Pepper Jack Cheese
- 1-1/2 cups finely chopped cooked chicken
- 8 slices OSCAR MAYER Bacon, cooked, crumbled
- 1-1/2 cups finely shredded lettuce
- 1 tomato, finely chopped

Direction

- Heat oven to 400°F.
- Unroll pizza dough on baking sheet sprayed with cooking spray; press into 15x10-inch rectangle. Bake 10 min.

- Mix mayo and 1/3 cup dressing until blended; spread onto crust. Top with half the cheese, chicken, remaining cheese and bacon.
- Bake 5 min. or until crust is golden brown and cheese is melted. Top with lettuce and tomatoes; drizzle with remaining dressing.

Nutrition Information

- Calories: 500
- Total Carbohydrate: 35 g
- Sugar: 6 g
- Fiber: 1 g
- Saturated Fat: 10 g
- Total Fat: 29 g
- Sodium: 1140 mg
- Protein: 25 g
- Cholesterol: 70 mg

326. Spicy Buffalo Style Chicken Salad

Serving: 4 | Prep: 15mins | Cook: | Ready in: 15mins

Ingredients

- 1 pkg. (6 oz.) OSCAR MAYER CARVING BOARD Hot Buffalo Chicken Breast Strips
- 2 tsp. hot pepper sauce
- 1 pkg. (10 oz.) torn salad greens
- 2 stalks celery, chopped
- 1 carrot, chopped
- 2 green onions, sliced
- 1/2 cup KRAFT ROKA Blue Cheese Dressing

Direction

- Toss chicken with pepper sauce.
- Combine remaining ingredients in large bowl.
- Add chicken; mix lightly.

Nutrition Information

- Calories: 200
- Fiber: 3 g
- Sugar: 0 g
- Total Fat: 14 g
- Saturated Fat: 2.5 g
- Cholesterol: 35 mg
- Total Carbohydrate: 0 g
- Sodium: 670 mg
- Protein: 13 g

327. Spicy Chicken Mac And Cheese Skillet

Serving: 0 | Prep: 30mins | Cook: | Ready in: 30mins

Ingredients

- 1 pkg. (7-1/4 oz.) KRAFT Macaroni & Cheese Dinner
- 1 Tbsp. olive oil
- 1 lb. boneless skinless chicken breasts, cut into bite-size pieces
- 1 can (14-1/2 oz.) diced tomatoes and green chiles, drained
- 1 can (14-1/2 oz.) diced tomatoes, drained
- 1 can (10-3/4 oz.) condensed cream of chicken soup
- 1/2 cup KRAFT Mexican Style Finely Shredded Four Cheese

Direction

- Prepare Dinner as directed on package.
- Meanwhile, heat oil in large skillet on medium-high heat. Add chicken; cook and stir 5 min. or until lightly browned. Stir in tomatoes and soup; cook on medium heat 5 min. or until chicken is done, stirring occasionally.
- Add Dinner; stir until blended. Sprinkle with cheese; cover. Cook 5 min. or until cheese is melted.

Nutrition Information

- Calories: 370
- Total Carbohydrate: 0 g
- Sodium: 1020 mg
- Protein: 20 g
- Saturated Fat: 5 g
- Cholesterol: 55 mg
- Fiber: 2 g
- Sugar: 0 g
- Total Fat: 18 g

328. Spicy Chicken Skillet Stew

Serving: 0 | Prep: 20mins | Cook: 10mins | Ready in: 30mins

Ingredients

- 1/2 cup KRAFT Lite House Italian Dressing, divided
- 1 lb. boneless skinless chicken breasts, cut into bite-size pieces
- 1 cup chopped onions
- 2 sweet potatoes, peeled, cut into 3/4-inch cubes
- 1 chipotle pepper in adobo sauce, chopped
- 1 tsp. chili powder
- 1 can (14 oz.) fat-free reduced-sodium chicken broth
- 1 can (15 oz.) chickpeas (garbanzo beans), undrained
- 1 pkg. (6 oz.) OSCAR MAYER Smoked Ham, chopped
- 1/4 cup chopped fresh parsley

Direction

- Heat 1/4 cup dressing in large deep skillet on medium-high heat. Add chicken; cook 3 min. or until lightly browned, stirring occasionally. Remove from skillet; cover to keep warm.
- Cook onions in remaining dressing in same skillet 3 min. or until crisp-tender, stirring occasionally. Add next 4 ingredients; bring to boil. Cover. Reduce heat to medium-low; simmer 8 to 10 min. or until potatoes are tender.
- Add beans, ham and chicken; cover. Simmer 5 min. or until chicken is done. Stir in parsley just before serving.

Nutrition Information

- Calories: 280
- Total Carbohydrate: 0 g
- Cholesterol: 60 mg
- Sugar: 0 g
- Protein: 26 g
- Sodium: 950 mg
- Fiber: 5 g
- Saturated Fat: 1 g
- Total Fat: 4 g

329. Spicy Chicken Stir Fry

Serving: 0 | Prep: 25mins | Cook: | Ready in: 25mins

Ingredients

- 1 lb. boneless skinless chicken breasts, cut into thin strips
- 1/2 cup KRAFT Asian Toasted Sesame Dressing, divided
- 1 tsp. hot pepper sauce
- 1 pkg. (16 oz.) frozen stir-fry vegetables, thawed, drained
- 1 can (8 oz.) pineapple chunks in juice, drained
- 1/4 cup PLANTERS Lightly Salted COCKTAIL Peanuts
- 2 cups hot cooked instant brown rice

Direction

- Toss chicken with 1/4 cup dressing and hot sauce; set aside. Heat remaining dressing in large nonstick skillet on medium-high heat. Add vegetables; stir-fry 1 min. Add chicken mixture; stir-fry 4 to 5 min. or until chicken is done.

- Stir in pineapple and nuts; cook 5 min. or until heated through, stirring occasionally.
- Serve over rice.

Nutrition Information

- Calories: 410
- Cholesterol: 65 mg
- Sugar: 0 g
- Fiber: 5 g
- Sodium: 500 mg
- Saturated Fat: 2.5 g
- Total Fat: 14 g
- Total Carbohydrate: 0 g
- Protein: 31 g

330. Spicy Hot Wing Recipe

Serving: 8 | Prep: 15mins | Cook: 30mins | Ready in: 45mins

Ingredients

- 2 lb. chicken wings, split at joints, tips removed
- 1/2 cup KRAFT Real Mayo Mayonnaise
- 2 Tbsp. Buffalo wing sauce
- 1 tsp. garlic powder
- 1/2 cup KRAFT Homestyle Ranch Dressing & Dip

Direction

- Heat oven to 450°F.
- Place wings in single layer in shallow foil-lined pan.
- Bake 20 min. or until browned. Meanwhile, mix mayo, wing sauce and garlic powder until blended.
- Brush mayo mixture generously onto both sides of wings. Bake 10 min.
- Serve with dressing.

Nutrition Information

- Calories: 310
- Saturated Fat: 5 g
- Protein: 13 g
- Cholesterol: 50 mg
- Total Carbohydrate: 2 g
- Sugar: 1 g
- Fiber: 0 g
- Sodium: 250 mg
- Total Fat: 27 g

331. Spicy Island Chicken

Serving: 6 | Prep: 15mins | Cook: 1hours40mins | Ready in: 1hours55mins

Ingredients

- 1/2 cup LEA & PERRINS Worcestershire Sauce
- 1/4 cup orange juice
- 2 Tbsp. olive oil
- 1 Tbsp. finely chopped jalapeño peppers
- 1/4 tsp. ground allspice
- 1 broiler-fryer chicken (3-1/2 lb.), cut up

Direction

- Mix all ingredients except chicken until blended. Reserve 1/4 cup Worcestershire sauce mixture. Pour remaining Worcestershire sauce mixture over chicken in shallow dish; turn to evenly coat both sides of all chicken pieces.
- Refrigerate 1 hour to marinate.
- Heat grill to medium heat. Remove chicken from marinade; discard marinade.
- Grill chicken 40 min. or until done (165°F), turning and brushing occasionally with reserved Worcestershire sauce mixture for the last 15 min.

Nutrition Information

- Calories: 270
- Protein: 28 g
- Sodium: 170 mg
- Total Carbohydrate: 0 g
- Total Fat: 16 g
- Saturated Fat: 4 g
- Fiber: 0 g
- Sugar: 0 g
- Cholesterol: 90 mg

332. Spicy Noodles In Peanut Sauce

Serving: 6 | Prep: 25mins | Cook: | Ready in: 25mins

Ingredients

- 1 cup fat-free reduced-sodium chicken broth
- 1/2 cup KRAFT Original Barbecue Sauce
- 1 tsp. crushed red pepper
- 1 cup PLANTERS Dry Roasted Peanuts, chopped, divided
- 2 tsp. oil, divided
- 1-1/2 lb. boneless skinless chicken breasts, cut into thin strips
- 1 onion, sliced
- 1 red bell pepper, cut into strips
- 1/2 lb. spaghetti, uncooked
- 1/4 cup chopped fresh cilantro

Direction

- Blend broth, barbecue sauce, crushed pepper and 3/4 cup nuts in blender until smooth.
- Heat 1 tsp. oil in large nonstick skillet on medium-high heat. Add chicken; cook 5 min. or until done, stirring occasionally. Remove from skillet; cover to keep warm.
- Add remaining oil to skillet. Add onions and bell peppers; cook and stir 5 min. or until crisp-tender. Meanwhile, cook spaghetti as directed on package, omitting salt.
- Drain spaghetti. Add to ingredients in skillet along with the chicken. Remove from heat. Add peanut sauce; mix lightly. Sprinkle with cilantro. Serve topped with remaining nuts.

Nutrition Information

- Calories: 480
- Total Carbohydrate: 0 g
- Fiber: 4 g
- Sodium: 600 mg
- Sugar: 0 g
- Protein: 36 g
- Total Fat: 17 g
- Cholesterol: 65 mg
- Saturated Fat: 3 g

333. Spicy Stir Fry Chicken

Serving: 4 | Prep: 30mins | Cook: | Ready in: 30mins

Ingredients

- 1 lb. boneless skinless chicken breasts, cut into 3/4-inch pieces
- 1 Tbsp. dry sherry
- 2 tsp. cornstarch, divided
- 1/2 cup KRAFT Asian Toasted Sesame Dressing
- 1 Tbsp. soy sauce
- 1/8 tsp. hot pepper sauce
- 1 Tbsp. oil
- 2 tsp. grated gingerroot
- 2 cloves garlic, minced
- 4 green onions, cut into 1/2-inch pieces
- 1/2 cup PLANTERS Dry Roasted Peanuts
- 2 cups hot cooked long-grain white rice

Direction

- Mix chicken, sherry and 1 tsp. cornstarch in bowl; let stand 15 min.
- Meanwhile, mix dressing, soy sauce, pepper sauce and remaining cornstarch until blended.
- Heat oil in wok or large skillet on medium-high heat. Add ginger and garlic; cook and stir

15 sec. Add chicken mixture; cook and stir 8 to 10 min. or until chicken is done. Push chicken to side of wok.
- Stir dressing mixture; add to center of wok. Cook and stir until thickened and bubbly. Add onions and nuts; stir to coat with sauce. Cook and stir 1 to 2 min. or until heated through. Serve immediately with rice.

Nutrition Information

- Calories: 480
- Sugar: 8 g
- Total Fat: 22 g
- Cholesterol: 65 mg
- Saturated Fat: 3.5 g
- Total Carbohydrate: 36 g
- Protein: 32 g
- Fiber: 3 g
- Sodium: 770 mg

334. Spicy Stuffed Grilled Chicken Breasts

Serving: 4 | Prep: 45mins | Cook: 10mins | Ready in: 55mins

Ingredients

- 4 medium boneless skinless chicken breasts, trimmed
- 1/4 cup KRAFT Zesty Italian Dressing
- 4 oz. (1/2 8 oz. pkg.) PHILADELPHIA Cream Cheese, softened
- 1/2 cup KRAFT Shredded Pepper Jack Cheese
- 1/4 cup canned diced green chiles
- 2 Tbsp. canned jalapeño peppers, diced
- 1 cup diced fresh tomatoes
- 1/4 cup pickled jalapeño peppers

Direction

- Heat grill to medium high heat
- Cut lengthwise slit in thickest side of each chicken breast, being careful to not cut through to opposite side.
- Place the chicken in a zipper bag, and pour the Italian dressing over the chicken. Marinate for 20-30 minutes.
- In a medium bowl, mix together the cream cheese, pepper jack, green chilies, and jalapeños. Remove the chicken from the marinade. Discard bag and marinade. Spoon the cheese mixture into each of the chicken breasts, being careful not to overfill; secure with wooden toothpicks.
- Grill the chicken 8-10 minutes per side, or until done(165°F).

Nutrition Information

- Calories: 0 g
- Sodium: 0 g
- Cholesterol: 0 g
- Fiber: 0 g
- Protein: 0 g
- Saturated Fat: 0 g
- Total Carbohydrate: 0 g
- Sugar: 0 g
- Total Fat: 0 g

335. Spicy Vampire Bat Wings

Serving: 12 | Prep: 20mins | Cook: 1hours10mins | Ready in: 1hours30mins

Ingredients

- 1 Tbsp. chili powder
- 1 Tbsp. minced garlic
- 1 tsp. ground red pepper (cayenne)
- 6 Tbsp. lime juice, divided
- 6 Tbsp. chopped canned chipotle peppers in adobo sauce, divided
- 12 whole chicken wings (3 lb.)
- 2/3 cup KRAFT Original Barbecue Sauce

- 1 cup BREAKSTONE'S or KNUDSEN Sour Cream
- 1 green onion, sliced
- 2 tsp. lime zest

Direction

- Mix chili powder, garlic, ground red pepper, and 5 Tbsp. each lime juice and chipotle peppers until blended; pour over chicken in large shallow dish. Turn to evenly coat both sides of wings. Refrigerate 30 min. to marinate, turning wings after 15 min. Meanwhile, mix remaining chipotle peppers and barbecue sauce until blended.
- Heat oven to 400°F. Remove wings from marinade; place in single layer on baking sheet sprayed with cooking spray. Discard marinade.
- Bake wings 35 to 40 min. or until wings are done, turning after 20 min. Brush with half the barbecue sauce mixture; bake 5 min., turning and brushing with remaining barbecue sauce mixture after 3 min.
- Combine sour cream, onions, zest and remaining lime juice. Serve with the wings.

Nutrition Information

- Calories: 150
- Total Carbohydrate: 8 g
- Sugar: 6 g
- Protein: 9 g
- Saturated Fat: 4 g
- Cholesterol: 60 mg
- Sodium: 200 mg
- Fiber: 0 g
- Total Fat: 9 g

336. Spicy Winter Chicken Soup

Serving: 0 | Prep: 55mins | Cook: | Ready in: 55mins

Ingredients

- 1 can (14-1/2 oz.) fat-free reduced-sodium chicken broth
- 10 dried guajillo chiles, stemmed, seeded and hydrated
- 1 small onion, quartered
- 1 clove garlic
- 1/4 cup KRAFT Zesty Italian Dressing
- 3 lb. chicken pieces, skinned
- 2 ears corn on the cob, cut into thirds
- 1/4 cup epazote leaves
- 3 zucchini, ends removed, cut in quarters
- 1 cup fresh green beans, trimmed
- 1 lime, cut into 6 wedges

Direction

- Blend broth, chiles, onions and garlic in blender until smooth. Press mixture through fine-mesh strainer into bowl.
- Heat dressing in large skillet on medium heat. Add chicken; cook 5 min. on each side or until evenly browned. Pour broth mixture over chicken; bring to boil. Add corn and epazote; cover. Simmer on medium-low heat 25 min., stirring occasionally. Add zucchini and beans; cook, covered, 10 min. or until chicken is done (165°F), stirring occasionally.
- Spoon into 6 soup bowls. Squeeze lime wedge over each serving.

Nutrition Information

- Calories: 240
- Protein: 25 g
- Sugar: 0 g
- Saturated Fat: 2 g
- Total Carbohydrate: 0 g
- Fiber: 4 g
- Cholesterol: 65 mg
- Total Fat: 8 g
- Sodium: 310 mg

337. Spinach Alfredo Lasagna

Serving: 12 | Prep: 25mins | Cook: 55mins | Ready in: 1hours20mins

Ingredients

- 9 whole wheat lasagna noodles, uncooked
- 2-1/4 cups CLASSICO Four Cheese Alfredo Pasta Sauce
- 3 Tbsp. lemon juice
- 1/2 tsp. black pepper
- 3 cups chopped cooked chicken breasts
- 1 pkg. (10 oz.) frozen chopped spinach, thawed, well drained
- 1 cup chopped roasted red peppers
- 3/4 cup KRAFT 2% Milk Shredded Italian* Three Cheese Blend

Direction

- Heat oven to 325°F.
- Cook noodles as directed on package, omitting salt. Meanwhile, mix Alfredo sauce, lemon juice and black pepper in medium bowl. Stir in chicken, spinach and red peppers.
- Drain noodles. Layer 3 noodles and 1/3 chicken mixture in 13X9-inch baking dish sprayed with cooking spray; repeat layers twice. Cover.
- Bake 45 to 55 min. or until heated through; uncover. Top with cheese; bake 5 min. or until melted. Let stand 15 min. before serving.

Nutrition Information

- Calories: 240
- Cholesterol: 55 mg
- Sodium: 440 mg
- Total Fat: 12 g
- Saturated Fat: 6 g
- Total Carbohydrate: 0 g
- Fiber: 2 g
- Protein: 19 g
- Sugar: 0 g

338. Stir Fry Salad With Rice

Serving: 4 | Prep: 20mins | Cook: | Ready in: 20mins

Ingredients

- 1 cup long-grain brown rice, uncooked
- 1 Tbsp. oil
- 1 lb. boneless skinless chicken breasts, cut into thin strips
- 3 cups cut-up mixed fresh vegetables (broccoli, carrots, pea pods and red peppers)
- 1/2 cup KRAFT Lite House Italian Dressing
- 2 Tbsp. soy sauce
- 1 pkg. (10 oz.) torn salad greens

Direction

- Cook rice as directed on package, omitting butter and salt.
- Meanwhile, heat oil in large skillet on medium heat. Add chicken; cook and stir 4 min. or until done. Add vegetables; cook and stir 2 min. or until vegetables are crisp-tender.
- Mix dressing and soy sauce until blended. Toss salad greens with chicken mixture and rice in large bowl. Serve with dressing mixture.

Nutrition Information

- Calories: 420
- Protein: 31 g
- Fiber: 6 g
- Total Fat: 8 g
- Saturated Fat: 1.5 g
- Sugar: 0 g
- Cholesterol: 65 mg
- Sodium: 930 mg
- Total Carbohydrate: 0 g

339. Stuffed Chicken Breasts With Parmesan

Serving: 4 | Prep: 20mins | Cook: 25mins | Ready in: 45mins

Ingredients

- 4 small boneless skinless chicken breasts (1 lb.)
- 1/4 cup KRAFT Shredded Mozzarella Cheese
- 1 slice OSCAR MAYER Baked Cooked Ham, chopped
- 1 Tbsp. finely chopped red peppers
- 1 egg
- 1/4 cup chopped fresh parsley
- 2 Tbsp. KRAFT Grated Parmesan Cheese

Direction

- Heat oven to 350°F.
- Make 2-inch-long cut in one long side of each chicken breast to form pocket; fill with mozzarella, ham and peppers. Press cut edges of pockets together to seal.
- Whisk egg in pie plate. Combine parsley and Parmesan in separate pie plate. Dip chicken, 1 breast at a time, in egg, then in parsley mixture, turning to evenly coat both sides of each breast. Place in 8-inch square baking dish sprayed with cooking spray.
- Bake 20 to 25 min. or until chicken is done (165°F).

Nutrition Information

- Calories: 190
- Sodium: 250 mg
- Fiber: 0 g
- Protein: 30 g
- Sugar: 0 g
- Saturated Fat: 2.5 g
- Total Fat: 7 g
- Cholesterol: 125 mg
- Total Carbohydrate: 0 g

340. Stuffing Topped Creamy Chicken Casserole

Serving: 6 | Prep: 10mins | Cook: 45mins | Ready in: 55mins

Ingredients

- 1-2/3 cups hot water
- 1 pkg. (6 oz.) STOVE TOP Savory Herbs Stuffing Mix
- 6 small boneless skinless chicken thighs (1-1/2 lb.)
- 1/2 tsp. each garlic powder and onion powder
- 1 can (14-3/4 oz.) cream-style corn
- 1/4 cup KRAFT Lite Creamy Caesar Dressing

Direction

- Heat oven to 425°F.
- Add hot water to stuffing mix; stir just until moistened.
- Place chicken in 13x9-inch baking dish sprayed with cooking spray; sprinkle with dry seasonings.
- Combine corn and dressing; spoon over chicken. Top with stuffing; cover.
- Bake 40 to 45 min. or until chicken is done (165°F), uncovering after 30 min.

Nutrition Information

- Calories: 240
- Fiber: 2 g
- Sugar: 0 g
- Total Fat: 4 g
- Cholesterol: 40 mg
- Sodium: 770 mg
- Total Carbohydrate: 0 g
- Saturated Fat: 0.5 g
- Protein: 16 g

341. Summer Chicken Salad

Serving: 0 | Prep: 30mins | Cook: | Ready in: 30mins

Ingredients

- 4 small boneless skinless chicken breasts (about 1 lb.)
- 1/4 lb. (4 oz.) 2% Milk VELVEETA, cut up
- 1/3 cup BREAKSTONE'S Reduced Fat or KNUDSEN Light Sour Cream
- 1/2 tsp. grated lemon zest
- 1/4 tsp. dill weed
- lettuce
- 1 medium tomato, cut into wedges
- 1/4 lb. (4 oz.) pea pods, blanched, cut in half crosswise

Direction

- Cook chicken in boiling water in covered skillet 15 to 20 minutes or until chicken is cooked through.
- Meanwhile, mix VELVEETA, sour cream, lemon zest and dill weed in medium saucepan; cook on low heat until VELVEETA is melted, stirring occasionally.
- Cut chicken into 1/4-inch-thick slices. Arrange on individual lettuce-lined plates along with tomatoes and pea pods. Drizzle with VELVEETA sauce.

Nutrition Information

- Calories: 240
- Total Carbohydrate: 0 g
- Saturated Fat: 4.5 g
- Cholesterol: 90 mg
- Sugar: 0 g
- Total Fat: 8 g
- Fiber: 1 g
- Protein: 32 g
- Sodium: 510 mg

342. Sun Dried Tomato Grilled Chicken & Vegetables

Serving: 4 | Prep: 30mins | Cook: | Ready in: 30mins

Ingredients

- 1/2 cup KRAFT Sun Dried Tomato Vinaigrette Dressing, divided
- 4 small boneless skinless chicken breasts (1 lb.)
- 1 each red and green pepper, cut into strips
- 2 cups hot cooked long-grain brown rice

Direction

- Heat grill to medium-high heat.
- Pour 1/4 dressing over combined chicken and peppers in shallow dish. Refrigerate 10 min. Remove chicken and peppers from dressing; discard dressing.
- Grill chicken and vegetables 12 to 15 min. or until chicken is done (165°F) and peppers are crisp-tender, turning and brushing occasionally with remaining dressing.
- Serve chicken mixture over rice.

Nutrition Information

- Calories: 310
- Cholesterol: 65 mg
- Total Fat: 9 g
- Protein: 28 g
- Sodium: 420 mg
- Total Carbohydrate: 0 g
- Sugar: 0 g
- Fiber: 3 g
- Saturated Fat: 1.5 g

343. Sun Dried Tomato Drumsticks

Serving: 6 | Prep: 15mins | Cook: 35mins | Ready in: 50mins

Ingredients

- 1/2 cup KRAFT Sun Dried Tomato Vinaigrette Dressing
- 1 tsp. smoked paprika
- 6 chicken drumsticks (1-1/2 lb.)

Direction

- Heat oven to 450°F.
- Mix dressing and paprika until blended. Reserve 2 Tbsp. dressing mixture; pour remaining over chicken in shallow dish. Turn to evenly coat drumsticks. Refrigerate 15 min. to marinate.
- Remove chicken from marinade; discard marinade. Place chicken in single layer in baking dish sprayed with cooking spray.
- Bake 20 to 25 min. or until done (165°F), brushing with reserved dressing mixture for the last 5 min.

Nutrition Information

- Calories: 130
- Saturated Fat: 2 g
- Cholesterol: 75 mg
- Sodium: 230 mg
- Fiber: 0 g
- Protein: 13 g
- Total Fat: 8 g
- Total Carbohydrate: 0 g
- Sugar: 0 g

344. Sunday Roasted Chicken

Serving: 12 | Prep: 30mins | Cook: 2hours | Ready in: 2hours30mins

Ingredients

- 1 large roasting chicken (6 lb.)
- 1 Tbsp. olive oil
- 1/2 cup each chopped carrots, celery and onions
- 2 jars (12 oz. each) HEINZ HomeStyle Classic Chicken Gravy

Direction

- Heat oven to 350°F.
- Brush chicken with oil. Tuck wings under chicken; place, breast side up, on rack in roasting pan.
- Combine vegetables; spoon into chicken cavity.
- Bake 1-1/2 to 2 hours or until chicken is done (165°F). Remove from oven. Let stand 10 min. before serving. Meanwhile, cook gravy in saucepan on medium-low heat until heated through, stirring occasionally.
- Remove and discard vegetables from chicken cavity. Slice chicken. Serve topped with gravy.

Nutrition Information

- Calories: 430
- Total Carbohydrate: 4 g
- Total Fat: 25 g
- Sodium: 350 mg
- Saturated Fat: 7 g
- Fiber: 0 g
- Cholesterol: 140 mg
- Protein: 44 g
- Sugar: 0.6877 g

345. Sweet And Spicy BBQ Chicken Wraps

Serving: 4 | Prep: 35mins | Cook: | Ready in: 35mins

Ingredients

- 4 small boneless skinless chicken breasts (1 lb.)
- 2 Tbsp. KRAFT Zesty Lime Vinaigrette Dressing
- 1/3 cup KRAFT Sweet & Spicy Barbecue Sauce, divided
- 2 green onions, chopped

- 2 Tbsp. chopped fresh cilantro
- 4 whole wheat tortillas (8 inch)
- 1 cup KRAFT 2% Milk Natural Colby & Monterey Jack Cheese
- 1 tomato, chopped

Direction

- Heat grill to medium heat.
- Brush chicken with dressing. Grill 6 to 8 min. on each side or until done (165°F), brushing with 3 Tbsp. of the barbecue sauce for the last few minutes. Combine remaining barbecue sauce, onions and cilantro.
- Cut chicken into strips. Spoon remaining barbecue sauce mixture down centers of tortillas; top with chicken, cheese and tomatoes. Fold in opposite sides of each tortilla, then roll up burrito style.
- Place, seam sides down, on grill grate. Grill 8 to 9 min. or until heated through and evenly browned, turning after 5 min.

Nutrition Information

- Calories: 420
- Sodium: 820 mg
- Total Fat: 13 g
- Total Carbohydrate: 0 g
- Fiber: 2 g
- Cholesterol: 85 mg
- Sugar: 0 g
- Protein: 37 g
- Saturated Fat: 4.5 g

346. Tasty Bacon Two Cheese Pizza

Serving: 6 | Prep: 20mins | Cook: 10mins | Ready in: 30mins

Ingredients

- 1 can (13.8 oz.) refrigerated pizza crust
- 1/4 cup KRAFT Mayo with Olive Oil Reduced Fat Mayonnaise
- 1/2 cup KRAFT Buttermilk Ranch Dressing, divided
- 1-1/2 cups KRAFT 2% Milk Shredded Colby & Monterey Jack Cheeses
- 1-1/2 cups finely chopped cooked chicken
- 8 slices OSCAR MAYER Bacon, cooked, crumbled
- 1-1/2 cups finely shredded lettuce
- 1 tomato, finely chopped

Direction

- Heat oven to 400°F.
- Unroll pizza dough on baking sheet sprayed with cooking spray; press into 15x10-inch rectangle. Bake 10 min.
- Mix mayo and 1/3 cup dressing until blended; spread onto crust. Top with half the cheese, chicken, remaining cheese and bacon.
- Bake 5 min. or until crust is golden brown and cheese is melted. Top with lettuce and tomatoes; drizzle with remaining dressing.

Nutrition Information

- Calories: 500
- Saturated Fat: 10 g
- Total Carbohydrate: 36 g
- Sodium: 1140 mg
- Protein: 25 g
- Total Fat: 29 g
- Sugar: 6 g
- Fiber: 1 g
- Cholesterol: 75 mg

347. The New Chicken Skillet

Serving: 0 | Prep: 20mins | Cook: 15mins | Ready in: 35mins

Ingredients

- 1 lb. boneless skinless chicken breasts, cut into bite-size pieces
- 1 Tbsp. dried oregano leaves
- 1 tsp. ancho chile pepper powder
- 2 Tbsp. olive oil
- 1 green pepper, cut into thin strips
- 2 Tbsp. sherry vinegar
- 1 can (14.5 oz.) no-salt-added diced tomatoes, undrained
- 1 cup KRAFT Mexican Style Finely Shredded Four Cheese

Direction

- Toss chicken with next 3 ingredients in large bowl until evenly coated. Cook in large nonstick skillet on medium-high heat 8 min. or until evenly browned, stirring frequently. Remove from skillet; set aside.
- Add peppers to skillet; cook and stir 2 min. Stir in vinegar; cook 1 min. or until vinegar is cooked off. Return chicken to skillet with tomatoes; stir. Cover; simmer on medium-low heat 15 min. or until heated through.
- Top with cheese; let stand, covered, 2 min. or until melted.

Nutrition Information

- Calories: 320
- Cholesterol: 90 mg
- Sodium: 300 mg
- Total Fat: 18 g
- Fiber: 3 g
- Saturated Fat: 7 g
- Total Carbohydrate: 9 g
- Sugar: 4 g
- Protein: 31 g

---

348. Three Cheese Chicken With Pasta

Serving: 0 | Prep: 10mins | Cook: 20mins | Ready in: 30mins

Ingredients

- 1/2 cup KRAFT Low-Moisture Part-Skim Mozzarella Cheese
- 1/3 cup KRAFT Grated Parmesan Cheese, divided
- 6 KRAFT Singles, divided
- 4 cups farfalle (bow-tie pasta), uncooked
- 6 small boneless skinless chicken breasts (1-1/2 lb.)
- 1 jar (24 oz.) CLASSICO Tomato and Basil Pasta Sauce, divided
- 2 Tbsp. chopped fresh parsley

Direction

- Combine mozzarella and 1/4 cup Parmesan. Cut 3 Singles in half. Cook pasta in large pot as directed on package.
- Meanwhile, cook chicken in large nonstick skillet 5 min. on each side or until done (165°F). Top each breast with 1 Tbsp. pasta sauce, about 1-1/2 Tbsp. of the mozzarella mixture and 1 Singles piece; cover skillet. Remove from heat. Let stand 3 to 5 min. or until cheese is melted.
- Drain pasta; return to pot. Stir in remaining pasta sauce and Singles; cook and stir 3 min. or until sauce is heated through and Singles are melted. Spoon onto platter; top with chicken, remaining Parmesan and parsley.

Nutrition Information

- Calories: 0 g
- Protein: 0 g
- Sodium: 0 g
- Fiber: 0 g
- Saturated Fat: 0 g
- Total Carbohydrate: 0 g
- Sugar: 0 g
- Cholesterol: 0 g
- Total Fat: 0 g

349. Three Cheese Pasta Bake

Serving: 0 | Prep: 20mins | Cook: 15mins | Ready in: 35mins

Ingredients

- 1-1/2 cups penne pasta, uncooked
- 1 pkg. (9 oz.) spinach leaves
- 1 lb. boneless skinless chicken breasts, cut into bite-size pieces
- 2 cloves garlic, minced
- 1 jar (24 oz.) CLASSICO Tomato and Basil Pasta Sauce
- 1 can (14.5 oz.) Italian-style diced tomatoes, undrained
- 1/2 cup (1/2 of 8-oz. tub) PHILADELPHIA Cream Cheese Spread
- 1/2 cup KRAFT Shredded Mozzarella Cheese
- 1/3 cup KRAFT Grated Parmesan Cheese

Direction

- Heat oven to 375°F.
- Cook pasta in large saucepan as directed on package, adding spinach to the boiling water for the last minute. Meanwhile, cook and stir chicken and garlic in large nonstick skillet sprayed with cooking spray on medium-high heat 3 min. or until chicken is browned. Stir in pasta sauce and tomatoes; bring to boil. Simmer on medium-low heat 3 min. Remove from heat; stir in cream cheese spread until melted.
- Drain pasta mixture well; return to saucepan. Stir in chicken mixture and mozzarella. Spoon into 13x9-inch baking dish; top with Parmesan.
- Bake 10 to 15 min. or until heated through.

Nutrition Information

- Calories: 410
- Sodium: 1180 mg
- Sugar: 0 g
- Cholesterol: 80 mg
- Fiber: 4 g
- Total Fat: 15 g
- Total Carbohydrate: 0 g
- Protein: 30 g
- Saturated Fat: 7 g

350. Thyme Roasted Chicken

Serving: 4 | Prep: 5mins | Cook: 35mins | Ready in: 40mins

Ingredients

- 4 small boneless skinless chicken breasts (1 lb.)
- 1/4 cup orange juice
- 2 tsp. WYLER'S Instant Bouillon Chicken Flavored Granules
- 1 Tbsp. chopped fresh thyme

Direction

- Heat oven to 350°F.
- Place chicken in shallow baking dish sprayed with cooking spray.
- Mix remaining ingredients until blended; pour over chicken.
- Bake 30 to 35 min. or until chicken is done (165°F), basting occasionally with orange juice mixture.

Nutrition Information

- Calories: 100
- Sodium: 340 mg
- Sugar: 0 g
- Saturated Fat: 0 g
- Total Carbohydrate: 0 g
- Cholesterol: 55 mg
- Fiber: 0 g
- Protein: 18 g
- Total Fat: 2 g

351. Tomato, Spinach And Chicken Pasta Bake

Serving: 0 | Prep: 25mins | Cook: 20mins | Ready in: 45mins

Ingredients

- 3 cups farfalle (bow-tie pasta), uncooked
- 2 cups tightly packed torn fresh spinach
- 1 Tbsp. oil
- 1 lb. boneless skinless chicken breasts, cut into bite-size pieces
- 2 Tbsp. chopped fresh basil
- 1 can (14-1/2 oz.) diced tomatoes, drained
- 1 cup cherry tomatoes, halved, seeded
- 2-1/2 cups CLASSICO Tomato and Basil Pasta Sauce
- 1 cup KRAFT Shredded Mozzarella Cheese with a TOUCH OF PHILADELPHIA, divided
- 1/4 cup KRAFT Shredded Parmesan Cheese

Direction

- Heat oven to 375°F.
- Cook pasta in large saucepan as directed on package, omitting salt and adding spinach to the boiling water for last minute.
- Meanwhile, heat oil in large skillet on medium-high heat. Add chicken and basil; cook and stir 3 to 4 min. or until chicken is evenly browned. Stir in tomatoes and pasta sauce; bring to boil. Simmer on medium heat 4 to 5 min. or until heated through, stirring occasionally.
- Drain pasta mixture; return to pan. Stir in chicken mixture and 1/2 cup mozzarella; spoon into 13x9-inch baking dish sprayed with cooking spray. Top with remaining mozzarella.
- Bake 20 min. or until heated through. Sprinkle with Parmesan.

Nutrition Information

- Calories: 440
- Total Carbohydrate: 0 g
- Sugar: 0 g
- Sodium: 720 mg
- Fiber: 5 g
- Cholesterol: 60 mg
- Total Fat: 12 g
- Protein: 32 g
- Saturated Fat: 4.5 g

352. Tuscan Garlic Chicken Skillet

Serving: 6 | Prep: 45mins | Cook: | Ready in: 45mins

Ingredients

- 2 Tbsp. olive oil, divided
- 6 boneless skinless chicken thighs (1-1/2 lb.)
- 1-1/2 lb. small red potatoes (about 9), cut in half
- 4 cloves garlic, minced
- 1/2 tsp. minced fresh rosemary
- 1/2 tsp. dried oregano leaves
- 1-1/4 cups fat-free reduced-sodium chicken broth
- 1/4 cup KRAFT Tuscan House Italian Dressing
- 1 cup frozen peas
- 1/4 cup KRAFT Grated Parmesan Cheese

Direction

- Heat 1 Tbsp. oil in large nonstick skillet on medium-high heat. Add chicken; cook 3 min. on each side or until thighs are evenly browned on both sides. Transfer to plate; cover to keep warm.
- Add remaining oil and potatoes, cut sides down, to skillet; cook on medium heat 7 min. on each side or until potatoes are golden brown, stirring in garlic, rosemary and oregano for the last minute. Add broth and dressing; stir to scrape browned bits from bottom of skillet. Bring to boil; cover. Simmer on medium-low heat 10 min., stirring occasionally. Return chicken to skillet; simmer

5 min. or until potatoes are tender and chicken is done (165°F). Transfer chicken and potatoes to platter with slotted spoon, reserving liquid in skillet; cover chicken and potatoes to keep warm.
- Bring liquid in skillet to boil on medium-high heat; cook 5 to 7 min. or until reduced to about 3/4 cup. Stir in peas; cook 1 min. or until heated through, stirring occasionally. Spoon over chicken and potatoes; sprinkle with cheese.

Nutrition Information

- Calories: 340
- Total Carbohydrate: 0 g
- Protein: 26 g
- Fiber: 3 g
- Total Fat: 14 g
- Cholesterol: 110 mg
- Sodium: 360 mg
- Saturated Fat: 3.5 g
- Sugar: 0 g

353. Ultimate Chicken Stroganoff

Serving: 4 | Prep: 40mins | Cook: | Ready in: 40mins

Ingredients

- 1/4 tsp. paprika
- 1 lb. boneless skinless chicken breasts, cut into bite-size pieces
- 2 Tbsp. butter, divided
- 1/2 cup chopped onions
- 2 cloves garlic, minced
- 1/2 lb. sliced fresh mushrooms
- 1/4 tsp. black pepper
- 4 oz. (1/2 of 8-oz. pkg.) PHILADELPHIA Neufchatel Cheese, cubed
- 1/2 cup fat-free reduced-sodium chicken broth
- 2 cups hot cooked noodles
- 1 Tbsp. chopped fresh parsley

Direction

- Sprinkle paprika over chicken. Melt 1 Tbsp. butter in large skillet on medium heat. Add chicken, onions and garlic; cook 5 to 6 min. or until chicken is done, stirring frequently. Remove chicken mixture from skillet; cover to keep warm.
- Melt remaining butter in skillet. Add mushrooms and pepper; cook and stir 5 to 6 min. or until mushrooms are tender. Spoon mushrooms to one side of skillet.
- Add Neufchatel to other side of skillet; cook and stir 2 min. or until melted. Gradually add broth to Neufchatel; stir until blended. Return chicken mixture to skillet; stir to combine all ingredients. Simmer on medium-low heat 4 to 5 min. or until heated through, stirring frequently. Remove from heat; let stand 5 min.
- Spoon chicken mixture over noodles; sprinkle with parsley.

Nutrition Information

- Calories: 390
- Sugar: 0 g
- Saturated Fat: 9 g
- Fiber: 2 g
- Protein: 33 g
- Total Carbohydrate: 0 g
- Sodium: 290 mg
- Total Fat: 17 g
- Cholesterol: 125 mg

354. Updated Chicken Parmesan

Serving: 2 | Prep: 10mins | Cook: 25mins | Ready in: 35mins

Ingredients

- 2 small boneless skinless chicken breasts (1/2 lb.)

- 1 Tbsp. flour
- 1 egg white, lightly beaten
- 1 large shredded wheat biscuit, finely crushed
- 1 cup cherry tomatoes, halved
- 2 Tbsp. KRAFT Lite Balsamic Vinaigrette Dressing
- 2 Tbsp. KRAFT Shredded Low-Moisture Part-Skim Mozzarella Cheese

Direction

- Heat oven to 400°F.
- Dip chicken in flour, then in egg and biscuit crumbs, turning to evenly coat both sides of each breast. Place in single layer in shallow pan sprayed with cooking spray.
- Bake 20 min. or until chicken is done (165°F). Meanwhile, bring tomatoes and dressing to boil in skillet on medium heat; simmer on medium-low heat 10 min. or until thickened, stirring occasionally.
- Top chicken with cheese; bake 3 to 5 min. or until melted. Serve topped with tomato mixture.

Nutrition Information

- Calories: 220
- Total Carbohydrate: 0 g
- Fiber: 3 g
- Sodium: 200 mg
- Sugar: 0 g
- Protein: 28 g
- Total Fat: 4.5 g
- Saturated Fat: 1.5 g
- Cholesterol: 65 mg

355. VELVEETA Chicken Curry Pot Pie

Serving: 8 | Prep: 15mins | Cook: 25mins | Ready in: 40mins

Ingredients

- 1-1/2 lb. boneless skinless chicken breasts, cut into 1-inch chunks
- 1/2 cup chopped onions
- 1 Tbsp. curry powder
- 1/2 tsp. garlic powder
- 1 pkg. (16 oz.) frozen peas and carrots, thawed
- 1 cup ORE-IDA Diced Hash Brown Potatoes
- 1 pouch (8 oz.) VELVEETA Cheese Sauce
- 1 can (8 oz.) refrigerated crescent dinner rolls

Direction

- Heat oven to 375°F.
- Cook chicken in large skillet sprayed with cooking spray on medium-high heat 7 to 8 min. or until done. Add onions, curry powder and garlic powder; cook and stir 2 min. Add peas and carrots, potatoes and Cheese Sauce; mix well. Spoon into 12x8-inch baking dish sprayed with cooking spray.
- Separate dough into 4 rectangles; firmly press perforations together to seal. Place over chicken mixture.
- Bake 20 to 25 min. or until golden brown. Let stand 5 min. before serving.

Nutrition Information

- Calories: 340
- Saturated Fat: 4.5 g
- Total Carbohydrate: 0 g
- Protein: 26 g
- Cholesterol: 60 mg
- Fiber: 3 g
- Total Fat: 14 g
- Sugar: 0 g
- Sodium: 720 mg

356. VELVEETA® Cheesy BBQ Chicken With A Kick

Serving: 0 | Prep: 15mins | Cook: 10mins | Ready in: 25mins

Ingredients

- 1 pkg. (12 oz.) VELVEETA Shells & Cheese Dinner
- 1 can (12.5 oz.) chicken, drained
- 1 green pepper, chopped
- 1 cup frozen corn, thawed
- 1/3 cup BULL'S-EYE Original Barbecue Sauce
- 1/4 cup BREAKSTONE'S or KNUDSEN Sour Cream
- 1/4 tsp. ground red pepper (cayenne)
- 1/2 cup KRAFT Finely Shredded Colby & Monterey Jack Cheeses

Direction

- Heat oven to 400°F.
- Prepare Dinner in large saucepan as directed on package. Stir in all remaining ingredients except shredded cheese.
- Spoon into 8-inch square baking dish sprayed with cooking spray; top with shredded cheese.
- Bake 10 min. or until heated through.

Nutrition Information

- Calories: 280
- Fiber: 1 g
- Sugar: 7 g
- Saturated Fat: 4 g
- Sodium: 710 mg
- Total Fat: 11 g
- Cholesterol: 40 mg
- Total Carbohydrate: 29 g
- Protein: 15 g

357. VELVEETA® Chicken And Vegetable Skillet

Serving: 0 | Prep: 20mins | Cook: | Ready in: 20mins

Ingredients

- 1-1/4 lb. boneless skinless chicken breasts, cut into bite-size pieces
- 2-3/4 cups water
- 3 cups instant white rice, uncooked
- 1/2 lb. (8 oz.) VELVEETA®, cut into 1/2-inch cubes
- 1 red pepper, cut into strips
- 1 pkg. (10 oz.) frozen green beans
- 1/2 tsp. each black pepper and garlic powder
- 1/2 cup french-fried onions

Direction

- Cook chicken in large nonstick skillet on medium-high heat 2 min. or until no longer pink.
- Stir in water. Bring to boil. Add rice; cover. Cook on low heat 10 min.
- Add all remaining ingredients except onions; mix well. Cook 5 min. or until VELVEETA is completely melted, stirring occasionally. Sprinkle with onions.

Nutrition Information

- Calories: 430
- Total Fat: 13 g
- Fiber: 2 g
- Sugar: 5 g
- Cholesterol: 80 mg
- Total Carbohydrate: 46 g
- Protein: 31 g
- Saturated Fat: 6 g
- Sodium: 600 mg

358. VELVEETA® Spicy Buffalo Chicken Dip

Serving: 0 | Prep: 10mins | Cook: | Ready in: 10mins

Ingredients

- 1 lb. (16 oz.) VELVEETA, cut into 1/2-inch cubes

- 1/4 cup BREAKSTONE'S or KNUDSEN Sour Cream
- 1 cup shredded cooked chicken breast
- 1 stalk celery, chopped
- 1 Tbsp. Buffalo wing sauce

Direction

- Microwave first 3 ingredients in large microwaveable bowl on HIGH 3 min. or until VELVEETA is completely melted, stirring after 1-1/2 min.
- Stir in celery and hot sauce.

Nutrition Information

- Calories: 80
- Sugar: 2 g
- Protein: 5 g
- Saturated Fat: 3 g
- Cholesterol: 20 mg
- Total Carbohydrate: 3 g
- Total Fat: 5 g
- Sodium: 300 mg
- Fiber: 0 g

359. Waldorf Salad With A Twist

Serving: 0 | Prep: 15mins | Cook: |Ready in: 15mins

Ingredients

- 2 cups chopped cooked chicken
- 1 cup halved seedless red grapes
- 1 red apple, chopped
- 2 stalks celery, sliced
- 1/4 cup KRAFT Mayo with Olive Oil Reduced Fat Mayonnaise
- 1 Tbsp. lemon juice
- 4 cups tightly packed mixed baby salad greens
- 1/4 cup coarsely chopped PLANTERS Pecans, toasted

Direction

- Combine chicken, fruit and celery in medium bowl.
- Add mayo and lemon juice; mix lightly.
- Cover large plate with salad greens; top with chicken salad. Sprinkle with nuts.

Nutrition Information

- Calories: 190
- Total Fat: 10 g
- Sodium: 120 mg
- Protein: 15 g
- Fiber: 2 g
- Total Carbohydrate: 0 g
- Cholesterol: 45 mg
- Sugar: 0 g
- Saturated Fat: 1.5 g

360. Warm Chicken Salad

Serving: 0 | Prep: 20mins | Cook: |Ready in: 20mins

Ingredients

- 3/4 cup KRAFT Classic Ranch Dressing, divided
- 1 lb. boneless skinless chicken breasts, cut into strips
- 1 pkg. (10 oz.) torn salad greens
- 1 cup dried cranberries
- 1/4 cup PLANTERS Sliced Almonds, toasted

Direction

- Heat 1/4 cup dressing in large skillet on medium-high heat. Add chicken; cook and stir 8 min. or until done.
- Toss greens with chicken, cranberries and nuts.
- Spoon onto platter; drizzle with remaining dressing.

Nutrition Information

- Calories: 440
- Sodium: 530 mg
- Cholesterol: 75 mg
- Protein: 27 g
- Total Carbohydrate: 0 g
- Saturated Fat: 3.5 g
- Fiber: 4 g
- Total Fat: 23 g
- Sugar: 0 g

361. Weeknight Cheddar Chicken Soup

Serving: 0 | Prep: 25mins | Cook: | Ready in: 25mins

Ingredients

- 1/2 lb. boneless skinless chicken breasts, cut into bite-size pieces
- 2 Tbsp. flour
- 1 can (14-1/2 oz.) fat-free reduced-sodium chicken broth
- 2 cups milk
- 2 cups frozen mixed vegetables (carrots, corn, green beans, peas)
- 1/2 tsp. onion powder
- 1 cup KRAFT Shredded Triple Cheddar Cheese with a TOUCH OF PHILADELPHIA
- 2 Tbsp. snipped fresh chives

Direction

- Cook and stir chicken in large saucepan sprayed with cooking spray on medium-high heat 8 to 10 min. or until done. Stir in flour; cook and stir 1 min.
- Add broth, milk, vegetables and onion powder; stir. Bring just to boil on medium heat, stirring frequently.
- Remove from heat. Add cheese; stir until melted. Sprinkle with chives.

Nutrition Information

- Calories: 200
- Protein: 16 g
- Sodium: 320 mg
- Total Carbohydrate: 12 g
- Sugar: 6 g
- Total Fat: 9 g
- Fiber: 1 g
- Saturated Fat: 5 g
- Cholesterol: 45 mg

362. West Coast Chicken Wings

Serving: 8 | Prep: 20mins | Cook: 1hours30mins | Ready in: 1hours50mins

Ingredients

- 1 cup LEA & PERRINS Worcestershire Sauce
- 1/4 cup pineapple juice
- 1/4 cup honey
- 2 lb. chicken wings, split at joints, tips removed

Direction

- Mix all ingredients except wings until blended. Pour 1 cup over wings in large bowl; stir to evenly coat all wings with Worcestershire sauce mixture.
- Refrigerate 1 hour to marinate, turning occasionally.
- Heat oven to 350°F. Drain wings; discard marinade. Place wings on foil-covered rimmed baking sheet sprayed with cooking spray.
- Bake 45 min. or until done, turning and brushing frequently with remaining Worcestershire sauce mixture for the last 15 min.

Nutrition Information

- Calories: 170

- Sugar: 11 g
- Total Carbohydrate: 11 g
- Total Fat: 8 g
- Cholesterol: 70 mg
- Fiber: 0 g
- Protein: 12 g
- Saturated Fat: 2.5 g
- Sodium: 310 mg

363. Zesty Chicken Chili

Serving: 0 | Prep: 25mins | Cook: 15mins | Ready in: 40mins

Ingredients

- 3 onions, chopped
- 1 jalapeño pepper, stemmed, seeded and finely chopped
- 1/4 cup KRAFT Zesty Italian Dressing
- 1 lb. boneless skinless chicken breasts, cut into bite-size chunks
- 8 fresh mushrooms, sliced
- 1 Tbsp. flour
- 2 cans (15.5 oz. each) white beans, rinsed
- 1 can (14 oz.) chicken broth
- 1/4 cup fresh cilantro, chopped
- 1 bay leaf
- 1 tsp. each ground cumin and dried oregano leaves
- 3/4 cup BREAKSTONE'S or KNUDSEN Sour Cream

Direction

- Cook and stir onions and peppers in dressing in large saucepan on medium-high heat 3 to 5 min. or until crisp-tender. Add chicken and mushrooms; cook and stir 3 to 5 min. or until chicken is lightly browned. Stir in flour; cook and stir 1 min.
- Add beans, broth and seasonings; stir. Bring to boil; simmer on low heat 10 to 15 min. or until chicken is done. Remove and discard bay leaf.
- Serve topped with sour cream.

Nutrition Information

- Calories: 300
- Sugar: 0 g
- Protein: 25 g
- Fiber: 10 g
- Saturated Fat: 3.5 g
- Cholesterol: 55 mg
- Total Carbohydrate: 0 g
- Total Fat: 9 g
- Sodium: 430 mg

364. Zesty One Pan Chicken And Potato Bake

Serving: 4 | Prep: 10mins | Cook: 1hours | Ready in: 1hours10mins

Ingredients

- 1/4 cup KRAFT Zesty Italian Dressing
- 4 bone-in chicken pieces (1-1/2 lb.)
- 4 large baking potato es (2 lb.), cut into wedges
- 1/4 cup KRAFT Grated Parmesan Cheese

Direction

- Heat oven to 400°F.
- Pour dressing over chicken and potatoes in 13x9-inch baking dish sprayed with cooking spray.
- Sprinkle with cheese.
- Bake 1 hour or until chicken is done (165°F).

Nutrition Information

- Calories: 440
- Sodium: 380 mg
- Fiber: 5 g
- Sugar: 2 g
- Saturated Fat: 4 g
- Protein: 36 g
- Total Fat: 14 g

- Cholesterol: 120 mg
- Total Carbohydrate: 41 g

365. Zucchini Chicken Salad

Serving: 6 | Prep: 25mins | Cook: 3hours | Ready in: 3hours25mins

Ingredients

- 3 cups shredded cooked chicken
- 1 zucchini, chopped
- 2 thin carrots, peeled, thinly sliced
- 1 stalk celery, chopped
- 4 green onions, sliced
- 2 Tbsp. dried cranberries
- 1/2 cup KRAFT Mayo with Olive Oil Reduced Fat Mayonnaise
- 2 Tbsp. GREY POUPON Dijon Mustard
- 1 Tbsp. COUNTRY TIME Lemonade Starter Classic Lemonade Drink Mix
- 1/4 tsp. pepper
- 8 cups loosely packed torn mixed salad greens

Direction

- Combine first 6 ingredients in large bowl.
- Mix mayo, mustard, drink mix and pepper until blended. Add to chicken mixture; mix lightly.
- Refrigerate 3 hours.
- Serve chicken salad over salad greens.

Nutrition Information

- Calories: 240
- Total Carbohydrate: 0 g
- Sodium: 340 mg
- Fiber: 2 g
- Cholesterol: 70 mg
- Total Fat: 11 g
- Saturated Fat: 2 g
- Sugar: 0 g
- Protein: 22 g

Index

A

Almond 13,28,82,90,101,188

Apple 4,53,59,65,66,89,111,139,169

Apricot 3,4,13,62

Asparagus 3,45

Avocado 4,5,87,114,127

B

Bacon 3,5,7,15,17,19,20,27,30,35,37,39,43,45,46,50,58,60,64,66,72,105,106,117,127,135,141,145,151,153,161,165,170,181

Baking 36

Basil 3,8,13,24,25,33,34,44,54,55,56,67,68,80,86,88,96,97,100,102,124,146,182,183,184

Beans 4,5,6,31,47,66,125,156,167

Beef 29

Beer 3,25

Berry 3,26

Bread 3,4,6,28,57,59,168

Broccoli 3,4,5,14,29,43,66,67,76,78,82,105

Butter 3,6,32,46,59,110,125,137,181

C

Carrot 6,157

Cashew 122

Cauliflower 3,4,29,81

Cava 4,55

Champ 3,34

Cheddar 3,4,7,19,26,30,35,36,38,39,40,44,47,55,57,58,60,61,64,72,74,77,86,95,104,105,106,108,110,119,126,137,138,154,159,167,189

Cheese 3,4,5,6,7,8,9,10,12,13,15,16,17,18,19,20,21,22,23,24,25,26,27,28,29,30,31,33,34,35,36,37,38,39,40,41,42,43,44,46,47,48,49,50,51,53,54,55,56,57,58,59,60,61,63,64,65,66,67,68,69,71,72,74,76,77,79,80,81,82,83,84,85,86,87,88,90,91,92,93,94,95,96,97,98,99,100,101,102,103,104,105,106,108,109,110,112,115,116,117,118,119,120,122,123,124,126,127,128,129,130,133,134,135,136,137,138,139,140,141,142,143,144,145,146,149,150,151,152,154,156,158,159,160,161,162,164,165,166,167,168,170,171,175,177,178,181,182,183,184,185,186,187,189,190

Cherry 3,14

Chicken 1,3,4,5,6,7,8,9,10,11,12,13,14,15,16,17,18,19,20,21,22,23,24,25,26,27,28,29,30,31,32,33,34,35,36,37,38,39,40,41,42,43,44,45,46,47,48,49,50,51,52,53,54,55,56,57,58,59,60,61,62,63,64,65,66,67,68,69,70,71,72,73,74,75,76,77,78,79,80,81,82,83,84,85,86,87,88,89,90,91,92,94,95,96,97,98,99,100,101,102,103,104,105,106,107,108,109,110,111,112,113,114,115,116,117,118,119,120,121,122,123,124,125,126,127,128,129,130,131,132,133,134,135,136,137,138,139,140,141,142,143,144,145,146,147,148,149,150,151,152,153,154,155,156,157,158,159,160,161,162,163,164,165,166,167,168,169,170,171,172,173,174,175,176,178,179,180,181,182,183,184,185,186,187,188,189,190,191

Chickpea 3,14

Chipotle 4,5,70,94,131,158,166

Cider 4,71,89,111,139,169

Coconut 3,4,34,73,90

Cola 3,14

Crackers 34,68,77,145

Cranberry 4,6,75,147

Cream 3,4,5,7,12,21,30,31,32,40,43,44,46,47,49,50,56,61,62,63,65

,67,68,70,74,76,77,78,79,80,81,82,83,84,85,90,93,94,95,98,104,118,126,127,137,141,143,147,150,152,155,156,158,160,161,166,175,176,178,179,183,187,188,190

Crumble 18,19,21,27,28,29,30,31,35,71,72,93,100,101,108,109,110,115,117,128,133,134,135,142,155,159,161

Curry 5,7,121,130,186

D

Dijon mustard 32

Dumplings 4,6,63,160

E

Egg 5,128

F

Fat 8,9,10,11,12,13,14,15,16,17,18,19,20,21,22,23,24,25,26,27,28,29,30,31,32,33,34,35,36,37,38,39,40,41,42,43,44,45,46,47,48,49,50,51,52,53,54,55,56,57,58,59,60,61,62,63,64,65,66,67,68,69,70,71,72,73,74,75,76,77,78,79,80,81,82,83,84,85,86,87,88,89,90,91,92,93,94,95,96,97,98,99,100,101,102,103,104,105,106,107,108,109,110,111,112,113,114,115,116,117,118,119,120,121,122,123,124,125,126,127,128,129,130,131,132,133,134,135,136,137,138,139,140,141,142,143,144,145,146,147,148,149,150,151,152,153,154,155,156,157,158,159,160,161,162,163,164,165,166,167,168,169,170,171,172,173,174,175,176,177,178,179,180,181,182,183,184,185,186,187,188,189,190,191

Fennel 4,62

Feta 3,5,6,18,27,31,71,93,100,101,109,110,115,133,134,135,142,159

Fettuccine 4,49

French bread 9

Fruit 4,73

G

Garlic 4,5,6,7,56,82,103,108,114,128,154,159,184

Gorgonzola 5,108

Gouda 22

Gravy 45,57,61,180

H

Ham 4,5,59,64,74,113,123,124,167,172,178

Heart 5,118

Herbs 155,178

Honey 4,5,6,17,53,63,87,90,119,131,152,160,167

Hummus 6,93,133

J

Jam 3,5,11,124

Jus 14

K

Ketchup 89,126

L

Lemon 4,5,6,64,71,128,129,149,191

Lime 5,20,21,119,121,130,180

M

Macaroni 6,41,42,51,79,82,94,108,145,171

Mango 5,131

Marsala wine 53

Matzo 4,81

Mayonnaise 10,26,30,54,59,63,78,82,84,86,87,89,90,92,106,113,120,129,131,145,170,173,181,188,191

Milk 16,20,23,27,29,33,35,38,40,48,57,68,84,95,97,104,105,117,127,130,133,136,137,140,159,168,177,179,181

Mozzarella 3,18,23,25,26,27,33,34,44,46,48,53,54,56,67,68,69,79,80,81,83,86,97,102,105,109,112,116,124,145,178,182,183,184,186

Mushroom 5,6,33,114,139,140

Mustard 5,9,17,52,53,63,65,74,86,87,90,91,92,93,111,114,119,131,132,146,147,148,160,191

N

Nachos 3,11,24

Noodles 6,7,141,165,174

Nut 6,8,9,10,11,12,13,14,15,16,17,18,19,20,21,22,23,24,25,26,27,28,29,30,31,32,33,34,35,36,37,38,39,40,41,42,43,44,45,46,47,48,49,50,51,52,53,54,55,56,57,58,59,60,61,62,63,64,65,66,67,68,69,70,71,72,73,74,75,76,77,78,79,80,81,82,83,84,85,86,87,88,89,90,91,92,93,94,95,96,97,98,99,100,101,102,103,104,105,106,107,108,109,110,111,112,113,114,115,116,117,118,119,120,121,122,123,124,125,126,127,128,129,130,131,132,133,134,135,136,137,138,139,140,141,142,143,144,145,146,147,148,149,150,151,152,153,154,155,156,157,158,159,160,161,162,163,164,165,166,167,168,169,170,171,172,173,174,175,176,177,178,179,180,181,182,183,184,185,186,187,188,189,190,191

O

Oil 12,58,63,65,106,109,110,132,137,146,181,188,191

Olive 12,58,63,106,109,110,132,137,146,181,188,191

Onion 6,142,160

Orange 6,142

Oregano 109,110

P

Parmesan 3,4,5,6,7,10,13,16,19,24,28,33,34,35,43,44,48,49,51,53,54,55,58,63,67,68,69,76,79,80,81,82,83,84,87,88,96,97,98,99,102,112,122,123,128,129,133,134,142,144,146,149,154,161,178,182,183,184,185,190

Pasta 3,4,5,6,7,8,12,13,27,33,34,41,43,44,54,55,58,67,68,80,81,83,84,88,96,97,98,102,103,114,115,122,123,124,128,133,134,135,137,141,144,146,149,154,177,182,183,184

Peanuts 52,65,66,98,127,143,151,172,174

Pear 5,119

Pecan 4,6,75,145,188

Peel 145

Penne 4,69

Pepper 3,4,6,42,44,47,56,60,71,141,145,150,151,158,170,175

Pesto 3,4,6,13,55,56,63,86,124,146

Pickle 59

Pie 3,4,6,7,32,39,43,50,57,58,91,108,122,137,143,148,157,163,186

Pineapple 6,156,164

Pizza 3,4,5,6,7,17,18,28,36,46,48,80,106,108,142,170,181

Plum 58,137

Pork 6,147

Potato 3,4,6,7,35,61,78,148,153,186,190

R

Raspberry 73

Ratatouille 3,23

Rice 3,4,5,6,7,10,15,18,41,44,45,67,77,89,123,142,149,152,165,167,177

Ricotta 28

Rigatoni 5,98

Rosemary 5,6,129,154

S

Salad 3,4,5,6,7,26,27,28,29,31,32,35,36,48,50,53,54,58,59,63,66,71,72,73,80,82,84,85,92,101,107,108,110,112,113,114,115,117,119,125,127,128,129,130,131,133,138,144,147,153,168,169,171,177,179,188,191

Salami 58

Salsa 3,4,5,6,20,38,40,42,63,83,84,85,87,88,97,100,104,115,118,

127,136,150,151,153,156,158,159

Salt 127,172

Sausage 3,4,5,6,11,33,80,116,123,155

Savory 6,17,63,90,131,155,157,159,160,169,178

Seasoning 40,43,47,61,97,134,137,156,162,166

Soup 3,4,5,6,7,42,63,64,77,81,118,137,139,176,189

Spaghetti 4,54

Spinach 3,4,7,28,66,135,177,184

Squash 3,32,46

Stew 4,7,65,172

Strawberry 5,115

Stuffing
3,4,6,7,33,38,65,71,76,105,106,138,140,147,155,168,178

Sugar
8,9,10,11,12,13,14,15,16,17,18,19,20,21,22,23,24,25,26,27,28,29,30,31,32,33,34,35,36,37,38,39,40,41,42,43,44,45,46,47,48,49,50,51,52,53,54,55,56,57,58,59,60,61,62,63,64,65,66,67,68,69,70,71,72,73,74,75,76,77,78,79,80,81,82,83,84,85,86,87,88,89,90,91,92,93,94,95,96,97,98,99,100,101,102,103,104,105,106,107,108,109,110,111,112,113,114,115,116,117,118,119,120,121,122,123,124,125,126,127,128,129,130,131,132,133,134,135,136,137,138,139,140,141,142,143,144,145,146,147,148,149,150,151,152,153,154,155,156,157,158,159,160,161,162,163,164,165,166,167,168,169,170,171,172,173,174,175,176,177,178,179,180,181,182,183,184,185,186,187,188,189,190,191

T

Taco 3,4,5,6,16,40,42,47,61,97,116,127,137,156,162,166

Tapioca 62,162

Tea 129

Teriyaki 5,117

Thai basil 56

Thyme 7,183

Tomatillo 4,60

Tomato
3,5,6,7,8,13,25,33,34,44,54,55,58,63,67,68,69,80,88,96,97,98,100,102,103,112,122,124,137,141,144,145,147,150,179,180,182,183,184

Tortellini 4,63

Turkey 117

V

Vegetables 7,179

Vinegar 21,72,89,91,111,114,139,169

Vodka 123

W

Walnut 4,63,65,108,119,130,144

Wine 114

Worcestershire sauce 72,76,139,173,189

Wraps 3,6,7,37,133,180

Z

Zest
6,7,10,13,20,21,27,31,42,45,48,60,62,70,77,81,91,95,101,106,107,109,112,114,119,121,123,124,130,132,133,134,144,151,156,157,167,175,176,180,190

L

lasagna 33,177

Conclusion

Thank you again for downloading this book!

I hope you enjoyed reading about my book!

If you enjoyed this book, please take the time to share your thoughts and post a review on Amazon. It'd be greatly appreciated!

Write me an honest review about the book – I truly value your opinion and thoughts and I will incorporate them into my next book, which is already underway.

Thank you!

If you have any questions, **feel free to contact at:** *author@shrimpcookbook.com*

Norma Wells

shrimpcookbook.com

www.ingramcontent.com/pod-product-compliance
Lightning Source LLC
Chambersburg PA
CBHW082147080125

20114CB00010B/963